TABLE OF CONTENTS

To my wife, Chris, and my children,
Lawrence, Louise, Charlotte, and Richard

ACKNOWLEDGMENTS

For encouragement or direct help with this project, thanks to the City of Calgary Archives, the University of Calgary Archives, the late Denis Cole, Dr. Pip Farrar, Dr. Max Foran, Elaine Husband, Bruce Morin, the late Chris Murphy, David Scollard, Barbara Tate, Heinz Unger, Tom Yarmon, and Dr. John Willey. For his initial commitment of time and energy, thanks to Rod Sykes. For their understanding, gratitude to my wife and children.

Photo of Rod used in campaign literature for at least two of his campaigns

INTRODUCTION

I n the unruly narrative of our lives, some characters can walk on stage, grab us, shake us, and demand a special place in our spotlight. Rod Sykes, mayor of Calgary from 1969-77, was such a player in my life's performance. As a *Lethbridge Herald* reporter, assigned to cover a speech he made to that city's chamber of commerce while he was still with Canadian Pacific Railway's Marathon Realty, I reacted with shock to the bluntness of his message. The gist was, "You're a bunch of sleepy layabouts who'll never amount to anything if you don't smarten up." What verve, and what a thrill to see his audience squirm.

Two years later, as a *Calgary Herald* reporter, I covered Rod again as he ran for the mayoralty, and, after a smashing victory, launched into his hectic first term. I marvelled at the fearlessness, the unvarnished outrageousness of this ectomorphic oddball; not to mention his iron will to complete worthwhile projects. Going to work for him a couple of years later gave me first hand insight into the contrary passions seething within him. After three years, perhaps overwhelmed by the intensity of the experience, I left for other pastures—but I stayed in touch.

At a loose end in 1980, after selling a business I owned, I was asked to be on his team while he campaigned for the leadership of the Alberta Social Credit Party. That proved a disaster for all involved, and gave me further confirmation of this complex character's feet of clay. Still, we maintained contact over the decades, and met for social occasions

Then in 2009, he and a group of Calgary City Hall retirees decided it was time to tell his story, and I was the one to do it. I signed on with gusto. The untidy recollections in my mind of Rod's extraordinary public career screamed out for order and exposure. As the work began, the sifting of the archives revealed how much Rod had achieved through his single-minded resolve. It seemed increasingly worthwhile to create an accessible and permanent record of this remarkable man. There was even joy in making more tangible through a book his active role in Calgary's and Alberta's history over a significant twenty-year period. Giving credit where it's due, and where it hasn't necessarily been granted, was also a strong motivation.

The project expanded into observations as to how municipal governments—those closest to the people—order their affairs. That's hopefully a bonus for those who care about local government. More germane to casual readers, whether they lived in those decades or not, is the pleasure or piqued curiosity in just sitting back and contemplating a narrative arc that began inauspiciously and strangely, and then morphed into an improbable adventure of business and political derring-do.

While writing the manuscript, I spoke with University of Calgary professor and prolific chronicler of Alberta history, Max Foran. At the time, Foran was preparing his fourteenth book, *Development Derailed: Calgary and the CPR, 1962-64* (Athabasca University Press, 2013). Rod was a principal source for that book, so the Australia-born author knew him well. "Someone's got to write about Rod Sykes, and you're the one to do it!" he exclaimed during one visit. He later warned, though, "Don't have Rod as your only source for your stories."

Much of what follows in this book is corroborated by newspaper and magazine accounts, by memos, and by interviews with others. Occasionally, though, confirming evidence of Rod's stories wasn't possible. The other person in accounts had died, or no records were kept. That is why phrases like "according to Rod" or "from Rod's view of events" are dotted throughout the book. However, the narrative where Rod is the sole source still sheds light on the man he was and provides an idiosyncratic take on people and events.

Three years of archival research were interspersed with frequent and lengthy sessions with Rod, covering broad swaths of his life. Recreating personal history may always be a murky endeavour. Memory can't always be trusted, and even the official record can be ambiguous. Most people want to cast themselves in the best possible light, but Rod always told me to "tell the story, warts and all."

The process took a wrong turn when Rod was given a first draft and disassociated himself from it. "What you have produced and circulated is not at all what I had understood we were to collaborate on," he wrote in a May 2012 letter. "The story of Calgary City Hall in the 1970s in a period of growth and transformation has become what purports to be a personal biography!" Note the exclamation mark. Rod always liked those stylistic spears. He said it was too personal, and lacking in historical and institutional perspective. He denied details of some stories retold.

While disappointing, his response wasn't entirely unexpected. Although his life's story places him in a frequently favourable light, his darker side shows, too. He didn't want his earlier vulnerabilities publicly analysed. I describe his *ad hominem* attacks and occasional maliciousness; his inconsistencies; his ability to re-invent history with a virulence that defies reasonable disagreement. He probably didn't like the depiction of his black-and-white division of people into good guys and bad; his sometimes misplaced loyalties and occasional disloyalties; or the odd time he went missing in action when the going got tough.

Rebuffed in this way, I gave up publishing the manuscript and let metaphorical dust gather on it. But I couldn't shake the conviction that this was a worthy story. Thanks to friends' encouragement, I blew off the dust and got to work again. I was able to renew my appreciation for Rod's eye for human foibles. I sifted through the upside-down caricatures spilling out of Rod's world, just like those inhabiting Lewis Carroll's *Alice through the Looking Glass,* which Rod read at such an early age. Through his stern and satirical eye, they came alive in weird and wonderful ways. Did he always hold fast to the truth? That's a hard riddle to solve. Truth, after all, is an elusive character, like Rod Sykes himself. If he's an enigma, he's a darn fascinating one, and one that Calgarians, indeed Canadians, can properly celebrate. Whether his exploits thrill you or anger you, whether you nod vigorously in agreement with what he said, or shake with rejection, you will taste a scintillating slice of this region's history. But delight even more in a full-on revelation, certainly not a hagiography, of one of this province's most compelling and controversial players of the past. Appreciate the outrageous, gutsy, and downright hilarious lengths people will go to pursue their goals.

1

STILL PROVOCATIVE PAST EIGHTY

Rod Sykes was the target of invective for much of his life, and it didn't let up in old age. At eighty, he was publicly branded as "crazy as shit" by the then mayor of Calgary's grandly titled chief of staff, Marc Henry. What had Rod done to deserve such rudeness? His sin was to publicly articulate his sharp-tongued version of the truth, just as he had done four decades before as Calgary's mayor, and before that as a chartered accountant and successful land developer. He was following a life-long inner insistence to tell things as they appeared to him, and to tread on the tender toes of the high and mighty. In this case, he'd pointed out in radio and newspaper interviews that the mayor of Calgary of the time, Dave Bronconnier, was leaving behind a $2.5-billion debt when he decided not to run again in the October 2010 civic election. With Rod's forbidding demeanour and meticulous way of speaking, his comments to the media came across like scolding a dog for a nasty deposit on the front steps. This massive and unprecedented debt constituted such a mess of finances, Rod explained, that the City would have a hard time digging itself out and cleaning up.

"Calgary can't borrow any more from the Province because we've hit our borrowing limit," Rod told the local media. They were apparently still eager to quote the now physically frail but mentally on-the-ball former mayor, who had stepped down after three terms at Calgary City Hall more than thirty-three years before.

He had done again what had tormented so many during his time in office, likely the most tumultuous years City Hall has ever experienced. In this case, dispassionately and with authority, he had scorched an outgoing mayor whom he had never much respected. This is how Rod Sykes operated, by casting a bare-bulbed light into the darker corners of the City's operations and revealing evidence that affairs were not as they should be. At the same time, he was quite aware of the provocative nature of his comments and the aggravation they inflicted. When the stakes were significant and the issues pressing, Rod could pounce with the speed and guile of a veteran fighter. He was a lightweight at less than 140 pounds, but backed by remarkable analytical skills built up since boyhood, the force of his precisely enunciated verbal assaults belonged to a much heavier class. *Calgary Albertan* cartoonist Lance Rodewalt called it "Thin Power," invariably drawing caricatures of Rod wearing a button bearing those words.

Rod was inclined to grimace at street-fighter or boxing analogies. With disarming informality, he liked to describe his approach as cutting through the bullshit, or applying strong disinfectant to the grime arising from the entitlement, corruption, and incompetence that he spotted among the ranks of those with entrenched power. Former Chief Commissioner Denis Cole said Rod found sin under every table. Let's say he enjoyed digging into people's affairs and offering an emphatic public assessment, whether entirely accurate or not. That was Rod's way of dealing with those he disagreed with, and those who disagreed with him. "I try to assess the facts in an objective way and present a fair view of the state of affairs," was his version of this approach. "That's what accountants do." Was he smirking while he said that? He sure appeared to savour this verbal sparring and the controlled release of judgmental outrage.

When Rod saw what he interpreted as dishonesty, mismanagement, laziness, cronyism, injustice, or a lack of transparency on the part of politicians, bureaucrats, or corporate bosses, his hawk-like eyes took on a weary look, like a stern cleric confronting yet another transgression. His relentless sense of moral rectitude informed his careers as a chartered accountant, property developer, big-city mayor, provincial Social Credit Party leader, newspaper columnist, candidate for federal parliament, and property consultant, as well as his family roles as a father, grandfather, and husband. Doing what he thought was the right thing — and winning, of course — were paramount. But, he usually only clawed those with the wherewithal to defend themselves. The afflicted and the vulnerable were spared from his swooping attacks.

Rod divided up the world into good guys and bad. Heaven help you if you were on the wrong side. Maybe that habit originated with his regular reading of *Boys' Own* or *Chums Annuals* that influenced his moral compass and that prompted him to ask, "Who needs parents when you have these publications to guide you?" I wondered about other reading at a precociously early age of Charles Dickens, Lewis Carroll, and other nineteenth century classics. His childhood years and highly unorthodox upbringing in Victoria, B.C., obviously helped determine the man he became. His rebellion against the stuffy and stultifying smugness of Victoria's English ghetto where he grew up left its mark on his character.

The pain from the detached cruelty of his early school years, followed by the growing confidence and self-understanding of his later school years during the 1940s, were important influences. They taught him about bullying, both as the inflictor and the victim, and they instilled an edgy sense of justice too. It was miraculous how he evolved from a shy, confused introvert to an intensely curious and skeptical man on a mission, ready to engage all manner of people in intellectual conversation and combat. The estrangement from his father, leaving home and assuming independence at an early age, and his relationship with influential mentors, played their part in shaping this self-sufficient and driven man.

Rod's bosses recognized his sharp intellect and ability to hack through the tangled undergrowth of obfuscation. They also sensed inner steel that gave him the resolve, and arrogance, to resist those who challenged his judgments. At the same time, he understood the art of negotiating outcomes without spilling blood. After his successful years with Price Waterhouse on the West Coast and in Montreal, CP Rail and its senior officers put a lot of faith in this Smart Alec, who was so confident of his views. They hired him and put him in a unique position of power and trust. They sent him west to figure out how to relocate the railway lines out of downtown Calgary and handle some foaming-at-the-mouth CPR critics there in the process. He didn't actually succeed with the relocation part, but instead, instigated and led one of the greatest periods of investment Alberta had ever seen. In a few dynamic years, he learned all about land development. He lifted his sights skyward with projects like the Calgary Tower, his concrete legacy for the city.

Calgary offered fresh and broad horizons for the skinny but ambitious businessman with his grey suit and colourful intent. While in Montreal during the 1950s, Rod met, fell in love with, and married Gisele Seguin, a gracious, humorous, and spirited woman who could be his match during verbal tussles. After settling in Calgary, their family grew to three sons and two daughters. Rod's involvement with CP Rail's economic study of Calgary, through its real estate subsidiary Marathon Realty, gave him unmatched access and insights into the workings and characters of the city.

Increasingly aware of incompetence and corruption pervading City Hall, Rod decided in 1969 to run for alderman. When confronted with the full scope of wrongdoing he suspected had permeated local government, he burned all career bridges and ran for mayor, defeating the incumbent, Jack Leslie, in one of the most lop-sided mayoralty races ever seen in Calgary. Aiming to clean up the less-than-savory ways of City Hall, keep taxes down, and open up local government to the citizens, he pursued an aggressive agenda and met, predictably, with hostile resistance.

Eight tumultuous years and two more elections followed, taking their toll on him and those he came into contact with. No foe was too big to tackle. From the Stampede Board to Alberta Premier Peter Lougheed, from the Calgary Police Department to city planners; they all came under his withering fire. Veteran *Calgary Albertan* columnist Fred Kennedy said he had never met a Calgary mayor who had experienced such a rough apprenticeship.[1] *Alberta Business Journal* headlined an article about him: "Hurricane Sykes Hits Calgary."[2]

A *Vancouver Sun* profile by Jack Nightscales referred to Rod's "damn-the-establishment sense of humour." Nightscales captured his subject's persona with delightful clarity: "It is typical of Sykes that he appears to be and sounds like something he isn't, but which his entire background has prepared him to be—chairman of an Establishment board. He is over six feet, so thin his white collar appears a size too large. His single-breasted, light grey suit, grey socks, black shoes, and black waistcoat give him the appearance of the head of a firm of chartered accountants or a slightly swinging undertaker. His voice is soft, clipped, precise, and vaguely English. At first he sounds like a private school master talking down to a boy; later the impression softens as his language dips into the gutter on appropriate occasions, still beautifully enunciated." With exquisite detail, Nightscales described Rod's thin black hair combed squarely from right to left over a balding, forty-year-old pate, his tortoise-shell glasses, and his slim and restless hands.

"He sits behind the desk and talks. And talks and talks and talks. He listens, too. He's really a hippie square rig, but his record shows he can do more than talk. 'I can produce,' he says, and you believe him." When Nightscales, soon after the article appeared, left journalism to join Prime Minister Pierre Trudeau's advisers as head of his western desk, he brought this oddball mayor to Trudeau's attention, although the prime minister was already aware of him. Trudeau and Rod hit it off and enjoyed a personal friendship for many years.

Albertan columnist and managing editor Don Peacock, friendlier with Rod than most journalists, wrote about "Calgary's turmoil of change." Since Rod Sykes became mayor, "he has made it plain he is no average, ordinary citizen … His critics and some of his supporters, will tell you that at best he talks too much and at worst employs far too sharp a tongue. Perhaps they are right. Even friends suggest he could have achieved goals more readily if he showed more diplomacy."[3]

Significantly, Rod used his mayoralty powers to their fullest and bemoaned after retirement how subsequent mayors squandered that ability. He did indeed open up City Hall to greater public scrutiny. He deliberately trod on toes, as he had promised, and made a sustained attempt not to "hear a rich man's voice any louder than a poor man's voice." Although a constant champion of the underdog and able to establish rapport with the hotel doorman or the self-effacing receptionist, he got along with the rich and famous too, including leading Canadian politicians and British royalty. He handled his formal duties with flair.

Under Rod's watch, Calgary got a new airport and a convention centre complex. The foundations for light-rail rapid transit were laid. He oversaw the building of three thousand lower-cost housing units and two seniors' complexes. He took credit for building up the city's physical infrastructure—sewers, water treatment facilities, and bridges—to standards that allowed subsequent mayors to coast for twenty more years of benign neglect, as he called it, before catch-up became necessary again. He ensured his administration kept the streets clean and the snow cleared, - unlike later mayors and councils, whom he scorned for hiring consultants to tell them how to do it.

He helped establish law and medicine faculties at the University of Calgary. During eight years in office, not a single day was lost to strike action by any of the City unions, this at a time when labour strife was rampant across Canada. He fought hard to hold the line on taxes or keep hikes at a reasonable level.

A review of the records points to other significant achievements during the Sykes years. On his watch and through his efforts, the city's downtown became a viable and successful commercial hub, Calgary established itself as a head office city, and new industrial parks were developed that would provide valuable jobs for years to come. City committees were opened up to fresh influences, and transparency was introduced to the budget processes. Calgary's evolving community, enriched by ever increasing immigrant newcomers from across the world, enjoyed access to and a welcome at City Hall they hadn't had before. Chinatown took shape, and other established neighbourhoods found new life from his efforts. The planning department was challenged to be responsive to the needs of the community, the relation-ship with the federal government was strengthened, and Francophone ties were restored.

At the same time, Rod was branded a "headline rustler", abusive, irre-sponsible, malicious, tight-fisted, misinformed, overbearing, pathologically mistrustful, and cantankerous, but never dull or slow-witted. Others have used words like brilliant, scrappy, and outspoken. How about annoying, as his friend Roy Farran called him? In frustration, Rod once turned the tables and called a *Herald* reporter "chicken shit." Shortly before he retired as mayor, *The Herald* said he "excelled as a news-maker, the master of the cutting barb, the cruel putdown."[4] The paper added, "At his best, Sykes can be effective, ener-getic and persuasive." This was grudging praise from a committed adversary.

Writer Frank Dabbs described Rod's eight years as mayor as "littered with the political and career corpses of those he shoved aside in an atmosphere of tension, anger and uncertainty."[5] Peter Miller said he used political craftsman-ship, intellectual brass knuckles and an acid tongue to survive his eight years in office.

His influence extended far beyond Calgary. While participating in the Edmonton Klondike Days Parade, he created headlines when he told his hosts they didn't know how to party like Calgarians. He took on Montreal Mayor Jean Drapeau for siphoning off taxpayers' money for his 1976 Olympics overspending. He publicly backed Pierre Trudeau in the prime minister's decisive efforts to fight Quebec terrorism during the early 1970s. He opposed the separatists and countered overspending by any government. He also stood up loudly for Canada and battled western separation. These sentiments prompted him to condemn Alberta Premier Peter Lougheed for what he considered flirtations with separatism in the late 1970s and early 1980s. It was Rod who provided the classic answer to the ugly Alberta bumper sticker that gave us a bad name during the 1973 oil crisis: "Let the Eastern Bastards Freeze in the Dark." Rod's response: "That Eastern Bastard is My Brother!"

So-called political correctness left him unmoved. Toward the end of his third term, he raised a furor with his pointed remarks at Mr. Justice Thomas Berger and his Mackenzie Valley Pipeline inquiry. He described Aboriginals as "simple" people manipulated by other self-interested people, and branded the Berger hearings a "charade".

Rod's interventions prompted intemperate reactions. A Stampede and Exhibition Board insider warned him early during his mayoralty that the board was plotting to provide a horse for his first Stampede that would bolt and buck and, some members hoped, set him on his pointy head when he rode down Ninth Avenue in the famous annual parade.

Rod had made clear during the campaign and his first few months in power he would rein in the powerful group and their overly ambitious expansion plans into Victoria Park. Unspooked by the warning and correctly anticipating the offer from the Stampede board, he had already arranged with a rancher friend for a gentler mare. He had, after all, hardly met a horse, let alone mounted one, during his growing-up years near Victoria. In subsequent years, he accepted a ride in flamboyant rancher and oilman Bill Herron's convertible with the gigantic Texas bull horns in front.

Another of Rod's weapons was a biting and acerbic wit that not everyone appreciated, especially those who felt its sting. After Rod's election in 1969, aldermanic outbursts became a regular agenda item, and intent by some on council to sabotage proceedings was apparent. One of the prominent "rat pack" members, the heavy-set Alderman Ed Dooley, publicly complained that during his turn as deputy mayor, he had been excluded from assignments to represent the City at public functions. Rod's public response was to commit the man of portly frame, as he described him, to an upcoming two-day fast by a charitable group, enroll him in a Red Cross blood donor clinic for a quart of his blood, and assign him to a charity slave auction planned by another organization. To his credit, even Ed Dooley later laughed at the prank.

When he was elected in that landslide win of 1969, Rod fully grasped another reality about the position that previous and subsequent mayors failed to exploit and that was shamelessly and surreptitiously taken away by the Ralph Klein Conservatives in Edmonton in the mid-1990s. The loss of authority in the mayor's office and the downloading of responsibilities from the City to the Province reflected in today's Municipal Government Act are shocking when compared to the prior situation, as chapter 6 will show.

The Rod Sykes who was such a controversial, achievement-driven, much liked, and much despised man during his mayoralty years seems to have little connection with the withdrawn and isolated boy growing up near Victoria in the 1930s. How he became a successful developer, builder, corporate doer, and political practitioner offers a remarkable story of determination.

That sense of duty that drove Rod to assume the Social Credit Party leadership quickly lost momentum when the wheels fell off the Socred bandwagon, as I describe in chapter 18. His Socred leadership days were a swim in shark-infested seas, but Rod managed to emerge from those stormy waters and carry on with good humour, incongruously writing columns for the *Calgary Sun* and helping farmers and ranchers around Calgary stand up to the imperious annexation ambitions of their city neighbours. He relished his David-against-Goliath role in the annexation hearings. Thorough and coolly analytical, he did well with his financial and property investments, building up a substantial portfolio in retirement.

Later in life, Rod retained his powerful appetite for political discourse, speaking publicly at forums, and offering articles and letters to the local media. He wrote to bureaucrats and politicians at City Hall, and some contacted him for advice. He kept reading and commenting on local issues, and he still clipped articles, marking a trail of underlining, ticks and crosses in the margins, like the droppings from hungry mice in a well-stocked pantry. Words like "wrong" or "bullshit" littered the edges. The writing eventually became more spidery, the sparkle in his eyes dimmed, and his voice sometimes turned hoarse and weary. But, the inner spark of rambunctiousness, rebellion, and rectitude still burned at most provocations.

A column by *The Herald's* man-about-town, Johnny Hopkins, just after Rod's retirement as mayor in 1977 summed up Rod well. Normally, the purveyor of superficial bonhomie and idle social chitchat, Hopkins captured the essence of the Rod Sykes enigma. A prominent member of *The Herald* band of committed imbibers who most work days travelled the back corridors from the downtown *Herald* building, opposite the Bay, to the former Empress Hotel on Sixth Avenue for late-morning, alcoholic fortification, Hopkins stood apart from his peers and their dour hostility to Rod.

"He (Rod) had and has the ability to establish a rapport with anyone. But he can't abide the foolish and the witless, and there's no reason to believe he should," Hopkins wrote. "I have known few men of such contrasts. I have winced on occasion because of his needless rudeness. I have also seen him walk into a room full of people he did not know personally and charm them to the point that he might well have hypnotized them … I don't know if any other Calgary mayor took more in the way of criticism and abuse … I would like to say he took the criticism and abuse with good grace. But I don't think he did … Sykes preferred to use the heavy artillery. He had a hand in some top men leaving the civic administration …And only rarely did he ever feel the need to explain his actions. Probably the best way to sum it up is to say he was easy to quarrel with. There was little point in debating him unless you were sure of your facts … He might not be remembered with love and affection but he won't be forgotten."[6]

2

FORMATIVE INFLUENCES

II **I arrived with the** Depression," was Rod Sykes' sardonic description of his coming into the world in May 1929 in Montreal. He was the first child for Leslie and Muriel Sykes, married just over a year earlier in what was still the undisputed economic and cultural centre of Canada. Leslie Sykes, then 31, was an electrical engineer, working at an entry-level job for Northern Electric. Muriel was the daughter of a merchant banker and adopted the role of stay-at-home mother, as many women of that day did.

The baby Sykes received three names and hence three initials: James Rodney Winter–J.R.W. James and Rodney were conventional enough, and as it turned out, Rodney was the name that stuck. That later morphed into Rod as his public persona evolved in his business and political careers. He remained Rodney for family though, and for Gisele, his wife, throughout their fifty-two years of marriage.

However, it was Winter that caught Rod's active imagination when he learned of possible ancestral connections to a murky character called Thomas Winter, who in the early 1600s was among the inner group of plotters recruited to help Guy Fawkes blow up the British Houses of Parliament. Winter and the other conspirators were caught before they acted on their dastardly plans and for his efforts, he enjoyed the fate befalling traitors of the day. He was hanged, drawn, and quartered. Rod felt Winter was an appropriate character to have in his genealogical portfolio.

The Sykes' more recent forefathers were Yorkshire folk. Rod's great-grandfather, originally an electrical engineer and the first of three generations of Sykes to achieve that designation, operated a wool mill in the industrial west

Yorkshire town of Huddersfield. He later specialized in textile and uniform manufacturing. The company did well, winning contracts to supply the British Army with uniforms. By the 1870s, great grandfather was "very solidly in business," according to Rod's research.

On the crest of that family success, great-grandfather Sykes sold the business and moved to Dublin in Ireland, where he set himself up as a consultant, invested in real estate, and enjoyed a life of greater leisure. He died in 1895, leaving a substantial estate to two sons.

Leslie Sykes was born in Dublin in 1898 into the well-off circumstances his father, James, had inherited from great-grandfather Sykes. Immersion in the privileges arising from commercial success understandably impacted Leslie Sykes' outlook. From Rod's strong impression, his father grew up as a dilettante, dabbling in numerous hobbies and personal interests, but not really applying himself to the disciplined pursuit of a career. He tasted the life of a Victorian era gentleman when most people were buckling down to full-time work. Seeking to be the third generation of electrical engineers in the Sykes family, Leslie attended private engineering school in London. After later moving to Canada, he received his qualifications from Trinity College in Toronto, but never fully practised his profession.

Two generations of the Sykes family returned to England, and then to Quebec, after the upheavals of the First World War before finally settling in the Saanich area of Victoria in 1921, where other well-to-do English people had also bought homes. Throughout this period, according to Rod, Leslie Sykes maintained his faith that the family's material success would last forever and continued to live off inherited capital.

Rod's mother, Muriel, also came from a comfortable background. Following her marriage to Leslie in Montreal, they travelled and enjoyed life at a time when the world economies were collapsing around them and dark anxieties gripped the population. "Then I showed up," as Rod dryly put it. When he was just seven months, the family returned to the Victoria area, with his father vaguely looking for work but remaining confident of ongoing help from his parents.

Leslie and Muriel Sykes found a place in Mills Landing, near Sooke, on Vancouver Island. Leslie Sykes eventually found work with Northern Mines in the Yukon and, apart from rare visits, left Muriel to look after the children with the income from her parents-in-law. During that time, Molly, one year younger than Rod, and Anne, five years his junior, were born. Rod remembered seeing little of his father after that. "He had an idea that he wouldn't have to look after the children when more interesting things caught his attention," was Rod's explanation. Rod tried to trace the family history, talking at length with his mother, but information tended to be "personal, emotional, and incomplete." Almost eight decades later, Rod was still uncomfortable discussing these difficult times.

Vividly he recalled an isolated but free boyhood in the rural area outside Victoria during the Depression. His mother, left largely on her own to raise the family while his father was away, taught him to read, write, and do his arithmetic. Apart from the chores of country living, chopping firewood, looking after the chickens and his rabbits, and, in Rod's caustic words, "doing what he was told in the best traditions of nineteenth century child-raising," he enjoyed considerable freedom.

At six, Rodney was learning to tend to the garden, sparking an interest in plants he turned to throughout his life, especially in retirement. He also took up stamp collecting, a passion that he stuck with for decades after and that he believed greatly expanded his knowledge about the world. He remained a keen member of the American Philatelic Society throughout his life. Late in retirement, he still liked to organize his collection and read philatelist publications. "I used stamp collecting as a relaxation," he said. Late in his last term, he told a fellow philatelist, "Stamp collecting is probably the most popular hobby in the world, and it has enormous value literally from the cradle to the grave."

All these experiences left him with mostly contented memories of his childhood. "You can't miss what you have never known, and these were happy times for a small boy with a great bump of curiosity." That bump of curiosity swelled within the young Rodney's psyche as prodigiously as the champion pumpkins in the nurtured Victoria area gardens—thanks to applications of an extraordinary fertilizer. That was the intellectual stimulation ignited by his reading at an early age. By five or six, this precocious boy was reading the *Boys' Own Paper* and *Chums Annual* editions piled in his home in stacks higher than himself and dating back to the turn of the century. Rod's floor-to-ceiling, book-lined study at his Elbow Park home is brimming today with back numbers of these once-popular and long-discontinued publications, qualifying him as one of their most prolific collectors in Canada.

"*Boys' Own* and *Chums* influenced me more than anything else during my formative years," Rod said. "They promoted good behaviour, independence of thought, honesty, and standing up for what is right. The Good Guys always won; the Bad Guys were always utterly contemptible."

Another circumstance of boyhood, critical to the man Rod became, was the freedom and independence he enjoyed as a youngster. His father was mostly absent; his mother pre-occupied with the struggle of raising a family on her own. Life was unstructured, and he didn't go to formal school until he was almost eight. He was isolated, making judgments about the world around him based less on what adults told him than on what he read. "Who needed parents when I had *Boys' Own* and *Chums*?" he asked. This was more than flippant or rhetorical.

The unambiguous morality Rod discovered in *Boys' Own* and *Chums* imprinted itself on his character and informed directly how he responded to situations throughout his later careers. For him, the world comprised just the good and bad, and both were easy to spot. This world view prompted him to tackle whatever he saw as wrong without regard for expediency or equivocation. His prevailing philosophy was to confront evil head-on and have faith he'd survive the collision. "I have defined personal views on morality and integrity," he said. In a hardly startling revelation, he added, "I would have said myself that I am highly opinionated." Many examples of that to come.

His reading of these publications also fostered an instinctive sympathy with underdogs. A sense of justice and fairness caught fire within him and burned all his life. Rod experienced adventures and came across characters that could well have been featured in those enticing publications. Later, to survive turmoil he became embroiled in, I suspect he often viewed himself as the central hero in a *Boys' Own* or *Chums* escapade. Seeing his real-life opponents in similar terms to these exaggerated and preposterous villains gave him a chance to find humour in tight situations. That gave him ammunition for his later mockery of adversaries.

While sparse, his parents' book shelves contained popular literature from the Victorian era. That exposed Rod, at a young age to books like *Vanity Fair* by William Thackeray or the *History of David Grieve* by Mrs. Humphry Ward. At six or seven, he was devouring *Pickwick Papers* and other works by Dickens. "If you're a lonely boy in the country, that's what you did; you read," was Rod's explanation. These satirical books, with their complex and sharp social commentary, introduced the young Rodney to wicked, foolish places, full of humbugs and pretensions. Rod clearly relished the memorable characters with exaggerated personalities and idiosyncratic villainy that Dickens depicted. I've wondered how a young boy could absorb all that irony. What would he make of those human caricatures? My conclusion was they helped build the jaundiced outlook, the gifts of skepticism and wit that became hallmarks of his later life.

Growing up, Rod became increasingly aware of how insular the Victoria of the pre-war period really was. "It was heavily influenced by English customs and attitudes from an earlier time when the now-retired military and civil servants of a vanishing colonial empire grew up and worked," he said. His scatological outbursts in adulthood—Rod often uttered the words "bullshit" and "chickenshit" during informal conversation—were in sharp contrast to the well-modulated and precise manner in which he otherwise spoke. They were likely symptoms of a rebellion against the stilted and restrictive language of the cliquish Victoria society his family was an integral part of.

Rod's isolated and bucolic life in Mills Landing came to a rude end in 1937 when his father found a job as a draftsman with an engineering firm in southeast England and decided to uproot his family to Kent. He enrolled Rod in a school called St. Dunstan's in the Canterbury area. It was called a preparatory school, a private institution considered a step-up from state school. "That was my first school. I was totally unprepared for it—and it for me," Rod said. The learning routine and having to sit still for long periods were penance enough.

After one year, Leslie Sykes decided the family should return to Victoria. His own father, James, had died, meaning the family home in Saanich was available. Once in Victoria, with war about to transform their lives, Leslie Sykes summoned the resolve to volunteer for the Victoria-based Canadian Scottish Reserves, where he qualified for a commission and prepared for service overseas. An already absent father now disappeared to the theatre of war in Europe, never to return on leave for six years. He persuaded Rod's mother that because Canada was at war, he couldn't come home. From his selfish perspective, he was enjoying a life of adventure. "My father seemed not to know how to handle his responsibilities," was Rod's conclusion. This set off in an already independent lad a period of estrangement and rebellion that made adolescence much harder and likely affected later relationships with authority figures.

In the meantime, his mother was again alone, raising with meagre resources her three children. "I don't know how she handled it," Rod said. "She had no car, no appliances, and little money." So hard was the impact that she suffered what people called a nervous breakdown and spent time in a nursing home. For about a year during that war period, young Rod and Molly were cared for in a foster home. Even toward the end of his life, he was loath to discuss that period.

His later enrollment at Victoria's private University School proved another shock for the slight, introverted Rodney, then nine. "I was the smallest boy and I was bullied." He despised bullying throughout his life, though some critics later suggested Rod could be one himself. However, there's no record of him pushing around the vulnerable or the defenceless. He was consistent in treating harshly only those in positions of authority.

During his one year at University School, Rod was mostly unhappy. He remembers the inhuman conditions and occasional sickness. "Hardening, it was called, making a man of me," Rod said ruefully. "They say that adversity moulds the character. I used to say I must be very mouldy."

His next school was Malvern House, a small private boarding school in Oak Bay close to the residence the family had inherited following the death of

Grandfather James Sykes. The proximity of the school allowed Rod to be what was termed a day boy, returning home each afternoon. "I had no friends, no sympathetic school mate," Rod remembered. "I had more detentions than anyone else, mostly because I didn't know what I was supposed to be doing." The school rule was: Five detentions, then the stick. When this first happened, eyeing the hapless waif, the master didn't thrash him. Instead, he handed Rodney some small scissors and ordered him to clip the grass around the playing fields. The thrashings came later. Rod agreed he was mischievous. He claimed, not without pride, that he had the record for canings and detentions.

Another bitter memory was being thrown in the pool, although he couldn't swim and had to be pulled out. He called the treatment at Malvern "thoughtlessly brutal". The Headmaster was the Rev. G.G. Scarrot. "He had a mail order ordination and was a really nasty piece of work," Rod noted. Much worse than Mr. Bumble or Bill Sikes in *Oliver Twist*. The school, he said, was "filled with hypocrites and liars who took advantage of their position."

An abiding fear afflicted him that he only had to turn a corner and trouble would be ready to pounce. As an understandable defence mechanism, he spent a lot of time in hiding, a tactic he practised years later whenever events grew particularly tense. He also forced himself to handle oppressive situations. The inner resilience that later served him so well began to form.

At thirteen, with his mother's urging, he began piano lessons. His sharp intellect gave him a natural aptitude to read music, and long, nimble fingers provided the ability to play it. "I enjoyed it and improved a lot," he said. "Bach was my favourite—so mathematical and intellectual." However, the teacher's habit of tapping a ruler on his hand if he made a mistake created a sour note. So, before his school days were over, he abandoned lessons and didn't touch a piano until the mid-1990s when he was semi-retired.

Moving to Oak Bay High School represented a positive step for the fast-growing and increasingly garrulous Rod. "I started to find myself," he said. He met first-class teachers, and for the first time in his life, realized there were some who took a direct interest in him. He needed a year to catch up academically from the lost years at Malvern, but he recalled the efforts of one teacher in particular, R.B. Bennett, to take him in hand. Rod described Bennett as tweed-jacket-and-pipe, no-nonsense type. "He spoke to me as a father should. He opened doors for me." Bennett became his math teacher during that first challenging year when Rodney failed the subject he later became so good at.

He played cricket and soccer. After leaving school, he pursued his enjoyment of cricket with the Christchurch Cricket Club as a wily, spin bowler. Rugby was different—he lacked the size, weight, or desire to succeed. He remembered one example of schoolboy cruelty when he was thrown into a scrum, and the players used him as a ball for a few frightening moments.

His voracious reading habits continued in his teen years. After devouring almost everything Dickens wrote, he soaked up Anthony Trollope's broad collection of Victorian novels and their glimpses into upper-middle-class English life. He became familiar with the works of Conan Doyle. This literary immersion spawned a disgust for the superficiality of the assigned school textbooks. "Conventional education provided a lot of information, not excitement or insight," was his damning judgment.

With more positive experiences in high school, Rod still didn't forget the effects of earlier bullying. After becoming a prefect in his last year at Oak Bay, he went out of his way to help the younger boys, particularly the bewildered ones. "I was aware of misery, the despair that people feel," he said. "Bullying is a less obvious form of torture." There is a consistent pattern through his life of helping the afflicted, whether they were citizens overwhelmed by the machinations of bureaucracy or young people bumping up against overbearing law enforcement authorities.

Because he lived an isolated life and was left largely to his own devices as a boy, he learned to be his own critic. Missing out on mature advice from parents, he adopted a habit of conducting post-mortems with himself on scrapes he had got into. It was an internal dialogue, or an examination of conscience, to use the Catholic Church term for it. "I made lots of wrong moves. I have lots of things to regret and be ashamed of."

His gregariousness awakened in high school and continued to flourish, its roots nurtured by his expanding self-confidence arising from his tangible achievements at school and in his work life. He revelled in the joy of his intellectual prowess. At school and afterwards, he learned to ask others for help. He began to lose his sense of being alone. At the same time, he developed a powerful streak of self-reliance. He trusted his own instincts in ways that were breathtaking for those around him. His faith in his own judgments and his willingness to articulate them became Rod Sykes hallmarks. Discarding his youthful guilt as an adult, he rarely wrung his hands in regret.

Otherwise, he stuck to a newly-discovered plan to get on with things to the best of his ability, using the facts at his disposal. Another lesson drilled into him from childhood stayed with him: "Do your homework."

Becoming more socially active at high school didn't mean Rod abandoned his fundamental reserve. He had difficulty revealing private thoughts. "I was brought up to believe you don't talk about internal emotions," he said. Yet he later developed the skill of engaging with people from all backgrounds, from humble immigrants to prime ministers and members of British royalty. He remained an enigma, though. "There are many more aspects to my personality that I have not paraded in public," he said. "People see the tip of the iceberg."

His increasingly judgmental mind stoked its share of youthful conflagrations. "When you start asking questions, boy, do you get slapped around," he said. A crisis came when, during his teens, the time came for confirmation into the Church of England in the Dominion of Canada, as the Anglican Church was called until 1955. In one of his first acts of open rebellion, Rod refused to conform to a ritual to which he felt no affinity. "I learned religion when I was young, the same way I learned multiplication tables. The noise was there, but not the meaning." Although he had to face the local minister, he held firm. "That cast me into outer darkness," he said. "I wasn't an atheist. I just didn't feel this [the Church of England liturgy or the presentation of its faith] was put to me in a constructive and believable way."

His stand against confirmation reinforced his status as a rebel. Rules were rules, he was told. In the wake of this family crisis, he began to assume an interest in Roman Catholicism. He took the initiative of asking a friend at school if his Catholic priest could talk to him. Those regular conversations lasted until Rod moved to Vancouver several years later. He met other Catholic adherents along the way who responded openly and wisely to his inquiring mind. The result was that at age twenty-five, Rod was confirmed as a Catholic and has maintained an association with the church ever since.

His political interests also blossomed while he was still at school. A world at war was an obvious subject for his sharp curiosity. He began his deep interest in history of all kinds. Among Rod's mementos from his formative years is a photograph of a former commissioner of B.C. Provincial Police called T.W.S. Parsons, who was the father of a school chum. "This is the picture of a man who saved me from being a juvenile delinquent," he said. "I had no father available during the war, so he appointed himself to that role. He provided support and discipline."

When the war ended, with Rod approaching seventeen and his last year of high school, Rod's father finally returned from Europe. Their estrangement erupted into outright conflict when Leslie, now in his late forties, showed up at the family home with the attitude that he was once again in charge. In the first seventeen years of Rod's life, his father had spent just two years at home, according to Rod's estimates. After so many years of not having an engaged father around, Rod wasn't going to knuckle under to his controlling ways now.

Bolstered by his academic success at school, young Rod had aspirations to be a lawyer. His logical, tenacious mind, his retentive powers, and his ability to pursue arguments with an orderly and impressive marshaling of facts made him suited for legal training and a profession in that field. But his father said it was out of the question. The only process Leslie Sykes knew about was the Inns of Court School of Law system in London for training young barristers, which could mean many years without an income. The prospect for studying law seemed financially impossible. It was hard for Rod to acknowledge his father was not interested in his son's future. Rod's mother was the parent pushing him to strive for professional qualifications.

In the interim, Rod took a business course at the private Sprott-Shaw Community College in Victoria, where he learned book-keeping, typing, and short-hand. Then he'd figure out how to earn a living. The arguments with his father became one row too many, and Rod, with hardly a penny to his name and still only seventeen, moved from the family home, cutting ties for several years.

Rod's first temporary jobs intensified his education in the school of hard knocks. Working on a Vancouver tug boat exposed him to people he called "tough men, the scum of the waterfront interested only in getting drunk or screwed." He lasted one month. There followed a stint as a choker man in logging camps, where he learned to wrap huge cable around felled trees so that they could be dragged and loaded onto trucks. It was dangerous, and "I was a skinny kid," but it was one more step in the toughening-up process. He was fired from there too. Next, he was a rod man with a survey crew. He wasn't trained or ready for that, either. The chief lesson from these experiences was self-reliance. "I also learned to recognize unfairness and injustice, and not let them consume me."

A major breakthrough for Rod's professional ambitions was hearing about a new system of articling in accounting. He could study, article, and get paid all at the same time. Learning and earning, they called it. "That sounded like a bonanza. I found I could survive," Rod said. His positive experiences with articling certainly instilled long-lasting support for the apprenticeship system that allows young people to learn a profession or a trade while being financially self-sufficient. "Apprenticeship is often a better decision than university," he said later.

With this in mind, he set out to find a chartered accounting firm that would indenture him. His quest led him to what he called a "bottom-of-the-heap" firm. It was a small practice with just three other articling students and the principal. Keen worker that he was, Rod received his articles within three months. The small firm provided him with a solid grounding in many aspects of accounting. It also brought him together with Tom Fleming, one of the other articling students, who became a lifelong friend. Tom offered good counsel as well as friendship, and they later worked together at Price Waterhouse.

At the end of his first year, when he was barely nineteen, Rod had a falling-out with the principal, which provided another lesson that served him well in later life. One of the principal's clients was a plumber having difficulty acquiring a loan for his business. Rod was directed to prepare an account for submission to persuade the bank to give the client the loan. Using the facts at his disposal, Rod realized he had no option but to show a poor outlook for the business. The principal, fearing the loss of a client, changed the figures in the report to paint a rosier picture, and told Rod to present it to the bank with his revisions. "I was upset and frightened," Rod remembered. "I would have to go along with patent fraud or burn my bridges at the firm." Just as his career was beginning to find traction, it could soon go off the road. When he met with the bank manager to make the presentation, his heart raced. Outwardly poker-faced, he handed over the doctored accounts, then coolly announced, "These figures have been changed. I don't think you can rely on them. These are not the accounts I prepared."

After Rod reported the incident to the Institute of Chartered Accountants in Vancouver, the response was immediate. Within two weeks, the principal was charged with what was called a disciplinary complaint, and he didn't speak to Rod again. The institute arranged for Rod to continue his career at another practitioner, which turned out to be Price Waterhouse. "They helped me find the best job available." The punishment for his original boss was a ban on taking in any more articling students.

Rod felt even more confident his feet were now on the right path. "Life became very different. There was a bright future at sea," he said. "I was working with people I could respect, honour, and obey. I became a learner in an environment with rigidly high standards. Besides, there's nothing like a little money and hard work to keep you out of trouble." Price Waterhouse brought him into contact with people like Allan Harris, a principal at the firm who became a significant mentor, and in Rod's words, "was a man of considerable integrity." His friend Tom Fleming was already at the firm, which helped secure his transfer. "They helped me settle in, and everything went well from there."

For the first sustained period since attending high school, life was good. He was living in rooming houses and meeting all kinds of people, young and old. His voracious reading habits from school continued. "I was always accumulating piecemeal information. I was very curious," Rod said. Memoirs and history were of particular interest. He learned to play chess and bridge. "I had a very lively and satisfying interior intellectual life," he said.

His reading about British royalty, the Indian partition, and the founding of Pakistan gave him insights into prominent figures including Earl Louis Mountbatten of Burma. That knowledge later led to extraordinary access to Mountbatten and the British Royal Family. So struck was Mountbatten with Rod's understandings that, when he came to Calgary, he would often ask his staff: "Find me a room where we can have a chat with Rod." This gave Rod direct access to a participant in some of the major events of the twentieth century.

With his relentless curiosity, Rod tended to associate with people who knew more than him. He learned that older, retired people were particularly rich sources of wisdom and knowledge. He met many Hong Kong immigrants, which enhanced his knowledge about China and Southeast Asia. This was useful in his later dealings with the Chinese community in Calgary.

In the meantime, putting his slender shoulder to the wheel, he achieved his Chartered Accountant designation. He travelled widely throughout Western Canada on behalf of Price Waterhouse. Then, after a seriously unconventional boyhood and equally idiosyncratic passage into manhood, his birthplace, Montreal, beckoned.

The original career plan with Price Waterhouse was for him to be transferred to Montreal for a short period before moving to the firm's Zurich office. "I wanted to see the world, but, first, I wanted to learn French," he explained. With his growing sense of wellbeing, he was keen to taste the social and cultural life of this vibrant bilingual city. The firm made the arrangements, and he lived there from 1954 to 1962.

During those initial years with Price Waterhouse, Rod put in painfully long hours completing assignments and preparing financial reports. Like a marathon runner, Rod could maintain a steady pace for long periods without wavering. "I worked more overtime than anyone else," he said. Discipline, performance, and getting on with the job were his guiding principles. Such was his reputation that he was chosen for many oddball investigations by the firm, ones that required relentless and fearless questioning. He learned to play the role of hatchet man, which proved useful later at the CPR and at City Hall.

He honed another attribute that would mark him out from the crowd. "I learned to tell clients things they might not want to hear," he explained. "There was no room for fudging, being nice, or deception. My job was to bring in audit work for Price Waterhouse."

This was the kind of drive he brought to Calgary City Hall. When you're in positions of responsibility, you have to be able to deliver bad news. Few have the stomach to do this. In politics, as in business, there's a tendency to believe you must get along, and therefore, go along with the prevailing or conventional wisdom. "That promotes fraudulence," said Rod. He learned to stand up for what he believed was right even if no one else in the room agreed with him. "I was the only politician I knew who could say 'no,'" Rod remembered. This approach later put him into all kinds of hot water. Suffice to say, his training in chartered accountancy reinforced what was a natural tendency to speak his mind, no matter the consequences.

Once in Montreal, he felt released from those boyhood years in Victoria where he had been constrained by the inward-looking world of his family and their contemporaries. Whereas he had grown up with a feeling he graphically described as "like a fly in the soup," he was now drying off and taking flight into exciting new territory. Rod continued to soak up information through his formal studies, his widespread reading, as well as his informal contacts with others. He built on his ability to engage people and draw them out in lively conversation.

His religious curiosity, already piqued during his years in Vancouver, found further stimulation when he connected with Father John McDonald, a Jesuit priest in Montreal. Throughout his life, Rod shared with the Jesuits a commitment to the principles of social justice and a belief in the power of education.

As an information sponge, Rod had taken correspondence courses in mineralogy while at school. The learning he acquired likely helped years later when he advised the CPR on resource development. While articling, he took extra-curricular courses in German and Spanish. He launched himself into Toastmasters and continued to perfect his life-long facility for the precise verbal articulation of the tide of judgments and thoughts that swept through his active mind.

In Montreal, with the letters CA behind his already well-initialled name, Rod enrolled in an economics degree program at Sir George Williams University, in the centre of the bustling city. He was motivated by the conviction that to get ahead required amassing the most qualifications possible.

Rod was living and working in Montreal during the last of the Maurice Duplessis years, when traditionalism and a resistance to more contemporary values prevailed. The so-called Quiet Revolution, led by Jean Lesage from 1960-66, was still in the wings. In the late 1950s, when Rod was immersing himself in Montreal, a dichotomy between the French and English communities, the Catholics and the Protestants, plus a mutual suspicion and resentment, still characterized much of the city and Quebec society in general. They remained two distinct societies, as first noted by Governor-General Lord Durham in Canada's pre-confederation years and then immortalized by Canadian historian Hugh McLelland. However, Rod was comfortable in both.

Through meeting, falling in love with, and then marrying Gisele Seguin during this period, Rod sailed headlong into these stormy waters of bicultural complexity. Gisele was from a long-established Montreal family with deep French Canadian roots. When Rod and Gisele first dated, her brother Richard did his best to protect her from this English interloper. But the courtship continued, and Gisele's parents were friendlier. Within a year of meeting Gisele, Rod knew he had found his love match, as well as an equal for his wit. "Being married was the best thing that happened to me," he said. The welling tears and the hoarseness of his faltering voice reinforced the sincerity of those sentiments.

Rod had kept in touch with his mother back in Victoria, but made little contact with his father. When news of Rod's engagement to Gisele spread, his distraught father showed up in Montreal, confronting Rod and announcing his intention of preventing this marriage "to an inferior person with the wrong religion." For the entrenched English, Rod's liaison was like collaborating with the enemy. The meeting ended whatever relationship the father and son had. Rod, of course, was adamant about his course of action, and his father would have no influence at all. The breakdown between them was irrevocable.

At the same time, the reaction to the engagement by some Price Waterhouse colleagues stunned Rod. He was considered a good company man with an excellent career ahead of him. However, a partner at the firm warned him that marrying Gisele was not a good career move, that he needed a wife who would be more helpful in his advancement. "All my elementary emotions boiled within me," Rod said. "The idea that I would dump this girl for career reasons repelled me."

Gisele's family connections in Quebec go back four centuries, according to research by her sister Clare of the church records. Because the Catholic diocese still kept good documentation, Clare spent a long time learning about the Seguin family and their arrival from France in the 1600s. Gisele's father was an accountant who worked hard to see that all his six children received a solid education. He made sure they then pursued respectable professions— Gisele had trained in social work, the others in chartered accountancy, engineering, teaching, law, and government. "He was modest, serious, religious, and respectable," said Rod with pride.

Because the family, as well as Rod and Gisele, had modest means and couldn't afford a big wedding, the ceremony was conducted in a chapel at the Jesuit Loyola College, with Father McDonald officiating. The reception was similarly low-key. However, thanks to the generosity of a major client at Price Waterhouse who had taken a shine to Rod, the newly-weds enjoyed a five-day honeymoon at the upscale Park Plaza in New York. After driving down in Rod's older Chevrolet, they were delighted to find an expensive bottle of champagne in their room. "Gisele drank half and passed out," recalled Rod. "That champagne didn't receive its due appreciation." In his own defence, "we were both nervous."

The negative reaction to their nuptials provoked turmoil at a critical stage in Rod's career. The upheaval gave momentum to life-changing personal developments. Until then, Rod thought he would stay at Price Waterhouse all his working life. He was happy there, did challenging work, and liked most of the people.

One of the largest accounts within his responsibility was that of Canadian Pacific Railway, a celebrated business success intricately involved in the history of Canada. With his growing confidence, Rod wasn't afraid to criticize CPR's handling of its varied resources across Canada, including its oil and gas, forestry, real estate, chemicals, and metals holdings. This was a time when CPR was poised to better exploit these assets and become much more than a railway company. Ian Sinclair, then second in line to CPR's crusty president, N.R. (Buck) Crump, had taken a particular interest in this whiz-kid chartered accountant who rarely seemed at a loss for words. Sinclair later became CPR president in 1966 until 1972, and served as chairman and chief executive officer until 1981. Born in Winnipeg and a lawyer by training, Sinclair sat for five years as a senator, appointed by the Trudeau Liberals in 1983. He certainly made a favourable impression on Rod, then approaching thirty and ready to assume all kinds of responsibilities following his marriage to Gisele and the arrival of two sons.

Sinclair decided Rod was going to join the massive railway and transportation conglomerate. "You are going to work with me. You said we're poor resource managers, so you're going to help us," Rod recalled Sinclair telling him. "If you're not going to come and work for us, you're not going to stick around here doing the company's accounting." Rod at first demurred, but he was starting to realize he didn't want to be an accountant all his life. Besides, that sounded like an offer he couldn't refuse. By 1959, Sinclair proceeded to draw up a contract that would give Rod undefined but broad powers to serve the company's interests. Ready for another challenge, Rod accepted. "I was put in a situation where I wasn't sure of my authority," he said. But he knew he had backing from one of the company's most influential officers.

Rod's title was supervisor of economic projects in CPR's research area for non-transportation matters. His duties were to evaluate potential CPR assets and offer strategies to better exploit them. An early major assignment was to meet with McMillan Bloedel chairman Jack Klein and appraise the British Columbia forestry company's lumber assets that CPR was interested in acquiring. "I saw my position as an earnest seeker after the truth," Rod said caustically. He also appreciated that he had landed a good job with plenty of scope for his curious, lively, and combative mind. When he joined CPR, other new interests of the burgeoning company included potash development in Saskatchewan and land development in Calgary.

By then, Rod had long established a reputation for bold opinions. He could write and speak clearly. Lacking confidence growing up, he had learned to cope with his new career challenges. He still tried to maintain a modest air, however, and sought help from others when he didn't know the answers. "If you don't know, don't guess," became a mantra. "When you ask for help, it's amazing what help you'll receive."

The tough, experienced Sinclair became an important mentor for Rod, both in Montreal and later in Calgary. From 1960-62, Rod spent half of his time in Calgary on land issues or in British Columbia on resource matters. That meant long stretches away from home while Gisele looked after the growing family. The determination to get ahead drove him to even higher levels of work activity. His goal, however, "was always to find security for my family." He also acknowledged his commitment to CPR "was not a good formula for married life."

Although Rod had entertained thoughts of taking Gisele and the family to the West Coast to live, Calgary attracted him too, with its newness and aura of unfulfilled possibilities. Moving the railyards out of Calgary's downtown was a simmering topic in the city during the early 1960s. Utilizing its extensive downtown land holdings to better economic advantage was becoming a CPR pre-occupation, and Rod was acquiring a growing role in the company's land-use project. In fact, when he moved permanently to Calgary with Gisele and their now three children in 1962, Rod received the vague title of project manager for what the CPR called their Calgary land use study. CPR's inducement to Rod, particularly that of Sinclair, was, "You think you're so smart, show us what you're made of."

Harry Hays, then Calgary's mayor, was giving the CPR a particularly hard time, publicly accusing the company of being a poor citizen. Hays, like others in Calgary, saw the extensive network of tracks through the downtown area as a serious impediment to the commercial development of what they considered a blighted area. One Montreal evening at five o'clock, Rod was told, "You're on tomorrow's 7 a.m. Empress of Vancouver [train] to Calgary." The strict order: "Get the mayor off Mr. Crump's back." Becoming one of the main players in the push to shunt the CPR tracks out of central downtown catapulted Rod into the public limelight and sparked a controversial episode in Calgary's history that is still discussed today.

As well as giving a lot of advice that stuck with the still impressionable Rod, Sinclair demonstrated utmost confidence in the ambitious young executive, and exposed him to as much corporate inside information as possible. Rod clearly remembered Sinclair telling him, "You have all the authority you can take and hold. If you hit the rocks, give me a call, and I'll get you off. Once anyway."

Here Rod was, in his early thirties, virtually handed the keys to the company safe. He immediately appreciated that a man with undefined authority can do much more than someone with a specific job description. "This gave me far more authority. No title meant no limit to my powers," he said. How he used those powers and boosted his career to impressively higher levels will be related in the next chapter.

The rise in Rod's public profile and reputation, along with the rapid expansion of his circle of friends, acquaintances, and business contacts, represented a remarkable transformation for the once shy and isolated young boy from Victoria who suffered such humiliation in his early school days. Still the slender workaholic with geeky horn-rimmed glasses and yellowing buck teeth, Rod manifested in a range of challenging circumstances an impressive fortitude under pressure, leavened by an occasionally biting sense of humour and a surprising charm. By 1962, this brash young man was indeed ready to go west and embroil himself in some life-changing and epic adventures.

3
ON TRACK FOR PROMOTION

As much as Rod liked Quebec, he wondered what kind of career future he would enjoy there. Starting in 1960, he commuted back and forth from Montreal to the West, spending considerable time in Calgary and feeling increasingly comfortable there. When the Canadian Pacific Railway decided in 1962 he should reside permanently in Calgary, Gisele and their three children, James, Henry, and Mark, joined him in the move.

As a British immigrant arriving in Calgary in the mid-1960s after a brief stay in Montreal, I shared his view, expressed in later conversations, that society in Calgary was less stratified than in Montreal, and relationships among people were more informal. Although Calgary's reputation as a superfriendly, hospitable city was partly bombastic vanity, many newcomers like Rod were—and perhaps still are—able to enjoy a prevailing sense of opportunity waiting to be grasped. As an energy and high-tech centre, it is still a place of possibilities. It certainly was in the 1960s as the oil patch blossomed and the population rose as dramatically as the Bow River in spring. Despite the cowtown image, Calgary then had a high proportion of affluent, white-collar workers. A more cosmopolitan population was evolving, and the economy was humming. That Rod had a new and challenging position with a major Canadian company undoubtedly fired his cylinders too.

All was not sweetness and light, however. Rod quickly became aware of what he saw as a narrow, self-satisfied parochialism among some of the city's leaders. The smell of entitlement was hardly distinguishable from other odours emanating from places like the Stampede Grounds. Rod got the impression from some of the city's elite that the prairie town didn't necessarily welcome outsiders. He frequently told the story of the well-dressed, neatly coiffed, elderly lady stopping him one morning when he still worked for the CPR outside the Hudson's Bay store on Eighth Avenue. "I know who you are, Mr. Sykes," she said, "and I want to tell you I used to know everyone I saw on Eighth Avenue, and now I don't know anyone. We had such a nice little town until you came." From his perspective, she represented a large body of similar thought in Calgary at the time.

Moving to Calgary in 1963 was a huge change for Gisele. Already pre-occupied with the welfare of their three young sons, she had their first daughter, Marie-José, at the Holy Cross Hospital two years later. Ann-Marie was born three years after that to complete their lively quintet. As with so many young mothers uprooted to a new city, life for Gisele was initially isolating and challenging. "It was a rough start," Rod agreed. But her indomitable spirit and cheerful demeanor that I'm privileged to have witnessed soon attracted people to her as they settled into their spacious home in Elbow Park.

The CPR bosses assigned Rod to Calgary for the express purpose of, as he described it, cleaning up the CPR relocation mess by moving the main rail line out of the downtown, as well as investigating investment and development opportunities for the company on all its land west of Fort William, Ontario. This involved establishing a subsidiary called Marathon Realty, with its headquarters in Calgary and with Rod initially called assistant general manager. The name Marathon was Rod's choice. He may not have run a literal marathon, but he had read about them in British writer Alan Sillitoe's 1958 book, *Loneliness of the Long Distance Runner*. Perhaps not coincidentally, it's about a young man in a youth detention centre who finds solace in long-distance running with the encouragement of the institution's governor. Isolation, individuality, and rebellion are interconnecting themes.

The CPR 1960s relocation saga and the company's extensive development activities in the West raised Rod's profile in Calgary dramatically. His bosses considered him a good fighter, able to punch far above his weight. Although the rerouting of the railway track along the Bow River away from downtown did not occur in the end, as Rod's company and others in the city had intended, additional projects by CPR and Marathon Realty grabbed attention and had a huge impact on the city's and the province's economies.

The rail-line relocation effort, called the CP-City Project, began auspiciously enough. Harry Hays, mayor from 1959 to 1963, was among Rod's important early contacts. Enjoying a positive relationship with him, Rod was open about his respect for Hays' business acumen and political skills. He had less regard for Grant MacEwan, caretaker mayor who assumed the reins of power in 1963 when Hays won a Calgary federal seat for the Lester Pearson

Liberals and resigned from City Hall. Many notches lower in his estimation, though, was Calgary real estate appraiser Jack Leslie, elected mayor in 1965 and thrashed at the polls by Rod four years later in the most one-sided mayoralty race Calgarians had ever seen.

Rod's early impressions were clearly informed by the three civic leaders' responses to the rail line relocation issue. "You can't take away from Harry [Hays] that he got out and brought in the country's major investor (CPR) at just the right time," Rod said. "Nobody else did." However, an *Urban History Review* published online[1] suggested that, at the outset, a hefty majority of city council endorsed the proposal. Hays and Rod jointly unveiled the relocation plans in the spring of 1963. This followed extensive negotiations involving Rod between the City and the CPR over land matters, sharing of costs, taxation issues, and a host of other details. Calgary was an experiment to see if redevelopment around the blighted railway track area was possible. Removal of the tracks to the banks of the Bow River was incidental to that, Rod later claimed, and not the only option CPR had in mind. Whether that was the case or not, the south bank of the Bow River in Calgary had become, as the *Urban History Review* described it, "an eyesore, a decaying and derelict commercial site. A greasy zone of light industry."[2] It certainly seemed a favoured option for the track relocation.

A minority led by then Alderman Leslie remained adamantly opposed to any dealings with the CPR, however. When Harry Hays won the 1963 federal by-election as Liberal and entered the cabinet as federal minister of agriculture, the then alderman Grant MacEwan had to carry the ball for the city, first as acting mayor, then, following a municipal election, as mayor in his own right. Initially, he was a tepid supporter of the railway relocation scheme, insisting that ratepayers should approve any final agreement in a plebiscite.[3] Unlikely and awkward in the role of real estate developer, according to Rod's assessment, a diffident and bemused MacEwan had to handle the complex negotiations with the CPR, deal with the Province, and along with the City's chief commissioner, John Steel, persuade the public of the project's virtues. Rod critically felt that he didn't do a good job.

Substantial challengers to the proposal emerged. They included academics, planners, the local Council of Women, disaffected real estate interests, and others who instinctively distrusted the CPR, according to the *Urban History Review*'s account. The academics and planners condemned what they saw as piecemeal planning for downtown, biases in the studies justifying the economic plan, the city's apparent loss of control over CPR land development, lack of consideration to alternative routes for the rail line, and the misuse of the river bank for transportation links.[4]

The opposition by disaffected real estate interests was a particular sore point. Rod has long contended that former mayor Jack Leslie, with his real estate background, and others inside City Hall, had insinuated themselves into land speculation that, at best, was inappropriate. Some of their interests focused around the land along the banks of the Bow where the new track was supposed to go. The relocation would undermine their land profit plans, according to Rod's perspective. While still an alderman, Leslie fought hard against the relocation and proposed a motion for the city to abandon the plans. He was clearly no friend of Rod's. Things turned nastier with his election as mayor in 1965.

Rod offered a consistently scornful perspective of the Jack Leslie legacy to Calgary. He believed an inexcusable amount of historical revisionism has been perpetrated, particularly by Leslie's loyal wife, Jean, and by media such as *The Calgary Herald*, blinded by ignorance or an enduring maliciousness against Rod. He pointed to their rewriting of history again in stories about Jack Leslie that followed his death at ninety the end of 2010. "If it wasn't for Leslie's dogged efforts as an alderman in the early 1960s, downtown tracks would have run right along the Bow River's edge in Eau Claire, trampling Fort Calgary and forcing a costly tunnel as the public's access to Prince's Island," wrote reporter Jason Markusoff.[5] "Leslie would go on to be elected mayor a year after council killed that plan, and had a productive four-year term full of new highways, downtown redevelopment, and parks." *The Herald* quoted at length from Jean Leslie's 2005 self-published book, *Three Rivers Beckoned: Life & Times with Calgary Mayor Jack Leslie*. "Now, [referring to 1965 when Leslie became mayor] without a backward glance, Calgary went forward to the greatest five years in the history of her growth." This was just one example of Jean Leslie's wild imagination. Even *The Herald*, ever Leslie's sycophantic supporter, acknowledged less than two years before Rod trounced him in the 1969 election that Calgary downtown development was in the doldrums. "If Calgary is to keep up, it will have to snap out of its state of complacent lethargy and get some things rolling."[6] Just about the only thing rolling during Leslie's regime was CPR stock along its downtown tracks, together with CPR's urban renewal plans and other commercial, office, and industrial development, most of it spearheaded by the energetic Rod.

Even though Leslie was one of the most vociferous opponents of the rail relocation along the southern banks of the Bow River, Rod suspected other motivations beyond creating green space and a park along the riverbanks for the enjoyment of citizens. For a start, Leslie's "productive term," as *The Herald* called it in its panegyric, included his push for the delightfully named Downtown Penetrator, a multi-lane expressway the City wanted to build alongside the relocated tracks, originating east of downtown and dead-ending in the west. Also, one of the City's hired consultants, Van Ginkel Associates, reported quite emphatically, "the south bank of the river is not used at present. Indeed, this whole stretch along the river is completely lost to the community and in many instances is a disgrace."[7] There is little evidence of Leslie having tackled that issue. According to Jean Leslie, Jack was responsible for the clean-up of the Fort Calgary site at the confluence of the Bow and the Elbow Rivers. Rod's response was, "Fort Calgary was Sam Sanford's scrap metal yard in Leslie's time, and it didn't appear to worry him." With Alderman John Ayer's primary involvement, it was Rod who oversaw the development of Fort Calgary as a historic site in the early 1970s.

One account of the final demise in 1964 of the CPR track relocation saga[8] has the acrimonious controversy surrounding it wearing down both opponents and proponents of the plan. "Everyone's sick of it," Grant MacEwan, mayor at the time, is quoted as writing succinctly in his personal diary. Aldermen for the relocation even received death threats, according to the *Urban History Review* essay, "How Did Calgary Get Its River Parks?" But, as details of the plan came under closer examination, cost estimates soared. Apparently, at a council meeting on June 22, 1964, the mayor and aldermen voted ten to three against a continuation of negotiations with the CPR. The CPR downtown development was thus pronounced dead. As the same essay noted, the election of Leslie as mayor in 1965 might signify majority public backing for his determined and successful resistance to the project and council's rejection of it. Yet counter-intuitively, he was succeeded in the mayoralty in 1969 by Rod Sykes, the major proponent of the scheme.

Rod had a different, close-up view of the story, one that finds no corroboration in official accounts. Despite his contention that the Alberta government, after a rigorous review, okayed the relocation, council seemed not to know what to do. CPR vice-president Ian Sinclair then confidentially told Rod from Montreal that the City was demanding an additional $500,000 as a signing bonus for its approval. This was interpreted as a way of letting the City crow it had wrung an important concession from the giant corporation. The CPR, however, took the demand as a sign of bad faith at this stage of negotiations and rejected it out of hand. It was, as Rod called it, a classic shakedown. Rod was made privy to the demand "since after all I had been through and achieved in several hellish years, I was entitled to know that the project would be abandoned through no failure of mine."

Following the City-CP Plan collapse, there was no post mortem, said Rod. There was little or no media publicity, and City Hall behaved as if it wanted to pretend nothing had happened. No report was made to council or the public, as far as Rod recalled. In other words, citizens received no explanation for the episode. "As for me, my masters apologized for having to cancel the project," said Rod. "It was made clear that no black mark, such as usually accompanies failure, was attached to me. Small comfort." His job was to pick up the pieces, and the result was spectacular. It led to the building by Marathon Realty of Palliser Square, the Husky Tower, and other significant urban renewal schemes—all projects that Mayor Leslie, by any stretch of the imagination, could take no credit for.

University of Calgary professor and prolific author Max Foran recently completed a book on the CPR relocation and interviewed Rod extensively for it during 2011 and 2012. "Rod appears to shoot from the lip," he said in an interview. "But there is far more to him." While negotiating the relocation, he had to tread a fine line between his masters at the CPR and the public, according to Foran, who came to Calgary in 1963 and has written extensively on western Canadian urban, rural, and cultural topics. "My analysis of him is as much more of a diplomatic person than he's given credit for. He had to be a salesman. He had to be able to placate people. He wore many hats." With his auditor's mind, Rod also had the ability to grasp intricate details of a project and the big picture all at the same time. Foran marvelled at Rod's sense of certainty. However, "like a lot of people who are confident in their own positions, he has difficulty seeing other potentially valid motivations."

Meanwhile, Rod's suspicions about council members' land speculations and other land-assembly schemes by City Hall staff gave him an early insight into what he called the "greedy little people, dishonest public servants, incompetence and corruption in City Hall." The scenario was similar to that described by Mr. Justice Turcotte in his damning 1959 report on City Hall corruption. That report led to the end of then Mayor Don MacKay's career and that of some senior staff who were depicted in the report in a less than savory light. Among other revelations, the Turcotte Inquiry found that Mayor MacKay "borrowed" and never returned thirty-six bags of City-owned cement for a private construction project in Banff. It offered many other, more offensive examples of a mayor and senior City officials on the take. "And, here it was the early 1960s just as if the Turcotte Inquiry had never happened." Rod could only conclude: "What a mess."

Despite the derailing in 1964 of the track relocation plan, the next five years saw the construction by Marathon and various partners of projects throughout Alberta that far exceeded the already significant $90 million in development the CPR rail relocation was expected to generate. "Our investment and diversification in Alberta was the greatest in the country's history in any one province in a short length of time," Rod said years later.[9] So great was Marathon's influence—and, by extension, that of its ambitious and brash vice-president, Rod Sykes—that Rod was given the province's first Industrial Development Award in 1969 by then Premier Harry Strom. At the award ceremony, Strom noted that, directly or indirectly, CPR was involved in at least one-third of all industrial developments across Alberta during that period. The company invested hundreds of millions at a time when, in Rod's words, "a million was important money." With Marathon Realty projects all over the place, he rightly boasted.

"I helped kick off growth in Calgary and Alberta," Rod said. "CPR was investing more in this province than all other provinces combined." With his first-hand understanding of financing acquired as a Price Waterhouse auditor, combined with a quickly growing knowledge about zoning and other planning issues, Rod became CPR's go-to man.

Rod had a direct hand in farmland consolidation and development, Bow River Pipe Lines, Alta-Fresh Produce, CP Oil & Gas (now PanCanadian Oil), Great Canadian Oilsands (now Syncrude), Fording Coal, Cominco, Alberta Stockyards, CN/CP Telecommunications expansion, and the most modern, automated marshalling yard in the country right in Calgary. They provided thousands of jobs, and that added sturdy planks to Alberta's economic foundations. Other noteworthy industrial projects included the Strathcona Industrial park in Edmonton, as well as Calgary's Mayland Industrial Park and Ogden Industrial Park. "We planned, built, marketed, and developed them," said Rod. Marathon brought many industries to the city for the first time, like Bell Canada/Northern Telecom, now Nortel. "That was my job—to make it work," he added. "And I did."

In Calgary during the 1960s, Marathon was almost the only game in town. The Natural Resources Building on Ninth Avenue, One Palliser Square, and Mount Royal House behind the Palliser Hotel were just some of the other large projects they launched. Soaring above all these developments was the phallic Husky Tower, opened in 1968 as a daring symbol of Calgary's incipient confidence. Having the tallest tower in the Western Hemisphere at the time did wonders for the young city. To imply that, after 1967, Mayor Jack Leslie was the inspiration behind Calgary's building spurt, as Calgary writer Candis McLean suggested[10] or Jean Leslie wrote in her first self-serving book on Calgary's mayors,[11] is a perversion of reality.

Renamed the Calgary Tower two years after completion, the tower was built to provide impetus for further urban renewal in a stagnant downtown district, particularly along the rail tracks. It was Calgary's big dose of Viagra, as it were, for citizens having to endure what Rod saw as flaccid civic leadership during the mayoralty terms of Grant MacEwan and Jack Leslie. The intent was for a "spectacular attraction because we were in a blighted area," said Rod, responsible for the concept, the economic evaluation, the planning, and the construction. He was the mastermind behind it and deserves full credit for its dramatic appearance on the Calgary scene.

It was an expansive enterprise by a man bursting with ambition and at the height of his business career. He acknowledged later it was an "oddball" project. For example, he brought in a building contractor called AhlForm from the Ruhr region in Germany, a company that had never built a tower of this kind. However, it had constructed many of the high factory smokestacks that dotted the industrial heartland it came from and managed to transfer these skills quite appropriately to the Calgary project. In fact, the company helped pioneer what was a new-for-Canada continual concrete pour, slip-forming construction technique. With completion of the tower, Rod proved again he could get things done.

For a short time, the city by the Bow was home to the tallest structure in Canada until Toronto's TD Centre topped it. Today several Calgary office skyscrapers dwarf the tower, but its significance as a tourist attraction continues. During the 1988 Olympic Games in Calgary, a massive cauldron, fired by natural gas, was placed on the top, serving as the world's largest and highest Olympic Torch, burning for the Games' duration. The flame has been lit on other auspicious occasions since. The tower stands as testimony to Rod's successful years with Marathon.

It's also worth noting that the response by the City to the development application provided ammunition for what became a long-standing battle between the planning department and the single-minded maverick. "The planning department opposed approval on the basis, so far as I could tell, that if God meant us to climb so high, He would have made a zoning bylaw providing for such a structure," Rod said later in a typically sardonic sideswipe at the planners who initially bucked the structure.[12]

That the impressive torrent of activity described in this chapter stemmed from CPR's failure to relocate the railway tracks is further proof of Rod's resilience under fire. Rod liked to call his success "making lemonade out of lemons." Abandonment of the City-CP Plan "freed up capital that could then be invested in growth that we had identified as potential, if only capital could be attracted."[13] Front and centre throughout the hurly-burly of construction was this outspoken, some said arrogant, young hotshot with deceptively frail-looking frame. Almost half a century later, Rod was able to look back and say he was trying to encourage other business connections to follow Marathon's example. "Calgary was full of people who were asleep at the switch, afraid to take a risk, and ready to resent anyone who did." That's the type of Rod Sykes plain talk that either irked or thrilled people then as much as it does today.

CPR vice-president Ian Sinclair continued as an important mentor by offering advice and helping with introductions to a wide range of business and political leaders in western Canada. With Rod reporting regularly to him on the CP phone system, their communication was informal and personal.

Rod was by now a skilled negotiator, with the ability to improvise his plays, and they often discussed tactics. "Sometimes I didn't know what was going to come at me, but I was light on my feet," he said. It's hard to imagine, but Sinclair told him he was too soft in his approach. That surprised Rod, who by then didn't consider himself gentle. "When you have someone down, don't walk away with them still breathing," was Sinclair's counsel. "Especially if a man is a nasty piece of work, you should put him away." That fitted Rod's combative style, of course.

Rod developed other tactics for what he called "engaging the enemy." He learned to blindside people, or surprise them with his vehemence. Get them off balance, he said. "I wanted people to know I meant what I said. I'm not trying to bullshit you. That's how I dealt with all people, businessmen and unions. I was known as a head butter. I wasn't romancing people."

He consciously developed a style of plain, direct language. "Being outspoken offends people unaccustomed to straight talk. They resent their inability to cope with what they're being told," he said. "If I had been a really nice guy, I could have been even more successful in politics or business, but I would have had to deal with the difficulty of living with myself." He acknowledged the personal costs of being a prickly character. "I'm not abrasive socially," he said. But on the job, "I'm like an animal that bites when it's threatened."

Buck Crump, meanwhile, thought Rod talked too much. He complained about Rod having authority over the sale and purchase of land. "We've given that man authority I never had," said Crump. Other vice-presidents learned to trust him, though. That was important for Rod. Later at City Hall, it was much more important for people to trust him than to like him.

As part of the CPR expansion of its Calgary operations, Rod conducted an economic base study. He applied his usual thoroughness to this huge task, meeting with countless citizens, community groups, labour union officials, local and provincial politicians, other working people, and business organizations. "I was trying to plot and forecast future growth and I had to understand what it might be and how the city could cope with it," he said. As a result, his grasp of Calgary flourished as quickly and as powerfully as the sturdy balsam poplars in the city's river valleys. Through face-to-face contact and written information and reports, he became familiar with Calgary's neighbourhoods and their unique characteristics.

The McNally Commission on Metropolitan Growth in Calgary and Edmonton, released in 1956, became an important reference point for his discernment of Calgary's character and the dynamics of its growth. As mayor, he said he "used it, applied it, and quoted it throughout my three terms." Calgary was a prosperous and growing city surrounded by settlements that, from Rod's observations, shared the growth but not the prosperity. As a result of the McNally Report, huge tracts were annexed into the city from 1956 to 1961, boosting almost fourfold the city's area.[14] This included neighbourhoods like Ogden, Forest Lawn, Montgomery, and Bowness where "the poor people, the newcomers, the strugglers lived without the level of municipal services enjoyed by other areas. They were looked on as slums, as substandard areas where you couldn't get the mortgages to build a house," Rod said during our conversations later in his life. "They were looked down on in very real ways, and life was made harder for the immigrants ... unpaved streets, poor water services, if any, poor sewage disposal, untested wells, and so on." Improving these standards became a condition for annexation following the McNally Report. But, according to Rod, city commitments were not honoured until he became mayor. "We were in default on every undertaking."

Rod directed much of his analysis to downtown neighbourhoods. For example, when the City-CP Plan for track relocation along the Bow River came up, the City pushed its own plans for a cross-town freeway—the Downtown Penetrator—to run parallel to the new track. The result would mean the destruction of an increasingly vital Chinatown to make way for ramps onto an elevated Centre Street Bridge, the raising of veterans' homes in Eau Claire, and the end of Inglewood on the east end. Under the plans, Inglewood was to be converted from a self-contained, small residential and business neighbourhood to a light industrial park from which truck traffic could feed onto the proposed freeway. "These plans made no accommodation for the older residents at all; they were to go elsewhere when their property was taken," said Rod. All these plans were official policy in 1969 when, as victorious mayor, he tore them up. But in the years leading up to his takeover of City Hall, Rod was already aware of all these matters and familiar with the people involved. He was immersed in community politics in the broadest sense. In his own words, he was "all over the place," having to justify CPR investment in the city. "I got enormous satisfaction out of this activity."

Another offshoot of this activity was his involvement with the Chinese community. Rod said he participated in the creation of the Sien Lok Society in the mid-1960s, as Chinese businessmen fretted about urban renewal, the Downtown Penetrator and the potential subsequent loss of Chinatown and its unique attributes. By supporting Sien Lok's mission to work for the betterment of Calgary's Chinatown and the city's Chinese community, Rod enjoyed positive associations with the Chinese Canadians throughout his business career and later as mayor. He was a frequent guest beyond the mysterious curtain that separated the Chinese community from the rest of the city. His first campaign manager was businessman George Ho Lem, also an early participant in Sien Lok. Chinatown has preserved its special identity for more than a century since it was first settled. With an estimated population of more than 74,000,[15] Chinese Canadians continue to exert considerable and favourable influence on Calgary.

While at Marathon, making speeches to many varied audiences became part of Rod's responsibilities. His well-modulated and precise speaking style came across as confident. It was surprising, therefore, to hear him relate what happened at one of his first speech assignments in Calgary while he was still commuting from Montreal. The Chamber of Commerce had asked him to address members at a luncheon in the sedate and grand Palliser Hotel. He wasn't the first to experience this terror and won't be the last. Still in his early thirties, as he stood at the podium and looked out at the sea of well-fed, smugly expectant faces focussing on his slight frame, he was aware of the classic symptoms of stage fright: his heart thumping, his tongue sticking to the roof of his mouth, dread in his stomach, and a blurring of the words on his note sheet. He stood there paralysed for what seemed like minutes, unable to deliver a sound. "It was a horrible experience," he said. Yet he somehow carried on, and vowed to never let that happen again. He was determined he would not make a fool of himself in this way. He had taken Toastmasters while in Montreal and continued to accept speaking invitations. "This all comes under the heading of survival," he could say with some levity, fifty years and thousands of speeches and presentations later.

"I just got into the habit of speaking," he said. "I knew what I was speaking about, and that made it easier." Just before Rod stepped down as mayor, I witnessed with trepidation his presentation at halftime during a Calgary Stampeders' football game. When he was introduced, the 30,000 people there booed lustily, just as crowds are wont to do when they have to listen to politicians at sports events. Rod stood there a moment, a lone, vulnerable, and gaunt figure surveying the crowd. "Well, that's recognition for you," came his cheerful words, instantly turning boos into laughter and applause. What aplomb, what nerve, what self-confidence! He'd come a long way since that Palliser speech in the early 1960s.

An active member of the civic affairs committee of the Calgary Chamber of Commerce, Rod spoke to many other chambers throughout Alberta during his pre-mayoralty years in the 1960s. Invariably, he conveyed a bluntness that was refreshing to some and shocking to others. He recalled going for a speaking engagement at Grande Prairie in northwestern Alberta and telling members "my first impression as I drove into town was that I should keep on driving." He was frank, he said, but he gave them specific recommendations too.

When I was a young reporter with *The Lethbridge Herald*, I was asked to cover a visit by Rod to the southern Alberta city in 1966. The CPR had a stake in Lethbridge, as it did in just about every city and town on the prairies.

The speaking engagement was an after-lunch affair for the local chamber. Attendees had enjoyed the usual roast beef and potatoes with gravy, and were settling into the routine of a second cup of coffee and a few soothing words from the guest speaker when Rod was introduced. The somnolent audience and a similarly drowsy reporter almost choked on their coffees when this earnest guest immediately began in his clearly enunciated way to castigate the Lethbridge chamber as one of the sleepiest he had ever come across. He told his stunned audience that the organization was stagnant, with members doing nothing about their problems and failing to grasp their opportunities. Reminded years later of this event, he said, "If people asked me to talk, they wanted straight talk, and they bloody well got it." As a then-wet-behind-the-ears reporter, I never forgot the occasion and this tough-talking, seemingly fearless businessman.

The 1960s was a decade of mostly successes for the brazen tycoon. "I was happy with my job. I had achievements, I had built a solid reputation," Rod said. "I was a workaholic, and I was in charge." The people he answered to were in Montreal, thousands of kilometres away. Negotiating CPR projects with the governments of all the western provinces, he knew first-hand the premiers and their senior staff. At the same time, he enjoyed a good relationship with many segments of the Calgary population. "It was an exciting, satisfying, and dynamic situation."

Intimations had occurred earlier in the 1960s from Herb Pickard, a colourful, energetic CPR manager, that Rod might be asked to return to the Montreal head office. Rod likened his situation to that of a governor called back to Rome after serving in a far-flung corner of the glorious empire. Montreal was the seat of power for the CPR. At the time, Rod had said no. After the tower project was done, Herb Pickard again suggested Rod would be expected to go to Montreal. "I was having fun … I said no again." He realized he could be transferred anywhere to help manage CPR's global holdings, from England to Bermuda.

A conclusion began to form in Rod's mind. He wanted to remain in Calgary, where he felt increasingly more at home and where his talents were publicly recognized. He was also aware you don't say no to Buck Crump several times and get away with it. "CPR was still a dictatorship and not always a benevolent one," said Rod. He knew he could be cast adrift as fast as an uncoupled rail car on a remote siding. However, by now Rod was confident in his knowledge of financing and municipal planning. Business opportunities were rampant. He told himself, "If you're so smart, why can't you stand on your own two feet?" But other pre-occupations were starting to invade his thoughts that would change his life and connections with Calgary more profoundly than he could ever imagine.

4
AN EIGHT-YEAR SENTENCE

Planting roots in Calgary had Rod digging around in a tangled weed patch. Aware of his ongoing obligations to the CPR and personal loyalty to people like Ian Sinclair, who had provided so much opportunity and encouragement, he sought to discuss with them his changing aspirations. Another confidant, Herb Pickard, had by now returned from Calgary to Montreal. However, the attention of these men was directed at expanding CPR operations, and they could spare little time to meet. "I had great difficulty getting advice, feedback, or counsel from my bosses," said Rod. They were not only unavailable; the idea that Rod could quit was incomprehensible. "I couldn't talk to them about my dilemma." Yet, he couldn't look for work behind their backs. They would be incredulous a man in his position would want to leave. From Rod's perspective, if he did leave, he wanted to go on good terms.

Rod wasn't clear whether he had hinted an interest in municipal politics, but Sinclair once told him, "You couldn't get elected as a dog catcher." Rod himself acknowledged he was not known as sensitive, and was not considered likely to become sympathetic and compassionate in public office.

What first brought Rod's political aspirations to light were Alderman Jack Davis and his engineering firm. Alderman Davis was by 1969 one of the most active and confident members of the Jack Leslie council. One day, according to Rod, Davis visited him in his Natural Resources Building office on Ninth Avenue. Davis got right to the point: "I'm taking over the Ninth Avenue parking lots." Rod wasn't sure whether he meant the City or himself. At the time, Calgary Parking, with manager Bert Stead, held a term lease, which was coming up for renewal. Rod had been talking with Stead, negotiating a lease increase, and described him as a "decent man who met his commitments." Davis had heard of the negotiations and saw an opportunity to insinuate himself into them. The ambiguity of whether Davis was acting for himself or for the City only heightened Rod's suspicions. "His manner and approach indicated shakedown for his own advantage. He got a short answer," said Rod. "I considered this obvious conflict. The man is competent, but arrogant. To say I chucked him out of the office was not far from reality."

That planted in Rod the seed to run for council as an alderman. He already felt uncomfortable about some elected and senior administration officials in City Hall. And of course, his Marathon dealings had given him an inside track on City contacts. "I felt angry. I thought I could send a message by sitting as an alderman, but I was not realistic. I believed I could do the job in my spare time." He managed to chat briefly with Herb Packard about his political plan, and the Marathon chairman said, "go ahead and run." Packard was constantly on the move, though, and had little time for in-depth conversation.

Interviewed by *Albertan* reporter Tom Kennedy, Rod explained his plans to run as alderman in the upcoming civic election less than three months away. "Frustrated by the general direction of local politics, he pledged to voice, within City Hall, the concern of the average taxpayer from a position that will not be aligned to vested interests of big business or to the labour vote of Calgary," Kennedy wrote. "Known for his outspoken criticism of many aspects of Calgary's situation, Sykes is determined to 'get things done.' "[1] He quoted a frequently-used metaphor: "There are always a few sore toes around me." For a citizen with a reputation for outspokenness, the time had come "to make good my words or eat them."

Planning to run for alderman in a City ward where the incumbent intended to resign, Rod picked Ward 6 in the city's southwest. Because of Rod's already high public profile, another declared candidate in Ward 6, Tom Priddle, who called himself a public relations consultant, laid traps for his for-midable opponent. Rod heard that eight community association presidents in the ward were planning to announce their endorsement of the Somersetshire, England-born Priddle for alderman. The only trouble was, Priddle himself had orchestrated the announcement, and the eight presidents had no mandate to offer such support anyway. After Rod attended the announcement meeting and called him out on this ruse, Priddle had to retract his claim of commu-nity backing and apologise for slurs he had directed at Rod.[2] The election race was off to a tough start. As Rod enjoyed warning foes, "You don't get into a pissing match with a skunk."

Rod had little respect for Priddle, who ended up serving two terms as alderman. When council voted themselves a salary increase in 1973, Priddle did some grandstanding, telling the media he would donate the extra money and not accept it for himself. At the time, there were suggestions his estranged wife was in difficult financial circumstances. This prompted Rod's terse message: "I note public statements to the effect you … are considering giving your salary away to charity. Don't you think it would be a generous gesture were you to make this increase … available to your wife and children?"[3] Rod had no compunction about wading into a personal family matter like this.

As the 1969 election drew closer, *Albertan* columnist Fred Kennedy, by then venerated as one of the deans of Alberta journalism and writing under the motto "I write as I please," proclaimed about Rod:

The top echelon of the local business community has not yet recovered from the shock of having one of their members deciding to run for council. Why, the fellow must be out of his tree. These jobs on council were for people who needed the money. How could he possibly spend all this time away from his very exacting business responsibilities and clubs to listen to the proletariat worry about stray dogs and cats? ... But Rod Sykes is not out of his mind ... He is merely one of the very few able businessmen in the community who has suddenly realized that unless something is done to halt uninspired planning and administration at city hall, the day will come when Calgarians will have to pay the bill in full ... If the voters of Ward 6 don't elect this man by an overwhelming majority, they are the ones who are out of their minds.[4]

It didn't hurt to have Fred Kennedy on board. He was sixty-nine by then, and had worked on and off in Calgary media for close to half a century, covering everything from sports to politics. He had closely chronicled Alberta's Social Credit years, angering Premier William Aberhart and acquiring a reputation for fearless reporting. He worked as publicity director for the Calgary Stampede for eight years before joining *The Albertan* in 1965. Short, stocky, and confident in his own wisdom, he was by this time losing his eyesight. His type-written copy was a jumble of misspellings and transpositions, but editors at *The Albertan* had orders never to change a word without his permission. I witnessed these edicts first hand as an *Albertan* editor. At first enthusiastically in favour of Rod, Kennedy later turned against him.

Rod had clear objectives for running for alderman, including the imposition of more transparency and accountability on council and administration, and tighter discipline over spending. But it was his earlier chat with Jack Davis and his anger over his perceptions of how some council members behaved in regard to downtown land investment that added fuel to the fire of Rod's political aspirations. He spoke widely about his candidacy. "I told people of the need to clean things up at City Hall." At this stage, however, he had not accounted for the involvement of incumbent Mayor Jack Leslie in the nefarious land dealings he'd heard about.

By then, Leslie had announced his intention of seeking another term as mayor. With what he considered abject naivety, Rod made an appointment to meet him. Once in Leslie's office, he told the mayor he would back him in his mayoralty bid, then added, "I think there are things you should know and do something about." He proceeded to outline his concerns about some aldermen's land dealings. The grey-haired Leslie was silent for a moment, then, according to Rod's account, turned and slowly uttered the words, "If you interfere in things that don't concern you, neither you nor your company are going to do business in Calgary."

One sentence dramatically transformed Rod's life. Confronting this out-right threat, Rod felt stunned, and rage boiled up. He hadn't faced such prov-ocation before. If he tackled the corruption at City Hall, he would have no future in Calgary. The conversation ended quickly, and Rod went home, his thoughts in turmoil. He chose not to tell Gisele about his encounter, but the realization overwhelmed him: Running for council would lead to retaliation, not only against him, but against his employer. A private gang is running the place, he said to himself. "To say I agonized over this is not an exaggeration. How could I face myself, how could I look myself in the mirror and avoid the issue?" Just as he had confronted the accounting firm owner who fudged financial records two decades earlier, Rod knew he couldn't turn back, what-ever the consequences. "I had put myself in an awful position. Leslie was an enemy to myself and my company. I had really put my foot in things."

That Thursday night around 10 p.m., a miracle occurred, and a lightning rod flashed from the clouds. Former mayor and now-Senator Harry Hays called from Ottawa. Media speculation previously had Hays, for whom Rod had considerable respect, returning to Calgary and announcing his candidacy for mayor against his old rival Leslie before nominations closed in the middle of September. Hays' tone was urgent. "I'm coming back to Calgary. The papers say I'm running for mayor, but I'm not. I want you to run and clean things up." He then offered money and people power to help. Rod was cornered. "I didn't know how this had happened, but here I was in this inextricable position. And here was Harry Hays telling me 'Don't run for council, run for mayor.' I didn't even know how people got to be politicians … I didn't know anything about campaigning."

The next day, Rod kept his own counsel, the dilemma still reverberating through his mind. On the Saturday, he told the few members present at the Calgary Press Club of his intentions. He had no campaign manager, no litera-ture, nothing. "As in a lot of things, I made a quick decision and had to stand behind it." Complicating the decision was the realization he would have to resign from his plum position with Marathon. That meant renouncing a good income and security for him and his family to enter a highly public competi-tion for a much lower-paying job—then $21,000 a year [about $140,000 in 2015 dollars]—that would involve a degree of public scrutiny he'd never expe-rienced before. He knew he would have to be seen as acting entirely indepen-dently of the company he'd had such success with for eleven years.

He sent a curt telegram to the CPR in Montreal: "I resign today." Herb Pickard, the Marathon chairman with whom Rod had got on well, was furious and didn't speak to him for years after. "He felt betrayed. I felt betrayed too, because I had tried for many months to talk to him about my career." Rod recalled in later life the shame he felt over resigning so quickly without warning. "I let my employer down badly."

Telling Gisele and the children after making the decision provoked similar remorse. "I treated my wife and family unfairly. I treated my company unfairly." Tears and recriminations were unavoidable. How could he have made such a commitment without at least talking with his family? Rod felt stunned, tired, a sense of fatalism churning through his skinny frame. "I was like the ship's crew member walking the plank."

There was little exultation in the Sykes household over *The Herald* headline "Sykes Steps In," and the every-hour announcements on the local radio stations regarding Rod's candidacy. "We are suffering from a lack of leadership, a lack of purpose, and a general confusion of priorities," Rod was quoted as saying.[5] "There must be drastic reform at City Hall in the conduct of the taxpayers' business." Adding to the drama was his gutsy prediction of holding the tax line for the following year. For the first of many times, Rod talked about "good housekeeping," and "cleaning up City Hall."

Wordy Fred Kennedy wrote, "Those burgesses of our fair city who have been yearning for years for a knock 'em down drag 'em out battle for the mayoralty in the annual civic elections are going to get their wish ... If there was ever a man born to raise 'hell', that man is Rod Sykes."[6] He added ominously, though, "I do not envy Mr. Sykes in his task of taking on the political machine which has ruled city hall for lo these many years." He warned that a weak council and a craven board of commissioners had reduced the role of mayor to "an almost honorary position." A stung Leslie "Comes Out Fighting," said another headline.[7] The battle was on.

Meanwhile, Harry Hays followed through on his assurances. Offers of money multiplied, and enthusiastic volunteers showed up for Rod's campaign. "I had unexpected help from all over the place." Provincial Social Credit MLA Roy Wilson also proved to be a pillar of strength. Wilson had been campaign chairman in Premier Harry Strom's successful Alberta Social Credit leadership quest a year earlier. While Hays could bring in money and people from his federal contacts, Wilson could do the same from his extensive connections within the provincial Socred political machine.

George Ho Lem, born in Calgary in 1918 as the son of Mary Ho Lem, the first recorded female Chinese resident of Calgary, came on board as campaign chairman. Involved in the Chinese Canadian community and the wider city, he was active for many years in land development, and the restaurant and laundry businesses. He served on City Council from 1959-65, becoming the first Chinese Canadian to achieve that distinction anywhere in Canada,[8] and in the Alberta Legislature during the early 1970s as a Socred MLA. Relying on his wits and guile, he was successful as a self-made business man too. As a

horse breeder, he won two Alberta derbies and was once declared thorough-
bred breeder of the year. He also served as a director of Stampede Park for
eighteen years.

Rod filed his official mayoralty nomination papers just five days before
nomination deadline, and was sharpening his public message that City
Hall under the Leslie regime was a private club that he was going to break
up. "That resonated with people," Rod said. When the campaign committee
started its regular meetings in an empty store on Eighth Avenue near First
Street S.E. (Nick Perry's store), Rod counted representatives from twenty-
one different ethnic and linguistic backgrounds sitting around the table. "I
had already established a position in the business community, in organizations such as the Chamber of Commerce and Rotary Club, and other levers
of influence. I had much better contacts than Leslie had," Rod said. "Leslie
regarded the CPR as the enemy, and he regarded me as associated with Harry
Hays (a long-time Leslie nemesis who had beaten him in a 1963 federal election). There was jealousy, rivalry, and hate going back a long time to the CPR
relocation issues."

Did Rod sense divine approval for this candidacy that had grabbed his
attention so urgently? "I don't believe in these sorts of things," was Rod's
response. "I felt I had a job to do." However, the old Anglican hymn reverber-
ated in his head: "Fight the good fight with all thy might." That he was already
replaced at Marathon by Fred Jaremchuk just days after filing nomination
papers also gave him the realization of bridges burned. The entry into the
mayoralty race of city lawyer Alfred Harris complicated matters somewhat,
but the main event was clearly Sykes vs. Leslie. Rod realized it was important
to attend all the open forums being organized. Leslie missed a couple of the
forums early on and noted his participation in the process might be limited,
thus undermining his cause. Still, he was confident he would win re-election.
Rod pounced on the chance to declare to the three hundred people packing
one forum: "He hasn't the guts to face the people … the mayor should have to
stand on his record."

The Herald gave Leslie credit for seeking a television debate when, in fact,
it was Sykes and Harris who pushed for it.[9] Rod was good on television while
Leslie looked shifty, and Harris was earnest and grumpy. The television forum
probably helped Rod the most. He came across as calm and in control on the
program that played on every Calgary television station—a first for the city.

Rod's promise of no property tax hikes was by now making the headlines.
It was called holding the tax line. Calgary's disgraceful housing record, suspicions hanging over a secrecy-obsessed City Hall, misspending on the Eighth
Avenue mall, botched urban renewal, and proposals for a public registry of
elected officials' land holdings to avoid conflict of interest concerns were

among other issues that put Leslie on the defensive. The planning department was also in Rod's sights.

The highly competitive Rod was eager to take any advantage he could. He easily won a sulky race organized at Stampede Park for the three candidates. George Ho Lem doubtlessly had a hand in making sure Rod had the most fleet-footed horse, but there's no mistaking Rod's gleeful grin after he crossed the finish line. Ho Lem stuck close to Rod in the first part of the campaign. "He served a useful purpose," said Rod. But the wily laundromat and dry-cleaning business owner didn't like Rod's propensity for washing dirty linen in public, particularly as it pertained to corruption and conflict of interest at City Hall. Ho Lem's style was much less direct, and he withdrew from the campaign team because Rod was antagonizing too many people for Ho Lem's sensitivities. "But that was the only way I could campaign," Rod protested. The media surprisingly missed reporting on Ho Lem's disappearance.

A shocking aspect to the campaign was a smear campaign directed against Rod and Gisele that prompted a request by Leslie for Police Chief Duke Kent to have the matter formally investigated. It must have irked Leslie, but he had no choice. Calls to Rod's campaign office reviled him for his Catholic and French Canadian associations. One person figured calling Rod a Jew would hurt his chances—a curious way of thinking because Rod made Jews welcome on his campaign committee. In fact, for his second campaign, I estimated that two-thirds of those around the table were Jewish. However, this was not long past the time when prominent clubs in Calgary and elsewhere practised a shameless no-Jews policy.

A call on the Sykes' phone line described Gisele as "a French Canadian whore." Catholic Bishop Paul O'Byrne denounced the smears on television as an "evil thing that came into our home." Vicar-General of the Roman Catholic diocese of Calgary Very Rev. John J. O'Brien also castigated the calls. "I'm sure these calls are being made by only a few bigots," said Monsignor O'Brien.[10] Senator Harry Hays described as "disgraceful" calls his wife received stating that Rod had been fired from Marathon and asking her to phone six others with that so-called information.[11]

Police never produced any formal conclusions on their investigations, but Rod said Mike Horsey, a public relations practitioner who had joined his campaign team and who would go on to be his bright and imaginative first executive assistant, called an acquaintance working in the Leslie campaign office to warn them the police were zeroing in on whoever was behind these nasty calls. That put a temporary stop to them, although the calls and the harassment returned after Rod became mayor. Rod and Mike speculated about the person with the seriously misplaced loyalty to Leslie who they believed initiated the ugly campaign. Rod never forgot Leslie telling him in private that he had no right to run for public office after such a short time in the city. Gisele, meanwhile, continued to be protective of the children, now aged from three to twelve. "I'm trying to ensure they don't lose their balance because of this [campaign]," Gisele told one reporter. "No matter what their father does, the children feel secure."[12]

Mike Horsey did a wonderful job during the campaign, according to Rod. "Mike was very sharp on public relations matters." His ability to analyse media coverage was particularly helpful. A former reporter with the Vancouver Sun, who had spent some time in public relations, Horsey just showed up at the Sykes' first campaign headquarters at age twenty-seven, just as how mythology had former waiter Rod Love appearing off the street in Ralph Klein's first Calgary mayoralty campaign more than a decade later. Horsey's wit, playfulness, and creative mind, plus his knowledge about the media and public relations, were excellent foils for Rod's business background. Horsey encouraged the creation of varied campaign materials, the likes of which Calgary had never seen before. Bumper stickers and buttons with cartoon caricatures of Rod's face quickly spread around the city.

The campaign team moved quickly to corral the key billboard and bench sign advertising space around the city. Thanks to Horsey and Karen Bell, another active volunteer, the campaign made extensive use of television advertising, including a half-hour paid program on CFCN that showed Rod riding a bicycle around the city. Rod and his team jumped at the chance for him to take part in an unusual joint television-radio debate carried simultaneously on the city's two television stations and several radio outlets. Horsey helped originate the idea of spending early mornings waving election signs at commuter traffic on busy Calgary streets. He would have Rod's hulking friend Don Luzzi, all-star Calgary Stampeder lineman, and a former Miss Canada pageant winner, Barbara Kelly (Mike Horsey's wife) among the group at his side. Despite his professed shyness, Rod showed flair for this kind of campaigning.

Albertan managing editor Don Peacock wrote early in Rod's campaign, "it looked as though [Leslie] would get in for his third term in a walk." Leslie assumed a detached confidence, an aura of electoral inevitability throughout the campaign. He openly wondered how this odd man who had led such a strange life and who couldn't know Calgary after such a short time could have had the nerve to think he could be mayor.

For anyone running for office, election day is unique. After weeks of hectic campaigning, the normal routine halts. Like jumping from an aeroplane, you're now suspended in space. The plane noise has gone, and all you can hear is the swish of air through your parachute. You enjoy that briefly before realizing you'd better prepare for the landing. You'd also better expect a crowd when you're on the ground.

For Rod, the routine up to election day was gruelling, even for the marathon man. As with any public campaign, he had to face the grind of endless canvassing, of anticipating the traps laid by opponents and some media, plus the frequently contradictory advice of his own supporters.

Rod never described it that way, but during campaigns, he could be testy, charming, evasive, and blunt. Who could blame him? Above all, though, he remained focused, rarely relaxing from his calculations as to how he could score points over his opponent.

Temperatures were around five degrees Celsius on that election day, Oct. 15, 1969, which is normal for that time of year. A light rain kept the carpet of leaves along the Sykes' elm-lined street in Elbow Park sticking to the ground. All was mellow in the season of mists and fruitfulness. There was a more leisurely start to the day for the Sykes household, although eldest son James was up at his usual 5.30 a.m. for his *Albertan* delivery round. The absence of appointments meant a little longer for the jesting between Rod and Gisele in their comfortable kitchen with the ribbed water radiators keeping the place warm. Caught in the electoral pre-landing, Rod went alone to eighty-eight cent day at Woodward's store, where he spent several hours and picked up a bargain or two from the garden section. He also washed his aging station wagon that day. Both activities helped appease the tentacles of fear and expectation tugging at his innards. Dinner was a more public affair as he joined almost four hundred people for a chow mein tea at the Chinese United Church.

The election night activities started at the downtown campaign headquarters, just a hundred metres east of the Leslie centre of operation. The place filled quickly; thirty-three volunteers had helped raise an estimated $25,000 for the campaign. Scores had helped with the canvassing and pamphlet drops. Scrutineers were in place for all the city's 491 polls. With Gisele at his side and dressed in dark blazer, grey pants, a light cardigan, and a shirt with the collar at least one size too big, Rod didn't wait long before a toothy smile brightened his face. Optimism reigned in the Sykes campaign headquarters from the moment the first advance poll results were announced and written up on the wall. As the pattern of winning polls persisted, Rod was able to declare, "It seems too good to be true." As *The Herald's* television columnist Bob Shiels wrote the next day, "the horse race almost everyone expected never materialized."

Herald political writer Don Sellar described the headquarters as bristling with activity, "as prominent Social Creditors, Liberals and even a smattering of Conservatives began to whoop it up."[13] There by invitation were Public Works

Minister Alberta Ludwig, a long-time friend, and Premier Strom's executive assistant Don Hamilton. One of the first calls of congratulation came from Strom. It was funny to see George Ho Lem back on centre stage, holding forth to the media and anyone who would listen with his explanations for what now would obviously be a victory. "We were warned not to peak too fast," he said, "but we always managed to get something new into the campaign and keep it going higher."[14] He obviously had no compunction about taking much of the credit despite his more than week-long disappearance from the campaign.

Gisele dared to yelp "Hooray!" as the overwhelming victory became clear, but she quickly drew back, saying "I'd better not gloat." Bless the politicians' wives who stand up for their husbands. The newspaper account described her as happy but numb. The win, she said, "takes a little while to register. It's all so new. Ask me in two years how I feel." What wise words. She told the media she still intended to spend most of her time at home with her children. "I didn't run for office, so they can't expect too much from me." Later, when Rod was leaving for a television appearance, well-wishers pushed him away as she grabbed his arm. "Listen, you be nice to me. Don't be a difficult mayor yet," she warned. While the two daughters were considered too young for the headquarters throng, the three sons were there phoning their friends with obvious and precocious glee. Rightfully, the evening had a strong family focus. Rod insisted later his family not be implicated in his political career. The one exception was the family photo on the cards he sent every Christmas.

Rod waited in vain for the defeated Leslie or someone from his team to drop by the headquarters and offer the customary concession. *The Herald* reported Leslie came over, but Rod had already left for a television interview. Rod vehemently denied this version of events, and nobody in his campaign headquarters reported seeing the incumbent. The effervescent Mike Horsey went by the Leslie headquarters instead not much more than an hour-and-a-half after the polls had closed. "Where's Mr. Leslie?" he asked the desultory handful of people there. According to Rod's version of events, the response was, "It's been a real nightmare. Mrs. Leslie had to be taken home in hysterics. Mr. Leslie's been vomiting in the toilet. We've had to clean up." What a way to go down. Earlier, Leslie had despondently told a reporter, "It looks glum. It's all over." He spoke of the "most vicious campaign that I can remember here." His opponent may have been the most hard-nosed candidate ever to seek the mayor's seat, but if calling for a clean-up of the Old Boys' Club at City Hall was vicious, then Leslie had overly precious sensitivities. Leslie's oldest daughter, Kathy Mackid, could only utter, "I just can't believe it."[15]

For Sykes fans, the party continued at the Danish Canadian Club on Eleventh Avenue S.W., a place where Rod felt comfortable and frequently ate. In fact, for the rest of his life, Rod was a regular at the modest restaurant, enjoying the relaxed ambiance and wholesome food. Noisy celebrations went on into the small hours.

Because of James' paper route, the whole family was up at 5.30 a.m. the next morning able to savour *The Albertan's* prominent headline: "Rod Sykes stuns Leslie with overwhelming win." Rod had won by the largest majority in Calgary's history—56,000 votes to Leslie's 32,000, taking virtually every poll in the city, except, ironically, the Elbow Park poll where he lived. He portrayed himself as the amateur who had knocked off the big political machine.

Later that morning, Rod, Don Luzzi and other supporters were back on Crowchild Trail waving "Thank you" placards and flashing broad smiles to motorists, despite little sleep the night before.[16] Campaign innovations like this originated mostly with Mike Horsey. It was Horsey, incidentally, who thought up the brilliant scheme three months after the election of having the outside door to the mayor's office removed to emphasize to citizens Rod's open-door philosophy. He left Rod after two years to launch a lively Calgary-wide weekly tabloid called *Sunday Express*. Many in Rod's campaign team and Rod himself invested varying amounts in the venture. But, the project was undercapitalized and collapsed in about six months, leaving the investors in the lurch and with a bad feeling in their wallets.

Losing his investment of time, energy, reputation and money devastated Horsey. Marital break-up with former Miss Canada Barbara Kelly added to his woes. However, moving to Toronto helped Horsey get back on his feet. He worked in public relations before the then B.C. Premier Bill Bennett lured him back to the West Coast in the early 1980s to take on the position of deputy minister of tourism. According to his obituary, "the flamboyant dealmaker and civic booster marketed British Columbia to the world during Expo 86 in Vancouver." Although some projects fizzled, he masterminded several sports franchise deals for Vancouver. He also contributed to other political campaigns, including those of MP Pat Carney and Prime-Minister-for-the-blink-of-an-eye Kim Campbell. He was only fifty-nine when he died of a heart attack while on a cruise ship.

Although City Clerk Harry Sales was quietly talking it up with colleagues about "new hope" at City Hall, the environment in the post-election period among most of the senior echelons was one of shock. Chief Commissioner Strong had been a particular target of criticism during the campaign. Rod had made clear his dissatisfaction with Strong and other staff in their handling of the finances, their failure to build public housing, and the inability to expand urban renewal. Rod's campaign had reinforced the notion he was not a man to mess with. "Sykes Plans Early Action," was *The Herald* headline a day after the election. Reporter Vern Simaluk said the new mayor was clearly interpreting his landslide win as a mandate to reshape civic policy.[17] Despite intimations of storms ahead, Rod was professional and calm in his first meetings with the commissioners. When he strode up the steps into the old sandstone building that housed the mayor's and the commissioners' offices, he sensed a strong rush of elation, foreboding, and excitement. He didn't yet realize how rough this job would be.

"It is going to take all the talents and the courage that Rod Sykes possesses to beat the system and the establishment," Fred Kennedy said in his column two days after the election.[18] "His first job will be to get the office and position of the mayor back to where it belongs." He went on to say that Rod will have to tell the city commissioners and the heads of departments that he is the duly elected chief magistrate, and that "they'll have to be content to do their work as civil servants and leave policy and planning to the mayor and council." He concluded, "There is a job ahead of the new mayor which would scare the average politician silly. But, friends, this man is one tough hombre, and I'm sure that you will get a real run for your money."

Rod was saddling up to ride his horse of idealistic hopes into City Hall, but once he took the reins, it bucked and tossed like the wildest Stampede bronc. We can't forget that what also drove him was disgust at the behaviour of some others with power at City Hall. Remember too that it was the threat from the former mayor against him and his company that had spurred him into this new and frenetic life that became eight years of aggravation, achievement, despair, and personal vindication. He had a job in mind, and he knew it might at times be a dirty one.

5

IN THE FIRING LINE

"Honeymoon" originally denoted the period of the moon after a wedding when relations between a groom and bride are at their sweetest. Observing Calgary's 1969 election, I depicted Rod as the frowning groom and City Hall senior administration as reluctant bride, taken to the altar with feet dragging the ground and a forced smile. It was as if the groom had warned his bride before the marriage that he was going to put her on a tough exercise regime, make sure she lost considerable weight, and order a makeover. That wasn't the best recipe for a long honeymoon. Few could have predicted how quickly relations would sour at City Hall.

"At first I felt awe that I received this huge vote that wiped out their whole system," said Rod. But within days of assuming office, "they were on the attack, telling me they'd drive me out in three months." Alderman Adrian Berry and his sidekick, Eric Musgreave, led the chorus. Rod heard that some of the bureaucrats, even people like parks department director Harry Boothman, were singing a similar refrain. Rod survived, but the hostility took its toll.

Within days of the election, Rod fielded questions about an investigation into thefts from the Calgary Transit System that had plagued the previous administration. One man had been convicted, and the arrest of three others on charges was still pending before the courts.[1] During his opening discussions with bureaucrats, Rod learned the losses were far higher than had been indicated, and that the City might have forfeited up to a million dollars from these thefts over a decade or more, mainly from transit cash boxes and parking meter proceeds. "That was one of many surprises once I took over. Once things started opening up, they never stopped," said Rod. "The cashiers' department, the police, and the transit office were all in turmoil. Some of the old-timers were trying to load these crimes onto the new mayor." The reality, he said, was that the police and the City administration had swept these matters under the rug and issued orders for people not to disclose the information before the election. That would have hurt incumbents.

Ten months later, at the City's request, the Alberta attorney general appointed Mr. Justice W.G. Morrow of Yellowknife to look into the debacle. While Rod based his push for the inquiry on the mismanagement of the previous administration that led to these huge thefts, the terms of reference were expanded to include issues such as Rod's responsibility for declining police morale, and other police matters to be discussed later in the book. The inquiry expanded its mandate to hear all kinds of City Hall gripes unrelated to the pilfering epidemic.

Chief Commissioner Ivor Strong even got some shots in, telling the inquiry that after an initial expression of desire to co-operate with the new mayor, an "air of hostility" developed between them that stemmed from the mayor's request for his resignation.[2] Strong said the mayor accused the board of commissioners of suppressing information, even though they agreed to co-operate with the police investigation into the thefts. Meanwhile, Rod took advantage of the inquiry to outline what he described as "quite improper and irregular" activities going on at City Hall and in the police department.

In his report released in May 1971, Morrow blasted the inadequacies of City Hall security that had led to the widespread thefts, which, according to his report, had reached "dangerous proportions" by 1969. He had heard evidence of City Hall employees jimmying open fare boxes, drivers intercepting coins and pocketing them as passengers dropped them into fare boxes, and bags of coins "treated almost with contempt" as employees in the cashiers' department regularly helped themselves to scoops of money. Some workers raked in up to $600 a month, the commission heard. Morrow's report suggested that the administration were to blame for lax supervision.

One middle manager who tried to raise the alarm was told he "worried too much" and that it was none of his business to interfere. The judge was "rightly appalled over the refusal of senior civic officials to prosecute offenders."[3] However, Morrow was surprisingly tolerant toward the police for failing to take a firmer stand on prosecution, said the *North Hill News* story carrying the headline "City Hall Whitewash of Scandal." In short, the transit theft issue fizzled out with a whimper. One employee was prosecuted, a few dismissed, and one known perpetrator transferred to another department where he had similar access to cash. So, one can hardly blame Rod for feeling revolted by this far-reaching scandal and the lack of resolve to deal with it.

Alberta Judge Mr. Justice Gordon Allen took Rod aside early in his term and told him the problem in City Hall was cronyism. Seeing people get away with embezzlement and dishonesty drew other people into dishonest activity, he said. As a result, Rod put his foot down and, in his eyes at least, his intent was noble. The area where Rod saw the easiest temptations for City employees to steal was in the building inspection and food inspection departments. There, kickbacks for licence approvals could be easy to get away with. "They are the quickies. You can only control that by setting an example and have consequences if dishonest practices are discovered," he said. Those principles got lost in Morrow's inquiry, he felt.

From his years with Price Waterhouse and the CPR, Rod was keenly aware of the need for tight internal controls in any organization where cash was handled. More resources have to be devoted to checking and cross-checking, he said in later life. He knew from experience the ingenuity of cheaters. Beware of employees, for example, who don't take their full holidays; they often stick around the office to maintain a watchful eye over their scams and make sure they remain undetected. Whistle blowing, where co-workers report illegal behaviour is, therefore, important for organizations to curb corruption. But if you receive information, "you have to assure people's willingness to talk won't come back to bite them." This was the kind of hard-nosed perspective Rod brought to City Hall, along with his zeal to pursue offenders. "I was attacked for creating turmoil and an atmosphere of fear," he said. "I was just trying to clean up a stinking mess ... After six months in City Hall, I had met more liars and thieves than in twenty years in business."

Although he wasn't on the City scene until 1971 as a city commissioner, Denis Cole recalled in 2011 Rod's propensity to dig into issues. "Rod was always looking for trouble and found it. He was inclined to see sin wherever he went," said Cole, who became chief commissioner in 1973. "He raised hell all around, and it was good for the City," he added. "[Rod's] impression of the

Leslie era was that you were either one of the 'in' people or not. Rod opened things up, and for that I greatly admired him." At the same time, said Cole, "Sykes used to see things under the table that I had never heard of. Maybe I was blind, but I never had an inkling of bad behaviour [after 1973]. My board of commissioners was as clean as a whistle."

Rod took issue with such insouciance. For example, he said Cole's colleague during the 1970s, Finance Commissioner Alan Womack, invested in Abacus Cities Ltd, a Calgary-based real estate developer that translated its tax-avoidance expertise into half a billion dollars' worth of assets before collapsing suddenly in 1979. Ken Rogers, one of two brothers who ran the company, had earlier worked in the planning department handling rezoning applications. Womack showed more than poor judgment with his Abacus investments, according to Rod, who did not hold the finance commissioner in high esteem anyway. In fact, when Womack tried to bluster about his involvement, Rod summoned City lawyer Brian Scott to the office. According to Rod's account, Scott bluntly suggested Womack could face charges under the Municipal Government Act if he didn't divest himself of the investments. He did just that soon after.

Within a week of Rod's election victory, *The Albertan* trumpeted, "Revolt brews at city hall." *The Herald*, meanwhile, stirred the pot with headlines like "Sykes 'Demotes' City's Old Guard"[4] following Rod's appointment of supportive Aldermen John Kushner and Bob Greene as chairmen of the finance committee and the community services committee, respectively. This kind of negative slant was common *Herald* practice. Another example was the unmistakable sour note in a *Herald* editorial two days after the election. The theme wasn't to welcome the new broom at City Hall, but rather bemoan the low voter turnout—it was 44%—and the implications that the result might have been "better" if only more people—that is, more Leslie voters—had shown up at the polls. The paper also wanted to make sure Rod didn't savour his victory too enthusiastically. The vote "was not a popularity poll," it huffed.

By making the appointments the way he did, Rod was following his prerogative and placing allies in important positions. We could hardly expect him to do otherwise, especially since the city's performance in money matters and in housing, which community services was responsible for, had been distressingly poor under the previous mayor. Also, Rod had emphasized these two areas in his campaign. "We have a clear mandate for change," said Rod when he announced the committee appointments.[5] "The people who campaigned for housing justice [which Bob Greene certainly did]ought to be able to work on these committees, and I have given them preference." That's being upfront about his motives, at least. Alderman Roy Farran, who had an on-off affable relationship with Rod, then reminded him he wasn't the only one on council with a mandate. The founder and owner of *The North Hill News*, who had served on council since 1961 and went on to be an Alberta MLA 1971-78, including a term as Attorney General, later commented to the media after one of the frequent council spats that characterized Rod's first term: "I hope he will also stop to listen sometimes. He is extremely intelligent, but should remember that only Superman could fly alone."

Born in England and educated in India, Farran served with distinction in the Second World War in North Africa, receiving the Distinguished Service Medal among several other military decorations. After the war, he was posted to Palestine with Britain's Air Service, where he was involved with counter-terrorism. Differing accounts exist as to whether the professional soldier was directly implicated in the murder of a sixteen-year-old Jewish terrorist, but when a mail bomb sent to "R. Farran" at his mother's English home killed his brother Rex, he decided to leave the Army and later immigrated to Canada. He wrote eighteen books, including the famous *Winged Dagger* about his Special Air Services experiences. Poker-faced and often with a pipe jutting out of his mouth, Farran managed to combine an avuncular look with the unblinking air of a reptile you shouldn't mess with. He was Rod's kind of man.

Also fermenting early trouble in Rod's regime were the incessant rumours that Ivor Strong, a commissioner of public works from 1952-57 and then chief commissioner under the Jack Leslie regime, was under pressure to resign. Rod was fingered as the instigator. Remember, however, that the Turcotte Inquiry into "certain matters connected with the good government of the City" a decade or so earlier not only pointed a wagging finger at Mayor Don Mackay and his thirty-six "borrowed" bags of cement. In his report to the Alberta attorney general, Mr. Justice Sherman Turcotte also had harsh words for Strong and a Commissioner Thomas. While Judge Turcotte was not asked to find evidence of Criminal Code offences, he did say that, in some transactions involving major City projects in the 1950s, "the close associa-tion between officials [of companies named in the report] and Mayor Mackay, Commissioners Strong and Thomas ... as evidenced by their friendship and by their gifts and work done, did have some effect on the course of action taken by the mayor and Commissioners Strong and Thomas." Later, Turcotte added, "I find that in some cases there were attempts to have an advantage accrue to those interests."[6] Quite damning findings.

After his first stint at City Hall and before returning for his second under Leslie, Strong had returned to private practice with his engineering consult-ing firm Strong, Lamb, and Nelson. Rod had concerns about the relationship of the firm with the City after Strong came back to City Hall under the Leslie regime. Strong's son was still with the firm when Rod became mayor.

Headlines following council's first full meeting such as "Row Erupts Over Strong" were unsettling, although hardly surprising. Rod had barely banged the gavel for the meeting's start when Alderman Adrian Berry was up on his feet on a point of order to clarify rumours about the replacement of Ivor Strong. One of Rod's most persistent adversaries on council, Berry was seen by Rod as the leader of a determined campaign to undermine his first term. The wooden gavel was close at Rod's hand for the whole meeting as Berry and other incumbents sought to embarrass him over his differences with Strong by calling for a vote of confidence in the by then weakened chief commissioner. The frequent banging of the gavel and his rulings that Berry was out of order were only met with more protestations and threats. The confrontation between the two was downright hostile, but if Berry had any sense that Rod was ripe for the picking, he was soon disillusioned of that by Rod's persistence under fire and by a supportive audience in council chambers applauding Rod's efforts.[7]

Anticipating uproar, Rod had earlier released a statement asking Berry to forgo his rumoured vote of confidence. Such a motion would be "destructive, creating needless stress and strain within council and within the civic administration. What we do not need is a return to pettiness and disruptive tactics. We need to work together—differences of opinion notwithstanding—to act on the City's urgent problems." Fine sentiments, but this prompted derision by the Berry bunch. It took Strong about another year and a half to quit and be replaced by Geoff Hamilton, who had become a commissioner shortly before Rod's election. In his letter of resignation, Strong extended thanks to the "former mayors and all members of council under whom I've served for their co-operation and support." Asked why he made no mention of thanks to Mayor Sykes, he replied, "I'd prefer to let the letter stand as it reads."[8]

Although media files show no record of it, Rod recalled that at the very first council meeting, normally an occasion for courtesy and introductions before the serious City business got under way, Berry told Rod he was an interloper to the line of succession that had been worked out with former Mayor Leslie and he was occupying a position he would soon be removed from. "You're sitting in my chair … we can drive you out," he repeated, according to Rod's uncorroborated account. Rod's assessment of Berry was that he was "a malicious, humourless man. His malice knew no bounds." Later he added, "He was too silly to be evil. He was just a fraud." Rod had kinder words for Eric Musgreave, who served as Berry's eager, chase-and-fetch puppy in the council shenanigans. Despite being an occasional thorn in Rod's side, he was still a decent man, Rod believed. "Eric had many good qualities." Serving as an alderman for three terms, he also worked for Imperial Oil for twenty-five years. Later, he was an MLA in Edmonton for four terms. Rod described him as trying to make his way in a system where to get along, you go along with what you're told; that is, he mostly tried to just fit in and be liked.

During Rod's second term, when he established the Citizens' Open Government Study (COGS) to explore proposals for a more accessible kind of local government, Musgreave wrote him a conciliatory, if rather unctuous letter. "There is no quarrel with your brilliance or your ability to stimulate people and institutions into a re-evaluation of their reason for existence," he said. "This letter is an attempt to help you, council and the board of commissioners to work more productively together." He went on, "Over the years, you and I have fought as bitterly as anyone on council … I think every alderman wants to do a good job, and he or she wishes to work with you. This is the spirit in which this letter is written … let us be known for our concern for people, our beauty, our vitality and our optimism for the future."[9] Musgreave meant well, and probably felt more intimidated by Rod than he cared to admit. Still some quite disarming if naïve idealism was on display here.

Uncharacteristically, Rod acknowledged he made a few bad decisions early in his first term. One mistake was to keep Kay Wood as the mayor's secretary. She had served three previous Calgary mayors, and he thought it would be smart to maintain continuity in the office. What he soon realized was that Wood was a Leslie loyalist and shared the former mayor's disgust for this upstart from other parts. Rod was suspicious that she regularly visited the Leslie house, reporting on Rod's activities and feeding Jean Leslie's constant harping that Rod had ruined her husband's career. Rod never had the chance to speak with Jack Leslie again. With their illusions in ruins, as Rod put it, the Leslies later moved to Invermere, B.C. "He was an amiable figurehead, not a malicious man, but someone out of his depth," was Rod's later assessment. "The practical effect of his defeat was to make his political viability a sham." Jean Leslie, on the other hand, was a "madly ambitious, unscrupulous wife. Her behaviour was really dreadful."

This apparent Leslie confidante, Kay Wood, with the title of executive secretary, was still lording over affairs in the mayor's office. "After my first few days in City Hall, I realized what a private club it was, with its ways of keeping foreigners out," said Rod. "I felt shock and disgust." Gail Rule was the first staff person Rod hired directly, and Mike Horsey came soon after. What a relief that was.

They were not yet fully settled in when Wood, deliberately in Rod's view, did not inform him of a Buckingham Palace note advising Calgary's mayor that the Duke of Edinburgh already had two white hats from the city and a third might be superfluous for his upcoming visit. New on the job and without this discreet background, Rod innocently took the hat Wood handed to him when he drove to the airport on a snowy, late October evening to participate in the greeting ceremony with other dignitaries. When Rod proceeded with the white-hat presentation Calgary had become supposedly famed for, a shivering Queen's Consort declared, "Not another one." Examining the hatband, Prince Philip added, "You must give out dozens of these." To which Rod replied, "Actually not, this is my first." Before handing the hat to an aide, Prince Philip continued, "I can always use it for carrying water ... or use it to put flowers in when I get home."[10] When a photographer asked him to put on the hat, he said, "I'm no clown." The whole affair was an embarrassment for Rod, although he maintained the duke was not as ungracious as the media made him out to be.

Only a few weeks after the Stetson saga, Rod went to Ottawa for what would be a first and crucial meeting with Prime Minister Trudeau. It was only because he called the prime minister's office the morning before to confirm the appointment that, to his shock, he was told he was expected that very day. After a mad scramble, he was able to arrive in time, but he remained convinced Wood had told him the wrong day deliberately. By now trust between them was rock bottom. She had to go.

"Job Loss Shock for Kay Wood," cried *The Albertan* headline.[11] After Rod tried to shop her around City Hall for a transfer, she ended up as secretary to research director A.H. Nicholson, which was hardly the glamour position she was used to. Some media commentators still painted Rod a villain for treating her this way.

Other annoyances dogged him. George Ho Lem was angry with Rod again because he hadn't received the appointment to the police commission he had assumed would be his. "George wanted a payoff," Rod said. "He never forgave me. I owed it to him."

An early surprise for Rod were the bribery attempts by developers. Rod said later that a five per cent share in projects was the figure presented to him on several occasions when developers hoped to entice his vote for projects. "They wouldn't directly pay me off, but they were conniving about it," he explained. Although Rod made clear he wouldn't own or invest in land in or around Calgary, the offers never stopped. "Throughout my three terms, I received subtle or not so subtle indications I could participate. I'd be told, 'We'd love to have you on board.' But corruption is hard to explain to people who don't understand the implications. Developers would then say, 'I'll hold an interest for you until you are out of office,' " Rod went on. "Do that once and they own you. I refused, of course, because I was outraged at the insult to my integrity." His practical side also prevailed. "There was no way this could be a workable scheme. After you've left office, how do you collect? Also, if you succumb, you don't know who else knows."

Corruption in public office became a pre-occupation for the rest of his life. "With the benefit of hindsight and experience, corruption, especially at the municipal level, is far more the rule than the exception," he said in later life. He made a special point in clipping an account of an insider trading scandal on the New York Stock Exchange in which a witness testified how he'd been seduced by a hedge fund founder benefitting from insider tips: "You work very hard. You are underpaid. People are making fortunes … so just keep track of your knowledge and share it with me,"[12] was the message the witness frequently heard. Rod kept the clipping, he said, because it repeated, almost word for word, what he heard so often from so-called friends and well-wishers during his time in City Hall. It was a tried and true formula for people approaching politicians to elicit useful information or insider help. "John Diefenbaker confirmed it to me when I asked him about it," Rod remembered. "He said that it succeeds more often than not, and nobody loses by telling a politician what he believes anyway. Most consider themselves underpaid and overworked." By extension, they feel deserving of more money than they legitimately earned.

As Rod pointed out, there are laws governing conflict of interest and other derelictions of duty, but apart from his own actions, he rarely saw anyone willing to enforce them. Former Chief Commissioner Denis Cole's comments about Rod finding sin under every table annoyed him. "Denis didn't want to see all the things going on at City Hall. How could he miss them?" Rod was bemused when Ralph Klein asked him in 1980, just as Klein was about to be mayor, how he made money from his time in that position.

A month after Rod's 1969 election, another train of events was set in motion that would cast a shadow over much of Rod's mayoralty. It became known as the Fortieth Avenue affair. It began with a meeting in the mayor's office five days after the election with City officials, Richard Baxter, developer of the Carma Shopping Centre (later to become Market Mall), and Carma's legal advisor Robert Fraser attending. Carma's plans to establish Fortieth Avenue as a main access route to the shopping centre through a residential area in which homeowners had been assured this would not occur had created a predictable furor among them. When Rod raised the matter at the meeting, he was certain that Baxter told those present that Fortieth Avenue was not essential to the company plans and should not be a deal-breaker.

When the matter went to the full council for a hearing in November, Rod had to excuse himself before the item came up on the agenda because he was committed to speak that evening to 700 members of the Mormon Church. The honouring of his commitment earned him the sobriquet of "social butterfly" from Alderman Ed Dooley. Imagine Rod's surprise when he learned the next day that Fraser, in his presentation to the aldermen, had described direct Fortieth Avenue access as critical to the project, and council had voted in favour of plans designating it as a main thoroughfare. At a press conference, Rod suggested Fraser had, by withholding the understanding reached in the mayor's office meeting, practised unethical and deceptive behaviour, contriving "in bad faith" to take advantage of Rod's absence from council.

An aggrieved Fraser initiated a $50,000 defamation suit against the mayor for his comments. This was clearly a blow, but Rod and his legal counsel, Reg Gibbs, felt reasonably assured that a defence of justification, fair comment, and qualified privilege for an elected official would carry the day. The news became more explosive, however. On November 5, 1970, Guy Fawkes Day, Mr. Justice S.S. Lieberman awarded Fraser $10,000 and full costs for Rod's transgressions. "Persons occupying positions of high office ... must realize that statements made by them are given wide publicity ... Notwithstanding the necessity for privilege extended by the law to such persons ... this privilege does not grant immunity to reckless and careless statements made without regard to accuracy," said the ruling.

Six days later, Rod issued a statement, noting, "the whole question of Fortieth Avenue involved vital principles of public interest. I cannot believe I could have acted otherwise in the circumstances."[13] Then he went to the heart of the matter. "An elected representative must weigh the facts and judge the alternatives open to him. When that is done, he must take a stand and vigorously defend what he believes is right." He said he would not ask council to have the City pay the bill and he thanked people who had already offered financial help. Even without an appeal, costs could be at least $16,000, which was still a lot of money then. His stoical and heartfelt conclusion was that, "The demands of office are heavy and the costs, both financial and in terms of personal and family life, are burdensome."

Convinced by the justice of his cause and keenly aware of the chilling effect such a judgment could have on political free speech, Rod and his legal advisors appealed the matter to the Supreme Court of Canada. That process dragged on for almost four years, costing considerable time, energy, and money. The final blow was a 4-3 Supreme Court vote upholding the Lower Court decision. It is testimony to his resilience and determination to speak his truth that this drawn-out court drama had no obvious impact on Rod's modus operandi. In similar situations where opponents might threaten legal action to shut him up or where similar restraints might prevail, he invariably stuck to his guns and spoke his mind. He backed aggrieved citizens no matter what the costs, and he spent a lifetime taking on underdog causes whether they landed him in hot water or not.

Regarding the Robert Fraser/Carma law suit, it's worth noting that when he took office, Rod's relationship with Carma was already foundering on a reef of mutual disregard. With his strong commitment to create more varied housing choices for Calgarians, Rod had judged early on that Carma, along with Nu-West, had the land inventory situation quite tightly locked up. "This was an intolerable position for my housing ambitions." As a result, he invited other major developers from outside Calgary to participate more actively in residential development. These moves caused trouble, as I shall elaborate on later.

After a short time at City Hall, Rod became curious about Commissioner Geoff Hamilton's relationship with Carma. He recalled going into Hamilton's office and spotting a solid silver tankard easily worth a thousand dollars. "What's that, Geoff?" he asked, picking it up and turning it over. Hamilton, whose florid face turned red at almost any provocation, was covered with confusion. "The tankard was from Carma," Rod said. "I then realized he had a closer relationship with them than I had thought."

Rod took many initiatives to consolidate his role as mayor and bring about changes at City Hall he considered he had a mandate for. Although he enjoyed an extraordinarily wide circle of contacts that provided him important information and offered their advice on matters within their expertise, he did not seem to have one or two consistent confidants giving advice on a regular basis. He absorbed all he could from the people around him, then took his own counsel. Some people he dealt with objected to inferences he took from their conversations. He occasionally drew implications and used language more drastic than the sources had intended. For him, that was his call a spade a spade principle at work, always digging for ways to advance his position and put his adversaries on the defensive .

Most of the torrent of activity, controversy, and adventure described so far occurred within the first one hundred days on the job., but the flood kept coming. Looking back at the headlines, the memoranda, the letters, and other material, make the pace of the action seem dizzying.

Another public controversy centred on Rod's struggle to persuade council to appoint three citizen members to the planning commission. That met with acrimony from some aldermen.[14] Rod's public criticisms of the planning department also sparked bitter recriminations from the local media and an open battle with planning director Mike Rogers that led eventually to Rogers' resignation, or ouster, depending on your perspective. This exchange in council offers a flavour of their relationship. During a discussion on the City's participation in the Calgary Regional Planning Commission, Rogers began, at the invitation of Alderman Eric Musgreave, to cite details from the planning department's upcoming budget.

Sykes stopped him. "I object to your pulling facts out of the air."

"They're not out of the air," Rogers replied.

"I don't expect to be answered back. I find the planning director's attitude negative, uncooperative, and hostile."

"I was attempting to answer the question. I object to being called a liar."

"I would ask the planning director to refrain from personal attacks," said Sykes.

"And I wish that were a two-way street," replied Rogers.[15]

And so it went on. You could almost hear the blue veins on Rod's pale temples throbbing. He was furious at the planning department because it had not only failed to produce any public housing, but had blocked housing initiatives with what he considered its elitist and obstructionist attitudes about what housing should be. The planning department's performance in encouraging urban renewal also met with his scorn, as did its planning for a hodge-podge Eighth Avenue Mall that Rod had criticized during the election. An *Albertan* editorial taking umbrage over Rod's attacks of the planning department speculated some of Rod's animus toward the department stemmed from his "unhappy experiences" while with Marathon.[16] Rod denied that strongly. "I never had conflict in the 1960s. The criticism was not personal on my part."

Rod loved to tell the story of having an announcement made over the intercom at the St. Louis Hotel bar, immediately east of City Hall and a popular hangout for City staff, at 1:30 one afternoon around Christmas time. The words rang out, "Will the planning department please return to City Hall." The only ones who hated the story were, understandably, the planners and the owner of the hotel. "If the department doesn't assert the normal discipline to produce to normal performance standards, then as mayor, I will find other methods, even if it means public announcements in taverns," Rod told media.[17] During a discussion about planners and his occasionally troubled relationship with them, he couldn't resist noting, "Planners are automatically experts the day they leave school."

Shortly before Christmas, two months after his 1969 election, Rod received news of his father's death at seventy-one. Leslie Sykes had been ill for some time, and Rod, after planning to visit his father, delayed travel plans to Victoria when told his father was progressing favourably. Rod spoke little about this incident, but participating in the funeral must have been difficult. The estrangement with his father from boyhood and the later clashes in values would certainly have been on his mind during the mourning period. After Rod's marriage to Gisele, he and his father had had almost no contact.

Rod's next swift action during those first hundred hectic days in office was to fire the complete management board for the city's three seniors' homes. His intention was to hasten government action on the building of a fourth home in Calgary. Hundreds of needy seniors crowded the waiting list for the partly subsidized homes, and Rod felt the management board had dithered long enough; not a single new building had come on stream in seven years.[18] He replaced the seven with two people he knew would take action immediately, and that's what happened—Murdoch Tower and Trinity Place were soon built in the downtown's east end.

Meanwhile, a death threat on his home phone compounded tensions. An anonymous caller asked his third son, Mark, if he'd like to find his daddy dead in the street. Rod, who already had a regular chat show on CHQR, had pricked the sensitivities of some aldermen by claiming on his broadcast that they voted as a block to prevent his reform initiatives. Alderman Ed Dooley suggested Rod suffered from a persecution complex, but assured him, "We do work for the city every bit as much as you do." Rod's quick rejoinder was that Alderman Dooley could accuse him of anything except working like he does. "That I cannot stand."[19]

With many of his efforts now directed at keeping taxes down, not only for the 1969-70 fiscal year but for 1970-71 as well, he took time to warn that the aldermanic budgetary "gravy train" was over, with particular references to Alderman Eric Musgreave's spendthrift proposals, and to take on the Chamber of Commerce for being "out of touch."[20]

Rod was past his first one hundred days when the sudden resignation of two General Hospital Board members in March placed him in the spotlight again. One of them complained Rod had made adverse comments about board operations, particularly the financial aspects.[21] The Herald crowed, "Sykes Under Fire for Criticisms."[22] Reporter Vern Simaluk wrote that the board chairman, Stan English, had blasted Rod for being "super-critical." English called for a provincial inquiry into the board's operations. In council chamber, he accused Rod of being at the root of the internal troubles plaguing the board since the fall. Although inquiries seemed to be the fad in those years, nothing came of English's request.

City Hall had sure seen a lot of action since Oct. 15, prompting the aging Albertan columnist Fred Kennedy to note, "In a lifetime of newspaper work … I cannot recall a mayor who has experienced such a 'rough' apprenticeship in the first five months in office as has Rod Sykes."[23]

The heat soon cranked up even further. "Sykes Draws Angry Blast," roared The Herald headline on April 4. Geoff Hamilton, city development commissioner, issued a statement publicly accusing Rod "of deliberately attempting to destroy the city planning department, scarring permanently the professional careers of several persons in the process." In a counter-attack to Mayor Sykes' frequent criticisms of city planners, Mr. Hamilton charged the mayor with attempts to "humiliate, degrade, and intimidate, thereby upsetting the home life of some planners, damaging staff morale to the point where the department is incapable of fulfilling council's instructions, and driving some senior civic officers to the 'breaking point.' "[24] This was intemperate language for a man hoping to take the place of Chief Commissioner Strong, and *The Herald* was gleefully determined to collect every ounce of mud to sling at the embattled mayor.

Meanwhile, Rod called Hamilton's statements "extreme, intemperate, and an emotional outburst." Rumours, encouraged by *The Herald*, of a non-confidence vote in council directed at the mayor prompted Rod to say, "I'll just ignore it." He knew well what his powers were and the limits of what council and the administration could do.

As the media storm continued, Rod called this his Pearl Harbor, an attack without warning "because he [Hamilton] had my confidence completely." Shrewdly, he deflected the spotlight from his commissioner and directed it on to the planning department and *The Herald*, whom he charged with cooking up the controversy in the first place. In the end, the storm subsided, with *The Albertan* able to report, "For all concerned, the one over-riding wish appeared to be that the whole affair be pushed into the past as quickly as possible."[25] Interestingly, a year after this commissioner kerfuffle, Strong was gone from City Hall, and Hamilton occupied the chief commissioner's office, his complexion ever more flushed. He wasn't there long, though.

A four-page profile on Rod in May's *Alberta Business Journal* with the headline, "Hurricane Sykes Hits Calgary," seemed in keeping with the tenor of the times. "Even in the supposedly rough world of private business, there has seldom been an administrative shakeup as thorough as the one Rod Sykes is giving the City of Calgary," wrote Don Sylvester. A defiant Rod was quoted as saying, "I tread on a lot of tender toes and kick a lot of sacred cows … and enjoy doing it." Ordinary people now have a champion, he said. "I don't hear a rich man's voice any louder than a poor man's voice, and it's important that it stays that way. That's the way I campaigned." Most of the interview for the piece appropriately occurred in the working man's St. Louis Hotel bar, east of City Hall, still with its deeply stained terrycloth-covered tables and a favourite hangout for Rod long before Mayor Ralph Klein claimed it as his tavern of choice.

Other council meeting stories invariably described scenes of acrimony and tumult. *Albertan* reporter Myron Johnson related one meeting where Rod had barely finished the session's customary opening prayer for peace and good will when the place erupted into accusation and counter-accusation. I wondered sometimes, though, whether Rod was deliberately having a bit of fun at the aldermen's expense. When he opened proceedings with the short version of a prayer from the *Soldiers', Sailors' and Airmen's Book of Prayer*: "Forgive us this day our foolish ways," it was hard not to sense mischief. The anger of some aldermen at the words was only compounded when he patiently, if not condescendingly, explained this was an official prayer. An equally appropriate prayer would have been, "O God, who knowest how often we sin against thee with our tongues; Keep us free from all untrue and unkind words."

The arrival of summer brought no respite. As if he didn't have enough on his plate in Calgary, Rod spoke out against federal subsidies for Montreal's 1976 Olympic Games bid. "Montreal is practising a kind of financial shake-down system with the federal government at the expense of cities like Calgary, and if they think Calgary is going to subsidize their Summer Games, they'd better think again," he said on his regular Sunday CHQR broadcast. Only a short time earlier, Montreal Mayor Jean Drapeau had participated in the Calgary Stampede Parade. "The Mayor of Calgary has a right to express his opinion," Drapeau responded, "but I don't care what he thinks. I know that if the people of Calgary had a chance, they'd throw him out and elect me mayor instead."[26] I sometimes questioned why Rod deliberately attracted these kinds of controversies, but taxpayers' money was at stake and that was what he was defending. He obviously savoured the public buzz too. Actually, Rod and Drapeau later became reasonable friends. That was the same Drapeau, inci-dentally, who later insisted a deficit for the Montreal Olympics was as likely as him getting pregnant. It had one, and he didn't, of course.

You could hardly top the courage (gall?) that prompted Rod, after joining his friend and fellow mayor, Ivor Dent from Edmonton, in that city's Klondike Parade, to unfavourably compare it with the Stampede Parade. He criticized the "joyless" Edmonton citizens and visitors. "During the parade, very few people cheered or showed enthusiasm. In Calgary, everybody cheered."[27] Although the remarks made headlines and provoked a storm of hostility on Edmonton's radio stations, that wasn't really his intention. He was merely fol-lowing an unavoidable inner insistence to say what he thought, no matter the consequences. A cheeky pleasure at tweaking Calgary's rival city undoubt-edly helped.

Rod took such delight in wrestling to the ground the people who thought they were heavyweight debaters. He remembered proudly the television debate he waged with Vancouver Mayor Tom Campbell, the man with the sobriquet Tom Terrific. *Vancouver Province* TV reporter James Spears, under the headline "Sykes Whomps Campbell," called it "one of the best pieces of TV debating I've seen in ages."[28] He said, "The reason the debate was such a brilliant piece of programming is that our mayor is never, but never outtalked … Sykes did the impossible, and Campbell … came out of the battle looking like a hurt little boy who's just been told that he's not big enough for the street ball team." While Campbell, with his long, bushy sideburns and gaudy suits, wanted to deal with his City's boisterous, counter-culture youth by getting them off the streets, the "grey-flannelled" Sykes sought to protect civil rights by ensuring the rights of minority groups, such as hippie youth.

On the national scene, the so-called 1970 October Crisis, triggered by two kidnappings of government officials in Quebec by members of the Front de Libération du Québec (FLQ), had captured the attention of the people and the media. Prime Minister Pierre Trudeau's hard-line response and his decision to implement the War Measures Act and deploy Canadian troops throughout Quebec and in Ottawa provoked controversy, as well as regard. Rod publicly praised the prime minister for his bold response and condemned the FLQ as common criminals. "Everybody across the country must be thankful he [Trudeau] has met the challenge as he did—with courage and wisdom. He's never appeared to more advantage than in this time of national emergency, and his leadership has never been more obviously right." Rod had already formed a good relationship with Trudeau. These words helped confirm their friendship, which lasted throughout Rod's three terms.

Rod faced more threats on the home front through a verbal rampage from Alderman Eric Musgreave in a speech to the Calgary Labour Council. Musgreave accused Rod of favouring his friends and supporters with City contracts and other benefits.[29] Although he mentioned no names, it was obvious Musgreave was referring to people like Albert Dale, who was the architect for Palliser Square when Rod was with Marathon, and who designed the Metropolitan Foundation seniors' high-rise. He would later oversee the building of the Calgary Convention Centre, among other City projects. Musgreave also had in mind architect Shelley Chandler, who had helped with the Variety Theatre renovation project, and accountant Bill Friedman, who received work from the City. Dale had long proven himself as one of Calgary's most active architects. Chandler and Friedman were on Rod's campaign team, but both had done City work before Rod came along and were successful in their own right. These were vague but discouraging charges. Where was the proof Rod had made any gain, other than the satisfaction of getting things done? He later contemplated a defamation suit against Musgreave.

While all this was going on, the police department continued to make the headlines with their attacks on Rod for destroying police morale. The pressure on him had been relentless from the day he had decided to run, and it was now at a crescendo. While the achievements had been many, he had taken no break from the unfolding chain of events. As the target of political attacks inside and outside City Hall, Rod had had enough. He even mused to a *North Hill News* reporter that he might not run again in the October 1972 election. "It's getting difficult to stand the strain," he said, barely past his first anniversary.[30]

Decades later, he was able to acknowledge how the public pressures affected him and Gisele. Alone at night, he wished many times he hadn't taken that precipitous step of running for mayor. When he worked for Price Waterhouse, he had done a lot of oddball investigations, but he had the weight and solid reputation of the company behind him. With CPR, he became their "hatchet man" to straighten problems out. Whatever he faced then, he was always able to call on resources at CPR to help. "I had that backing. But when I was at City Hall, I had never been so alone in my life."

Then one night, feeling particularly deluged by the flood of public approbation, he asked himself: "How can I get out of this?" This was his dark night of the soul when circumstances overwhelmed him. Fighting the good fight had lost its appeal, and for a moment, he could see no way out.

However, he summoned the defiance and resolve to keep his grip on the wheel and maintain his course. His practical, rational mind and a sense of *noblesse oblige* became again his compass. He concluded, "I can't get out of this mess. I have a duty and responsibility to ride it out." He continued on that stormy journey, showing flair, humour, fearless determination and a disregard for opponents' toes.

This chapter describes some of the tumults from his first year or so in office in roughly chronological order. I now take a detour to track a potentially explosive theme that ran through all his years as mayor and which still resonates at many city halls today: The power of the mayor and how it was weakened.

6

LOSS OF MAYORALTY MUSCLE

Tens of thousands of open-jawed Albertans watched when then provincial premier, Ralph Klein, blew up the Calgary General Hospital in 1998. Ralph didn't actually press the detonator button that turned to rubble the well-equipped, close-to-downtown, 960-bed hospital, but his stubby finger wasn't far away. Together with former Alberta Treasurer Jim Dinning, who helped hatch this modern-day gunpowder plot, Klein figured the Province would immediately save about $500 million through this action. In the frenzy of cost-cutting going on at that time, that was considered to be worth the price of destroying forever a conveniently-located hospital on which hundreds of millions of dollars had been lavished earlier in that decade.

With a chronic shortage of hospital beds since, many have come to regret that decision. It's staggering to learn that twelve years later, neither of these two political leaders had any prepared studies with clear rationales and economic evidence for their actions. According to Rod, in conversations he had with him in 2010, Dinning acknowledged there was no documentation behind this far-reaching decision that affected so significantly the delivery of health care since.

The General Hospital wasn't the only asset blown up during those halcyon days when King Ralph ruled the roost in Edmonton and hardly a fleck of chicken scat ever stuck to his glossy feathers. Other similar events took place under Klein's watch that reflected his damn-the-torpedoes approach. That was Rod's position and why he remained unenthusiastic about Klein's legacy for the province. I will focus now on one action under Klein that may seem, at first glance, relatively unimportant to the general public, but which ultimately has had considerable impact on the practices of locally elected municipal officials and how responsive they are to citizen needs.

The first place to look is Alberta's Municipal Government Act, a set of rules and guidelines for how local governments in Alberta operate. In 1994, two years after Klein became premier, the MGA, along with several other provincial laws, came up for extensive legislature review.

An important aspect of that process in the early 1990s, leading to the formal changes in the revised MGA of 1995, was that they were guided by Keith Ritter, hired by the government as a lawyer with supposed experience in government law. His title was chief parliamentary counsel.[1] The man who hired him was Calgary Progressive Conservative MLA David Carter, then speaker of Alberta's Legislative Assembly and an ordained Anglican minister. Ritter also spearheaded changes to other provincial legislation and advised provincial lawmakers on a variety of matters affecting Albertans, from conflict of interest guidelines to the constitutionality of proposed bills.[2] Ritter, still in his twenties, was given a remarkably free hand, in accordance with the "don't bother me with details" style of government Klein preferred. Ritter's proposals for a new MGA received little independent review before they were enacted. The oversight committee included two names from Rod's days as mayor: former Aldermen Ross Alger and Eric Musgreave, then MLAs. "With their new sense of status, they enjoyed cutting down others to size," was Rod's assessment of their involvement. In the end, "Ralph emasculated the legislation." To its credit, the Alberta Urban Municipalities Association (AUMA), representing the province's towns and cities, rang the alarm bell. "The AUMA was concerned that amendments to the MGA were taking place without adequate consultation or time for reflection on the part of the association ...

the process of approving amendments was eroding the spirit of the municipal act," said one commentator.[3]

As it turns out, Ritter, the architect of the MGA changes, was a fraud. It took more than a decade to find this out, but when he was convicted in 2006 on fraud and embezzlement charges related to an off-shore investment company he operated, evidence revealed that the credentials he had used while working in the legislature from 1988-93 were mostly made up.[4] He had never graduated in London, or studied in the prestigious Gray's Inn and the Université de Genève, as he had stated. The Swiss Bankers Association, where he supposedly worked, had no record of him. He had forged his credentials. Worse, the Alberta government did not acknowledge or even know this until his 2006 conviction. This was the man responsible for the MGA revamp passed with hardly a whimper in 1995 under Premier Klein. Ritter served only eighteen months of the maximum ten-year sentence the court handed down. The National Parole Board adhered to standard policy of releasing non-violent offenders after they served one-sixth of their time.

I want to highlight one specific aspect of the amendments that differentiated the role Rod was able to play as mayor from that of not only Naheed Nenshi, elected Calgary mayor in 2010, but Dave Bronconnier and Al Duerr before him. It's highly instructive, if not fascinating, to see how the duties of a mayor, or chief elected official (CEO) as the MGA calls the position, were transformed, and how that repositioned the roles of the aldermen in Calgary City Hall and other municipalities across the province.

In addition to performing the duties of a councillor or alderman, as they insisted until recently on calling themselves in Calgary, the CEO must, according to the revised MGA of 1995, preside or be the chairman at council meetings, unless a bylaw specifies otherwise, and perform any other duty imposed by any other bylaw. That could mean the mayor isn't even guaranteed the role of chairperson under the revised act. In addition, the CEO "is a member of all council committees and all bodies to which council has the right to appoint members … unless the council provides otherwise." That authority is also then not guaranteed—council can take it away. Section 3 states, "The chief elected official may be a member of a board, commission, subdivision authority or development authority … only if the chief elected official is appointed in the chief elected official's personal name."[5] The implication is that the mayor cannot transfer his official authority with him, which is another diminishment of the role.

Those words may seem innocuous, but when Rod was elected in 1969, the MGA read dramatically different. The act stated that the mayor was chief officer of the municipality. In other words, he was at the top of the municipal power pyramid. He presided at all meetings and, most significantly, had the

authority to "supervise and inspect the conduct of all officials of the municipality in the performance of their duties." In other words, he enjoyed a clear
and primary administrative role as well as a political one. In addition, he was
required to "cause all negligence and carelessness and violation of duty to be
prosecuted and punished, as far as it is within his power to do so, and communicate from time to time to the council all such information and recom-
mend such measures that he considers will better the finances, health, security, cleanliness, comfort, ornamentation and prosperity of the municipality."

Finally, the act declared in those days that "the mayor is *ex officio* [or automatically by virtue of their position] a member of all boards, associations,
commissions, committees, or other organizations to which the council has
the right to appoint members ... and the mayor when in attendance possesses
all the rights, privileges, powers, and duties of other members."[6] This is an
extraordinary variation from the modern-day mayor's duties. The importance
of the mayor having to "cause all negligence and carelessness and violation of
duty to be prosecuted and punished" cannot be understated. I'll show how
Rod applied these statutory powers. Similarly, his automatic membership
on city boards and committees was guaranteed in a far more substantial way
than the 1995 act allows.

Of course, Rod had done his homework and understood the legislated
powers he assumed in 1969. The assertive positions he took on many issues
should be understood in the context of the Municipal Government Act
of his era. Rod's harsh criticism of his predecessor, Jack Leslie, for being
a figurehead mayor and for failing to exercise his full powers, becomes
more understandable.

In retrospect, Rod pointed to the Klein years as mayor, 1981-88, as the
critical period when the rot of diminishment for the position set in. With
his modest background in the media and low-level public relations, and with
limited understanding of the inner workings of local government, Mayor
Klein signalled early to his chief commissioner, George Cornish, "You do
the administration; I'll do the public relations and the public glad-handing."
Ralph's formula was to enjoy the generalized application of the position
without grasping the intricacies of administration. He was able to blithely
abrogate those responsibilities as mayor as defined in the act. Ammunition
for the later demolition of the MGA was, in effect, installed during Klein's first
term as mayor. Through the changes in the act in 1995 when he was premier,
he formalized the unwritten agreement he made with Cornish more than a
decade earlier. From then on, the mayor didn't need more power than his
fellow councillors, except in his ability to be chairperson at council meetings
and the figurehead leader in social or ceremonial occasions. He wanted to be
the City's official greeter.

Al Duerr followed Klein as mayor in 1989. Rod branded him the "absentee mayor," more interested in appearances than ruling the roost. With his background as a city planner, he knew far more than Klein about the workings of City Hall and won four large majorities during his twelve years there. However, he put a primary emphasis on promoting consensus with his council and working collaboratively with others. His priorities, he explained in a *Herald* interview, were to push values, and "it's not necessarily what you do that counts, but who you are as a person."[7] In the same article he's quoted as saying, "Doing the right thing can mean so many different things to different people." Does he mean that ethical behaviour is a moving target, depending on the day and place? That's not the sort of philosophy that the plain-talking Rod appreciated. Little wonder that Rod was not a fan of the touchy-feely Duerr.

To this day, Rod is highly critical of the advantage that Duerr took of his position. By constantly striving to be cozy with council, he, like Leslie and Klein before him, failed to assume all his duties and responsibilities. That's when the influence peddlers—the businessmen, developers, and property owners seeking surreptitious advantages—came into their own. Duerr frequently pointed out he had no influence on council and could not be held accountable for what council did. However, there's no record of him pointing to the 1995 Municipal Government Act as the reason, even though those legislative changes occurred under his watch as mayor.

Rod claimed that when he left office in 1977, the City's infrastructure had been updated or plans were in place for their renewal and expansion over the next twenty years. Both Klein and Duerr squandered that advantage, according to Rod. By default, he argued, they were responsible for long neglect of basic City services. As importantly, they allowed the authority of the mayor's position to be diluted to such an extent that the revisions of 1995 became possible.

Ross Alger, mayor for a term right after Rod retired, has received little mention here, although his less engaged, Patrician manner certainly signified a reluctance to involve himself in the nitty-gritty of City Hall. When he announced his intention of running in 1977, he told Rod he looked at the position as a way "to cap my career." In other words, he was setting himself up to enjoy the well-deserved fruits of mayoralty status after a career in accounting, plus terms on the Calgary Public School Board and on council, where he served one term as an alderman. He had run unsuccessfully against Rod in 1974.

After Duerr, along came Dave Bronconnier in 2001. Already a nine-year council veteran, he was anxious to get his hands on the levers of power. The Calgary-born entrepreneur ran on a platform of addressing Calgary's neglected infrastructure needs and funding. He also sought to improve accountability among council, the city executive, and administration, according to his campaign literature. He was brash, bold, and ambitious. Within a couple of years, Mayor Bronconnier's big plans were bogged down in a quagmire of opposition from some aldermen. His reaction was to try to intimidate his opponents into accepting his way, restructuring City Hall, and granting him the authority to implement his policies. He failed. Charges of bullying came thick and fast, and confusion reigned over the lines of authority between elected officials and administration.[8] The failures and misunderstandings stemmed not only from the 1995 Municipal Government Act changes, but from more recent, so-called governance restructuring implemented in Calgary during the year Bronconnier was elected. The result was continuing dysfunction, and Bronconnier's frustration was palpable. The levers of power in his hands crumbled as though made from papier mâché.

At *The Herald's* invitation in 2003, Rod prepared for publication a lively analysis of City Hall cogently explaining the losses of mayoral authority and Bronconnier's subsequent frustrations. "City Hall is a mess," he declared with classic directness. "Council is blamed for frustrating the mayor … and the mayor is blamed for trying to intimidate council," he said. "As if this wasn't enough, the civic administration, the people who have to make the City work while all this nonsense goes on, is blamed for opposing the mayor."

The basis for Bronconnier's problems, Rod explained, lay in the loss of authority over council and administration brought about by the 1995 MGA amendments. Aldermen during Bronconnier's time were earning salaries approaching six figures, and enjoyed full-time staff and lavish expense allowances. This was in sharp contrast to the 1970s when they were considered part-time and access to the administration on ward complaints and issues went through the mayor's office.

The advantage during Rod's mayoralty was that "the part-time role allowed active business owners and professional people to run for council. In a later *Herald* column, he expanded on this theme. "We got better people when we paid much less … There was never any shortage of good candidates because council service was seen as a civic duty, a donation of time and effort by successful people."[9] Ironically, to make these points in later life, Rod depicted his councils in far more complimentary fashion than he did when he was mayor.

Rod went on to note that the evolution of the figurehead mayor system led to later councillors acting like fifteen independent mayors, interfering in day-to-day administrative matters and pursuing their self-interests. He concluded, "This is a major source of today's problems."

The mayor's loss of authority in policy matters, according to Rod, allowed aldermen to trade support for issues important to them in their wards.

Council votes would no longer be made on a basis of principle, but rather on ward-to-ward bargaining. Aldermen, at least the successful ones, became pre-occupied with making sure their fiefdoms received their "fair share" of publicly-funded projects. Rod claimed this reciprocal approach extended to planning matters, "as a result of which … many applications were decided before council heard the case: Thus does expediency descend to corruption of the democratic process."

It appeared to Rod that Bronconnier ran for a figurehead job at a cost of nearly $900,000—his spending in 2001, according to news reports—without knowing what the job was. Having to raise that kind of money may not only have compromised Bronconnier and created the potential for tainted relationships with business people, professionals, developers, and others dealing with City Hall, from whom he actively solicited campaign funds.

Fundraising has dominated much of councillors' activities in this century. Even aldermanic campaigns raised sums in six figures. A disturbing aspect of Alberta's weak campaign funding rules is the free hand for aldermen to raise money when and how they want, and then spend it with similar abandon. That allows them to create savings nest-eggs, all without being accountable to citizens. The result could be more than the "Bad Optics" that was the headline for Naheed Nenshi's April 2010 article in *Alberta Views*.[10] The flow of cash into aldermanic pockets with no accountability was an obvious recipe for possible corruption.

Rod's position is summarized in his introduction to *Take Back City Hall*,[11] "Our new-style council of professional politicians has deliberately reduced competition for their well-paid jobs by increasing the time taken to do the job, eliminating most employed or business people." At the same time, "we also make money the second major deterrent by raising the cost of election campaigns … How can voters tell a donation from a bribe? How can a newcomer compete? It's not possible."

Rod's final conclusion was clear about the legislative situation discussed in this chapter: "I can't imagine working in this system … I would never have run for mayor in such a system." In 1969, however, he did look at his job description and operated to the fullest extent possible within its much wider bounds. Here's how he managed that.

When Rod made that giant leap in early September 1969 to campaign for mayor, some in the media and the public understood the significance of that decision for City Hall. They were aware of the mechanics of mayoralty power. They certainly saw in Rod a totally different kind of political representative than the low-key, figurehead persona of the incumbent, Jack Leslie.

Rod frequently reminded people throughout his tenure and later in his life that he was not a real politician; he was quite different to others in political office. He called politics a "dirty business" to which he never became accustomed. To rationalize his status, he liked to say things like, "You have to swim in the sewer if you're going to clean things up." In a narrower sense, he wasn't a political professional, and he certainly hadn't run for political office before, but that assertion was disingenuous. During his time with Marathon, he had associated with a wide range of political leaders throughout western Canada, and, of course, he had read extensively about politics. He also was familiar with the people and the dynamics within Calgary City Hall. As he reminded people later, he had done his homework and knew the rules of engagement. He could "read" his constituency, had a great ability to capture the public mood, and had the skills to communicate what he considered important.

Graham Smith, editor of Roy Farran's independent weekly newspapers, *The South Side Mirror* and *The North Hill News*, stood apart from the mostly conforming journalists of that time. Born in England and a former RAF fighter pilot from the Second World War who immigrated to Canada in the 1950s, Smith flew his own vectors. He had figured out the lines of authority at City Hall where Mayor Leslie spent most of his efforts on meeting and greeting when he wasn't making decisions behind closed doors with cronies. It was obvious to Smith that Leslie had not seized the authority available to him but had handed it by default to the then Chief Commissioner Ivor Strong.

Smith was therefore able to describe a process whereby "decisions made by city commissioners and aldermen in committee take over from the open debate that formerly decided city policy ... the democratic processes have atrophied, communication between city hall and the taxpayer has been diminished ... the net result is a form of government as unsatisfactory as it is costly and impractical."[12] To bring transformation, "it will take a strong man, strong-willed and with strong backing from other members of council," he said with some prescience. He had the strong man and strong will parts correct, but the council backing idea later fell short.

Even *Herald* columnist Vern Simaluk understood what was at play. When Rod turned his sights on the mayoralty seat, rather than an aldermanic ward, it was obvious, Simaluk wrote, that "Mr. Sykes' scope of municipal political thought was much broader than that of any ward alderman ... the only seat of power available to effect any wholesale changes as envisaged by Mr. Sykes was that of the mayoralty, not that of an alderman. As an alderman, he would be only one of thirteen."[13] However, and here is the nub of the preceding discussion on mayoralty powers, "the man who sits in the mayor's chair has at hand levers of power unavailable to the alderman. How they are used depends on the disposition of the mayor. The feeling is that the full force of the office has not been applied since the days of Harry Hays." That was exactly Rod's point.

It was obvious that Rod would frame his campaign to tackle this discrepancy. He had confidence that people would understand and relate to
the City Hall role he had in mind. "Real leadership opportunities have been
lost because the present mayor feels he has no power," he told a community
group.[14] "But the mayor can act much more positively. He can perform more
significant roles than being a 'fitting representative of the city' at ribbon cut-
tings, civic receptions, and cocktail parties." He put the question quite simply
and rhetorically: "What do we need? A ribbon-cutter and figurehead, or a
worker, a doer, a leader?"

Columnist Fred Kennedy realized that Rod's election heralded a new era
at City Hall. "I personally believe that former Mayor Jack Leslie's apparent
acceptance of the minor role contributed greatly to his decisive defeat ...
There is one thing you can be sure of. The moment that Rod Sykes is sworn in
as mayor, he will be the boss. He'll lay out the game plan, call the signals, and
carry the ball."[15]

Indeed, that's what Rod did. He moved quickly, for example, to assert
his power of appointments to civic committees outlined in the Municipal
Government Act. He dealt expeditiously with Chief Commissioner Ivor
Strong, responsible in Rod's view for deficiencies at City Hall, and not as
neutral as he should have been during the election. We saw how, early in his
tenure, Rod took aim at what he called the "planning dictatorship." Although
he poked fun at them, the intent of his remarks was serious. He called the
department dictatorial and out of touch, unwilling to take direction.

Planning department boss Mike Rogers was clearly in the line of fire
and resigned within two years. Rod had warned during the election campaign that "Mr. Rogers would have to either follow directions or leave City
Hall."[16] Planner architect Harold Hanen was pushed out of the department
within a month of Rod assuming power under a cloud of conflict of interest accusations.

From Rod's perspective, these were challenging times. The lurid headlines
reinforced a superficial sense that City Hall was embroiled in havoc and
dysfunction as Rod went about the business of asserting his role as mayor.
"Sykes battles on in City planning commission scrap"[17] was typical. What he
was attempting to do, and succeeded at, was to have three private citizens
appointed to the City's planning commission, a move he considered essential
for his commitment to open civic government to the people and make City
Hall operations more democratic. Not long later, these three appointees were
actually stimulating debate, challenging unanimity at the commission hearings, and prompting headlines like, "Appointees add fire to planning debate."[18]

Despite contrary views by some observers, Rod did not see himself as a
demagogue. From my perspective, though, he was frequently prepared to

appeal unmediated to the public to establish important goals. As mayor, he could often circumvent the constraining bureaucracy of City Hall and reach out directly to affected citizens. As a consequence, he provoked extreme hostility from some not used to this new way of handling power. City Hall had not seen such boldness—they might call it brazenness—for a while.

Other City Hall watchers applied the term 'populist' to his style. While he stood for political ideas and activities that were intended to represent ordinary people's needs and wishes, and while he sought to enjoy direct, unmediated access to citizens to hear their concerns and present his ideas, he still worked within the traditional political institutions. He wasn't interested in blowing up City Hall or making fundamental changes to conventional political processes.

Rod's unequivocal language upset many in the media. They couldn't see beyond the tensions arising from the positions he took between himself and those who, by inaction or resistance, sought to sabotage his policy initiatives. As the media still invariably react, they were more interested in the public spats than in the principles at stake behind the issues. Rod called it the "let you and him fight" syndrome that motivated the media then and will always be a stock in trade approach by journalists. No doubt, Rod was often harsh in his assessments of people he considered had failed their responsibilities, but he was trying to get a lot of things done and he had to move quickly to succeed. In response, some in the media could only wring their hands. Regarding his criticism of planners, an *Albertan* editorial lamented, "The hypercritically derogatory approach Mayor Sykes has displayed can only fan public prejudice, on the one hand, while generating excusable planner resentment on the other ... it is time he began showing more common sense and courtesy."[19]

No matter. Rod, as U.K. Prime Minister Maggie Thatcher said a few years later about herself, was "not for turning." She became the Iron Lady, but the Iron Man moniker never stuck to him. Instead, Lance Rodewalt, then editorial cartoonist at *The Albertan*, always depicted Rod with a button on his lapel with the words "Thin Power." That struck me as a neat enough label to become the title of a book. So much fire and brimstone originated in a match stick.

When Rod was elected, the mayor was called the "chief officer of the municipality," as was explained earlier in this chapter. He had a responsibility to supervise and inspect the conduct of all municipal officials in the performance of their duties. Early in his tenure and in the spirit of those words, Rod spent a lot of time walking the halls of City Hall and meeting with all levels of City employees, from managers to front-line workers. He asked many questions, watched, and listened.

Rod more than once told the story of Peter Thompson, then with the title of personnel manager, entering his office to tell the new mayor how things

were run in City Hall. The essence of Thompson's message was that the City
didn't hire people with handicaps, but they told other employers to do so.
They didn't promote non-whites beyond supervisor levels. That was code for
people who weren't English or Scottish, and perhaps Irish. They certainly
could never be department heads. Some departments had many long-
term employees who were not permanent and had no pension rights even
after twenty-five years of service. To avoid these obligations, the City hired
workers, and then laid them off every twenty-three weeks, only to hire them
back again when needed.

Hearing these practices, Rod looked Thompson in the eye and told him
the rules had just changed. "We will hire the handicapped if they can do the
job. We will promote entirely on merit in future, regardless of racial origin."
He also ordered pension rights to be created for all long-term employees and
made retroactive to their original hiring. A startled Thompson stammered,
"You can't do that." Rod's curt response: "I just did."

Within minutes, according to Rod's account, Chief Commissioner Strong
and the finance commissioner were in Rod's office to tell him he couldn't
change personnel policies of long standing. He was overstepping his lines of
authority. "I listened to them and gave them a choice. Either accept my decision and follow it, or I will put these issues on council's agenda for public
debate at the next meeting, and I will let council and public opinion decide,"
said Rod. That was not an option the commissioners liked, so his message prevailed. For Rod, that became a way for handling administration recalcitrance.

So it was that people with less than white faces or non-Anglo-Saxon names
discovered new opportunities at City Hall. Seventeen years later, when Rod
wrote a column in the *Calgary Sun* on the stance he had taken on hiring at
City Hall,[20] he received in the mail a clipping of the column with the hand-
written comment: "Please accept a long-delayed thank you from an ever-
grateful 'ethnic' Hugh Quintilio." During a face to face meeting after that,
Quintilio, who ended up as director of engineering, told Rod that he had said
to a colleague at City Hall with similar "ethnic" background after Rod's new
approach became apparent, "Looks like we've got a chance now, Sam." The
Sam was Sam Humeny, who ended up as manager of streets before he retired.

Rod's control over the budget process and his determination to stick to his
hold-the-line-on-taxes promises further illustrated his take-charge approach.
His full immersion into his duties prompted this lament from Fred Kennedy,
who was by this time almost blind: "Ever since he took office he has been
engaged in a running battle with civic administration employees, individual
members of the board of aldermen, public school board trustees, the exhibition and stampede board, the General Hospital Board, the board of governors
of Mount Royal College, patrons of the arts, various ratepayers' associations

and at least one recreational group, in addition to incurring the displeasure of segments of the news media on matters of policy."[21]

Denis Cole, who joined the City as a commissioner in 1971 and became chief commissioner two years later, remembered well the dynamics created by Rod's view of his own powers. In a 2011 conversation, when he was a spritely ninety-one, Cole saw the situation this way: "I visualized council as the board of directors, elected by the shareholders who are the electorate. Rod was chairman of the board. The Chief Executive Officer (CEO) was the chief commissioner. Rod, however, saw himself as the CEO. We had differences, but we could work them out." Regarding Rod's interpretation of his powers, "He stretched things to the limit."

The two argued on finances, said Cole, who came to work for the City after eighteen years in Red Deer as the first director of the regional planning authority there, and then as city manager. Born near London, England, Cole enjoyed some unusual experiences during and after the Second World War, including training as a policeman in Jerusalem and then dealing with land management issues in the Middle East. He had earlier studied as a professional chartered surveyor, specializing in property appraisals and planning.

"Any time the City finished the year with a surplus, Sykes said we had overtaxed the people. But that didn't make sense to me." Sykes was the clear leader on council, although "he didn't always get along with the aldermen," he added. He did recall Rod once threatening, in a half-jovial kind of way, to reduce his salary to a dollar a year.

In one bold fit of independence, Rod declared a half-day holiday for Calgarians to celebrate the Stampeders' Grey Cup victory in Vancouver against Toronto in 1971.[22] Too bad the Calgary Board of Education trustees held an emergency meeting to try to block the holiday (three-quarters of students didn't attend school anyway) and that Chief Commissioner Geoff Hamilton still insisted that City Hall workers would have to remain on the job. "If people say I can't declare a holiday, let them try me," Rod was reported to have said.[23] The same newspaper report noted Rod made the decision after consulting with former Mayor Don MacKay, who had declared a similar celebratory holiday twenty-three years earlier after a previous Stampeder Grey Cup victory. Being carried on fans' shoulders around Vancouver's Hotel Georgia after the game may also have helped Rod in his decision-making. The community celebration and parade for the Stampeders was a happy occasion for tens of thousands of citizens, including many youngsters who remember the occasion to this day.

Throughout his eight years as mayor, Rod regularly reminded others, particularly the board of commissioners, of his specific authorities under the Municipal Government Act. Relationships with the commissioners were frequently fractious. He became frustrated by the trivia he thought dominated much of the commission's weekly meeting agendas, and he felt his positions on issues were not being reflected in commission minutes.

As the following memo hints, he was suspicious of commissioners' motives and ways of operating that seemed to exclude his participation in regular meetings. "From discussions with Kates Peate Marwick [the consulting firm was at the time conducting a management efficiency study at City Hall], I have the impression that their impression is that the board does not work effectively as a board. From my own experience, I know that the mayor, although a member, is for all practical purposes excluded from the board's activities. I believe that we must make the board system work and I intend to do my part. Therefore, please ensure that I'm included in discussions leading to collective decisions of the board in future."[24]

A year later, matters reached a sorrier state. It was time for Rod to once more yank the commissioners' chains. "I believe commission board meetings must be taken much more seriously than they have," Rod said in typical no-nonsense tone.[25] He laid out his reasons in his unmistakable, systematic manner. First, they should start on time and on a day that was convenient for him. He should be consulted on the agendas, which, he said, contained too much "administrative trivia." He also directed his ire at commissioners' practice of setting council's agenda on their own. "This must stop," he wrote. The latter sentence was underlined, with the intent of emphasizing the authority of the mayor and City clerk to decide on agenda items.

Rod flagged other problems too. Then, because he had left for a trip to Northern Europe, he concluded the memo with, "I am happy to discuss these matters when I return. In the meantime, I suggest you give them some thought. Either the board must work effectively as a board, or we should dispense with the illusion." No sugar-coating the issue here, and no chance of misunderstanding. He had got to the point without the niceties that often obfuscate communication within an organization like the City. His attendance at board of commission meetings became less frequent. In his place, he'd send his executive assistant Tom Yarmon to report on what went on. For Rod, the meetings were a waste of time.

Understandably, the commissioners bristled at these missives. Indeed, there was outright resentment and occasionally anger. Rod got along with Denis Cole and with George Cornish most of the time, but "I did lose my temper a couple of times with Denis," Rod recalled.

However, his view of Alan Womack, finance commissioner for most of Rod's tenure, bordered on contempt. He considered Womack inept, pompous, and verbose. When Rod questioned him, Womack, like Geoff Hamilton before him, had a florid face that turned an even deeper red. Womack was easily reduced to stuttering incoherence. There was no pleasure in witnessing that, but after all, he was in a position of considerable responsibility. Others in City Hall referred to Womack behind his back as "Captain Crazy", said City Director of Dental Services John Willey. According to his City Hall obituary, the U.K.-born Womack had once served as a fighter pilot with the Royal Air Force and earned a Distinguished Service Cross. As a commissioner, he tiptoed around Rod nervously.

No wonder. Take this tart note to Chief Commissioner Cole, one of several critical memos about Womack over the years. "When Mr. Womack returns from holiday I would like to discuss with you and with him some unsatisfactory responses to requests of mine. I refer specifically to the failure to take prompt action, and the inadequate, misleading, incomplete, and even rather 'flip' memoranda from him in response to legitimate queries of mine or requests for information. The situation is most unsatisfactory from my point of view, and I believe that Mr. Womack is not carrying out his responsibilities with respect to the mayor's office adequately." [26]

Here's another example of Rod's abrasive, no-nonsense push-back style. [27] He was responding to what he saw as inaccuracies in the board of commissioners' meeting minutes and a number of initiatives the commissioners planned to take without consulting him. He described a part of the minutes as ridiculous. "What the commissioners say is not always in accordance with the facts … get on with the job." On a matter of mileage expenses, he wrote, "Far too many people have car allowances who don't need them. The list should be drastically pruned. It's become a gravy train for the brass!" On a proposed downtown development: "The commissioners have so far failed to protect the public interest. I am disturbed to see further attempts at a hidden giveaway. You should stop this nonsense and either publish what you propose or treat these developers on merit like any others." The tirade continued in the same vein. At the end, for further emphasis, he added, "You will see other notes endorsed on the board minutes representing my views. They should remain on the record and not be in any way deleted or 'lost.' " This is a refreshing directness, and is more evidence of Rod's relentless interest in protecting taxpayers' money in City Hall.

Consider this memo regarding action by commissioners to boost department head salaries. Again, he wrote it in numbered, systematic point form. "Your salary increases exceed the guidelines agreed to by council, and the rationalization you use is merely playing with figures," he said. He pointed out he received no formal notice of the meeting, calling into doubt whether it was a proper meeting anyway. Further, he had received no personnel evaluations on which an intelligent decision could be based. Then he wrote, "Your recommendations in certain cases conflict seriously with your own evaluations of performance expressed to me… The implication is that (i) You didn't want to provide objective reports for objective evaluations. (ii) You didn't want to discuss these matters with me (iii) Your decisions are not objective, and you are looking after your friends. It is a cynical grab, and, for these reasons, I do not consider this matter confidential." [28]

Rod lined up his ducks and took good aim, arming his reasoning with an extra shell—the warning about going public with the information. While his communications with the commissioners may seem stern, Rod had every right to require accountability from them. That was his job. He wanted to make sure there was no weaseling out of their responsibilities. These missives certainly tested commissioners' patience.

Rod's hawk-eyed accountancy skills were ever on the lookout for what he considered spending abuses. A bill from a Calgary firm, McKinsy & Company, consulting to the City on its Management Information System, caught that eye. "I have just seen the bills for three days' consulting services … I must say that I think it inappropriate that an assignment of this sort should be entered into with outside consultants without some advice to the mayor and some discussion with him; and, furthermore, I consider the fees and expenses outrageous." [29] In the final months as mayor, he was still watching over the money and protecting his office's authority.

Another example of his vigilance was a minor matter involving the creation of a brochure for the City by public relations firm Francis Williams and Johnson. The firm, which did pro bono work for Jack Leslie during his 1969 campaign, quickly attracted suspicion from Rod over its long relationship with City Hall. The firm's ability to do most of the City's outside public relations work without any bidding process seemed to warrant further scrutiny. Rod went on the attack. "The last Francis Williams brochure is full of errors of fact and spelling and grammar, it should have been stopped and can do the City no good," said Rod after one job the company did for the City[30] "The question of excessive charge … will be investigated. All future advertising assignments will be made on a basis of quality performance, service, and price, and not on any other basis." The last statement related to the issue of untendered work. This memo signified an almost unheard-of involvement in day-to-day matters, certainly by today's standards. In retirement, Rod still maintained that Francis Williams and Johnson received considerable business from the City outside the tendering process. The result, he said, was "gross overbilling for crap." Small wonder he and principal John Francis were bitter enemies for years.

For willingness to take on all issues without apparent fear, see how he handled long retirement ceremonies at City Hall held during working hours. Note the timing, too—just after Christmas. "I believe retirements ought to be suitably recognized, and in most businesses it is customary to do so with a gathering of friends after working hours," he told commissioners.[31] "In City Hall this sensible practice is not followed." He mentioned two recent retirement ceremonies in the main concourse where the people pay their bills. "The public had no interest but were obstructed. Some eighty employees stood around watching and listening to speeches on working time for which the taxpayer foots the bill. The cost could not be less than $500 for the thirty-five minutes taken. What a way to celebrate retirements! Wasting public money in public! ... I sometimes wonder how we can be so out of touch with the real world ... let's do retirements after working hours in future, please." This order undoubtedly created resentment. And, because it received no publicity outside City Hall, the initiative gained no wider political points for Rod. He was just trying to do his job the best way he knew how, no matter what toes he stepped on.

A frequent target of his blistering missives was Dave Russell, Alberta Minister of Municipal Affairs from 1971-75. A former Calgary alderman and an architect by profession, Russell came across as effete and underhanded in his dealings with Rod. During his second term, Rod learned that Russell was planning a private meeting with some of council's more recalcitrant members to discuss City financing, and who knows what else. "I have always considered that such arrangements are properly made through the mayor," Rod said. "It is particularly interesting that you should take this action with some representatives of my political opposition with an election coming soon. Furthermore, your recent announcements through the press, without consultation or co-operation with the City, conflict with the government's announced policy of consultation and with common courtesy... In view of my satisfactory relationship with the government so far, I am asking for a meeting with the premier to discuss this apparent new policy of yours."[32] This was yet another effective shot across Russell's bow, and it proved successful. It was straightforward language laden with serious intent to injure. The meetings never went ahead.

Rod also showed up regularly at Public Utilities Board hearings when milk price increases were proposed. Because the dairy industry was protected against market forces through price regulation, it was within PUB jurisdiction to set prices. Before Rod was mayor, these proceedings were considered a formality. That is, the lawyers for the dairy companies just showed up, made their perfunctory presentations, and price hikes were approved without a hitch or much publicity. Imagine the dropping jaws when Rod entered the hearing room armed with nothing but a few brief notes and a confident smile to tell the board it must take consumer interests into account and should not simply rubberstamp the increases sought by the industry. He was actively standing up for regular families in the name of the City.

"Milk is essential food, especially for growing children," he said at one hearing, while most of the other participants bristled with hostility. "Many governments have accordingly arranged for subsidized distribution. Ours have not, and this exposes poorer infants and children, in particular, to the economics of the marketplace in a matter of health that will affect them all their lives." Accordingly, he announced the City of Calgary was asking that the application for a milk price increase be refused and that a "full public health study be undertaken with particular reference to the role of milk in child health and the effect of price increases on poorer families."

The study got side-tracked, but he gave the dairy industry and the board considerable food for thought. Of course, they hated this intruder exposing the sham of their pro forma proceedings. Initially, they hadn't prepared for these interventions. Rod thrived on this kind of tense situation, where he was the only one in the room setting up a rational, reasonable, humane perspective against much more narrowly defined self-interest. He spoke directly and seemingly without any sense of being intimidated. When he took part in these hearings, out of the media spotlight, I felt they were occasions to be proud of.

We've seen how effective Rod could be as mayor, combining his own personal, take-charge style with the formal assumption of all the legislated powers at his disposal. Because of his own unique character and the fundamental rule changes in the Municipal Government Act, it's safe to say there's never been a mayor since quite like him, and it's unlikely there will in the future—at least not without restoration of the powers mayors once enjoyed in Alberta.

However, the election of Naheed Nenshi in 2010 as Calgary mayor brought new excitement to the office that citizens hadn't witnessed since Rod's tenure. He couldn't resist making personal comparisons with Nenshi.

Rod, as he liked to remind people, scored the largest majority in Calgary's history, gaining 62% of the vote and remarkably topping almost every poll. Naheed Nenshi, on the other hand, split the vote, taking 40% of the ballots against a large field of candidates, including substantial opponents. Like Rod, who had lived full-time in Calgary only seven years before taking on high office, the latest mayor was considered by many as a newcomer, and certainly an outsider. That's wrong, of course; Naheed Nenshi came to Calgary as a babe-in-arms and lived here most of his life, playing an active role in civic and cultural affairs.

It's hard to ignore the physical disparities between them. First, you have the austere, aesthetic Rod with his stick-like figure, sharp nose on pale, ectomorphic face, thinning hair, sombre suits, and yellowing teeth. He is chalk and cheese next to the full-cheeked, unconstrained Nenshi with his constant movement, colourful clothes, thick shock of black, wavy hair, and dazzling white smile.

Their election victories both drew wide media interest. Nenshi was on national broadcasts right after the election, as was Rod back in 1969. "In both our cases, huge notice was taken," said Rod. The emergence of both men at a similarly youthful age (Rod was just forty, Nenshi thirty-eight) also encouraged hopes of a clean sweep through City Hall, a new way of doing business. This book examines how effective Rod was, though Nenshi's record needs the perspective of more time.

Both men came with stellar qualifications. Rod, the chartered account, was familiar with corporate boardrooms and diverse aspects of private and public financing. He had worked his way toward the top of one of Canada's toughest and most successful corporate empires. Nenshi's credentials were impressive too. A Bachelor of Commerce from the University of Calgary and a Master of Public Policy from the John F. Kennedy School of Government at Harvard University were among formal qualifications. After many years at the business consulting firm, McKinsey & Co., providing corporate strategy for a range of large firms, he formed his own company, consulting to non-profit groups, government, and the private sector. Before becoming mayor, he was Canada's first tenured professor in the field of non-profit management, working at Mount Royal University's Bissett School of Business. He had written extensively on municipal issues.

Like Rod, Nenshi enjoyed considerable enthusiasm from visible minority groups, who now make up a quarter of Calgary's population, according to Statistics Canada figures. Nenshi was a self-confessed "big mouth"; Rod a "smart arse". Rod said in his caustic way, that Nenshi "was much more oriented to the artsy-fartsy crowd."

Although communication technologies have obviously undergone huge transformations in the past four decades, both men's campaigns made excellent use of so-called new media available in their respective eras. Nenshi raised the political application of social media to unprecedented heights. Rod, as we saw, used television, campaign literature, billboards, and public appearances to their fullest potential with innovative techniques. Both men relied a lot on young, bright, behind-the-scenes advisors. Rod had Mike Horsey, and Nenshi had his own relatively youthful adviser constantly at his elbow in public relations hot shot Stephen Carter.

Voters likely saw in Naheed Nenshi a deep sense of the public interest and the strength to tackle wrongdoing, just as they had with Rod. Neither had direct political experience before aiming for the top job, but as Tom McMenemy, a Calgary citizen, pointed out in his support for Nenshi: "The idea that a candidate must have previous political experience to be a good mayor is incorrect. The great Calgary mayor, Rod Sykes, had no experience— and look at his achievements." [33] Rod increasingly questioned Nenshi's abilities to stand up against corruption, over-spending, and political expediency. History will elsewhere make its dispassionate judgment.

7
DOING TIME

I described in chapter 5 Rod's temporary sense of being overwhelmed by the frenzied activities of his first year in office. Efforts to undermine many of his initiatives raged on without respite. Despite a year of progress with his first-term agenda, he continued to swim in conflicting currents of praise and condemnation. Subsequent chapters will focus on specific areas where he put a clear stamp on city affairs, physical infrastructure, and the lives of Calgarians. Before going there, though, let's continue with the chronology of his mayoralty.

The challenges didn't ease up through Rod's three terms. The "loyal opposition" maintained their counterattacks. Two quite contradictory letters to *The Albertan* conveyed the dichotomous assessments of him. "I am unimpressed by his bullying of city commissioners, the planning department, and the police force," said one. "I really think he is showing signs of being 'Sykotic.' I would reiterate to ex-Mayor Leslie that I'm sorry I made an error at the last election, which will not be repeated next time." No name attached; just "Disillusioned, Calgary."

Beside it was Ben Bodenhoff's letter. Mayor Sykes "does not deserve to be the target of idle minds," he wrote. "We are lucky beyond comprehension to have such an able man in our midst, to have such an honest and dedicated man as our mayor ... the distinction between loyal opposition and insidious, incessant, and unwarranted criticism is all too often eluding the backbenchers ... Give the mayor a fair chance to work for the future of this city." [1]

This latter type of public letter gave Rod a predictable boost. It was clear to him he was committed to a long, wearing battle. Those on the sidelines, including the media, gleefully rubbed their hands at the conflicts unfolding before them. By early 1971, some were already anticipating the civic election in the fall. "Mayor Sykes has set the stage for a slam-bam election," said *Albertan* reporter Al Scarth.[2] "He has insured adversary-style politics a large chunk of the spotlight in this fall's civic election." Scarth then lined up comments from council members on their mayor, like cannons taking shots at the approaching enemy from fortress turrets. The ammunition was both surprising and predictable. Here's what some said.

Roy Farran: "A compulsive critic who prefers that role to one of being a leader ... If anyone could sober him down a little, say put him under a cold shower for a week, we'd have a pretty good man ... shoots from the lip, and three times out of ten that he's wrong, shoots someone on his side." Farran was hot and cold about Rod, but usually they were allies. He also had humour.

Bob Greene: "Brilliant financially. They may hate his guts, some of these guys, but they can't match his logic. Has brought more consideration for human rights into city planning. Too abrasive in lots of areas, prone to let personalities become involved too often." The Anglican minister usually considered himself a friend and admirer.

Tom Priddle: "Rod Sykes has spent a whole year shaking things up at City Hall, now let's see him put it back together and make it work efficiently. There is no more fighting in council here than in any other cities, but there are fewer in-camera meetings, and the conflicts are thus reported more fully." Priddle and Rod were frequently at loggerheads, so this comment was unusually mild.

Adrian Berry: "A constant barrage of unwarranted and unproductive attacks emanating from the mayor's office has caused a destructive alienation of council, community, administration ... the mayor's apparent fear of being wrong on any issue is his greatest weakness." This was typical of the negativity invariably emanating from Berry.

John Kushner: "Doesn't pussy-foot about things, one of the sharpest mayors ever. He is using a practical, common-sense approach and trying to live within what people can afford to pay ... he has brought government closer to the people." Kushner owed much to Rod for his political survival, so you'd expect sentiments like these.[3]

Albertan columnist Fred Kennedy, now turning decidedly grumpy as Rod continued to take on some of his buddies, including the police and the Stampede board, could only growl: "As the new administration ends its first year in office, it is obvious that things are not going well at City Hall. All during the year the mayor has been at loggerheads with certain members of council, and his co-operation with the commissioners has been something less than spectacular."[4] Several months later, Kennedy was still hammering away at the same message. "There are times when I feel like shedding a tear for the much harassed and often confused Calgary City Council," he wrote.[5]

"It seems that ever since Rod Sykes became mayor ... they have undergone one traumatic experience after another."

One of Rod's council opponents, already signalling he was going to challenge Rod for the mayor's seat in the October election, was the comical Ed Dooley. After Rod left the city for a few days in February to represent Calgary at the celebrated Winter Carnival in Quebec City, Dooley hatched a plot to occupy the mayor's office. Aldermen took turns every month to be deputy mayor and take on extra duties, and it was his month for the task. He told the media this was a "gesture" to indicate he intended to take on more responsibility than was traditional for deputy mayors. "His [the deputy mayor's] job is to take the place of the mayor in every way," Dooley told surprised media representatives. But, as was duly reported, the rotund alderman, brandishing no weapon more deadly than a determined smile and a partly-smoked cigar, failed to get beyond a locked door. The "one-alderman coup attempt," as Richard Bronstein of *The Albertan* called it, failed when "the absent mayor's lieutenant [executive assistant Mike Horsey] steadfastly adhered to his [Rod's] orders to keep the office locked."[6] Cooler heads prevailed when Dooley and Horsey met with commissioners and City Solicitor Jay Salmon. Dooley emerged to say he would not be entering the mayor's office after all. Contacted in Quebec City, Rod told the media, "I think it's all very silly."

As an aside, Rod attended Carnival several times and built a positive relationship with Quebec City's Mayor Gilles Lamontagne. Following that 1971 visit, the city's French-language daily newspaper, *Le Soleil*, surprised that a mayor from the West would be so fluent, reported that Rod spoke excellent French.[7] Rod shrugged off the compliment, noting that Gisele, his wife, had "taught him a thing or two about the language."

A pre-occupation during 1971 was yet another City Hall probe into possible impropriety by senior administration officials speculating in real estate property. This was the fourth such inquiry in twenty-six years. The repercussions continued into the fall when the names of two of the principal people involved, City Solicitor Jay Salmon and his assistant, Jim Low, came to light through a report by Edmonton lawyer Angus MacDonald on the land interests and private business practices of the two men and other City employees. As was soon disclosed, the two had formed a company called Ponderosa Land Development Ltd. in 1963 and had a history of transactions involving eight Calgary properties, with the intention of renovating them and selling at a profit. Encountering financial difficulties, they had recruited six other shareholders from City Hall. In a short announcement, Rod offered little information except that the two men were suspended from their jobs.[8]

When City Council heard about this, they sought to debate the matter in public. Even though Chief Commissioner Geoff Hamilton suggested the dealings of Salmon and Low were "inimical to the interests of Calgary," and Alderman Roy Farran said their actions were at best indiscreet, Aldermen decided by a 9-3 vote to re-instate the two officials. Rod was reported to have remained "strangely silent" through the debate.[9]

Within weeks, however, the two left City Hall permanently. If there was a cloud over their heads, they at least had bags of gold in their hands, in the form of a full year's salary for each of them. That settlement, coming after an 8-4 vote, predictably angered Rod. The settlement prompted Calgary Labour Council executive secretary Bill Paterson to suggest that all City unions should secure such a sweet deal in their contracts for any members let go by the administration.

In the latter half of 1971, another historic election set Alberta politics in quite a different direction. On August 30, the Progressive Conservative Party, led by the youthful and seemingly dynamic Peter Lougheed, broke the thirty-six-year dominance over provincial politics of the Social Credit Party. After the retirement of Social Credit Premier Ernest Manning three years earlier, his successor, honest but plodding farmer Harry Strom, had been unable to revive what was seen as a tired regime. With forty-six per cent of the popular vote, the Lougheed Tories won forty-nine of the seventy-five seats in the Legislature and formed a strong majority. The Socred's precipitous drop to opposition status and twenty-five seats was attributed to plunging support from the two major urban centres of Calgary and Edmonton, combined with the distortions of the first-past-the-post electoral system.

Rod enjoyed a friendly relationship with Manning and Strom. Through his massive building achievements with Marathon Realty, he had often dealt with them directly. *The Albertan* headline after the election reflected Rod's dilemma over their loss. "Rod Sykes offers congratulations, sympathy," it said. "Nobody who has regard for the solid achievements of Social Credit under Ernest Manning can see it pass without regret," Rod said in a statement. "My sympathy goes out to Harry Strom—a fine man who took on a tough job ... Unfortunately, he had poor advisers, and when a leader listens to poor advisers, he pays the price."[10]

For Lougheed, the glitzy lawyer, Rod obviously had congratulations too. "He has a tremendous opportunity ahead of him ... He is well qualified for his job, and I will work with him for the good of the people of Calgary," Rod said. Pointedly he added, "I look to him to implement his campaign undertakings." He referred particularly to Lougheed's promise to relieve homeowners of a portion of the burden of education taxes, to restore to cities a fair share of oil and gas revenues, and above all, to protect individual rights and liberties. Rod did not hit it off with the thin-skinned premier he considered quite vain, and years later, judged that Lougheed failed on all these undertakings.

In the meantime, Rod had to face judgment from the electorate within a month and a half. Frank Johns announced in early September he would take a leave of absence from his position of executive secretary with the Calgary Real Estate Board and stand for mayor.[11] Running under the umbrella of an amorphous but well-funded group calling themselves the October 13 Citizens Committee, (the date of the election) the fifty-three-year-old Johns set himself the goal of attracting five thousand campaign workers by the September 15 official nomination day. Reuben Hamm served as campaign manager and the executive director of the October 13 group. He later found a niche for himself as a "futurist" and new trends guru adviser to governments and private companies.

"I'm known for being a thinker," Johns was quoted as saying after a thirty-three-year career in real estate.[12] Things probably started going downhill from there for the tall, heavy-set man with dark hair brushed back from a high forehead. With his pencil-slim moustache and tight mouth, he gave off the air of a small-town band leader having trouble keeping his musicians on beat. He said a key to his approach to civic business would be to restore order and confidence in the civic administration and in the council chamber. He pledged constructive, positive leadership, and harmonious and morale-bolstering relationships with the administration. By that he meant, of course, that he wouldn't be a mean-mouthed cad like Rod Sykes.

With his ever-sharp competitive instincts, Rod sensed that the October 13 Citizens Committee, with its preponderance of real estate interests and its well-filled coffers, was vulnerable to public exposure. City Hall can't be bought, he said quite pointedly to a conference in Winnipeg five weeks before the civic vote. He made it clear that voters are too smart to be fooled by any group with unlimited funds that tries to "buy" City Hall in an election.[13] Although no direct reference was made, Rod's remarks were clearly a broadside against the Frank Johns machine. "Over the years, some special interest groups, often related to the real estate industry, gradually take over and dig themselves in ... This kind of government by crony or clique destroys public confidence in the democratic system, discourages participation, holds back civic progress, penalizes the poor and disadvantaged, and produces a host of other evils," Rod said. One could already hear the air hissing out of the Johns campaign.

Alf Harris, a mayoralty candidate in 1969, also declared his intention to run again. The dour, thick-set lawyer announced increased resource revenues and equitable taxation as his top priorities. He called for a swimming pool and an ice rink for every ten thousand Calgarians. He also wanted to shelve the convention centre project, introduce a "crash" program to involve women in politics by instituting a twenty-five-per-cent quota on civic committees, and push clean environment proposals. Rod was not independent, he said, because of the involvement of the Social Credit machine in the 1969 election.[14] Harris had only gained 5,670 votes then. He was destined to be a non-factor again in 1971.

About three weeks before the vote, *The Herald* declared Rod the front runner. He has "sewed up the 'little man' vote because of his Sunday radio chats," said reporter Gary Park. "While alienating segments of the middle class, he has consistently curried support of the 'little man' and ethnic minorities to hold a large, solid voting bloc."[15] Johns was still not well known, and Sykes was gaining ground by hammering at his opponent's real estate background.

Johns' get-rid-of-Sykes-at-all-costs campaign soon entered even rougher straits. Rod recalled that Harry Huish, then a community association leader later to be elected as an alderman from southeast Calgary, and mostly an ally of Rod's, organized a mayoralty debate at the Ogden Legion Hall. The expectation was that the audience would be mostly Sykes people. "It was packed when I arrived, but Johns was so fearful he didn't show up," said Rod. Then word came that, exhausted by the campaign effort, he had collapsed and had been taken to hospital.

Instead of commiseration, Rod responded as only he could. He reminded the audience he had been in the public spotlight for a couple of years, while Johns had for only three weeks during the campaign. "I wonder how he would endure the rigors of the mayor's position," he hinted. He also wondered aloud whether the story was true. "I don't think he's sick, he's just scared to show up," he told his friendly audience. He recalled in later years, "There was a kind of a love-in with the audience after that."

There was little surprise when the media described a smiling, relaxed, but obviously tired Rod Sykes savouring his second resounding win in the Calgary civic arena. In 1969, he drew sixty-two per cent of the vote, and this time it was fifty-eight per cent. As after his first election, the victory party frolicked well into the early morning at the Danish Canadian Club. Among the supporting cast was the quiet and modestly competent John Starchuk, who had served as a loyal campaign manager.

"John masterminded the successful Rod Sykes mayoralty campaign," said *Herald* columnist Brian Brennan after Starchuk died in 1997.[16] Brennan quoted former *Herald* columnist Johnnie Hopkins, asserting in an earlier column, "Everything considered, Starchuk probably will be remembered as the guy who got Rod Sykes elected." That was an exaggeration, but he certainly served as a dependable and well-liked campaign figure-head. Besides, he was better known as the owner of the St. Louis Hotel, east of City Hall, which Rod and other City Hall workers favoured as a hang-out, along with a fascinating mosaic of other Calgary people. Starchuk had run himself for public office unsuccessfully as a Liberal in Calgary Centre during the 1967 federal election. The year after the 1971 election, he sold the famous hotel and bar to the Blitt brothers, who maintained the place until selling it to the City in 2006 for east-end renewal plans.

At the post-election news conference, Rod couldn't resist a parting shot at the Johns campaign. His own campaign, he explained, had concentrated on advertising on bus benches and billboards, and more lightly on television exposure. "Bus benches and billboards don't indicate you have more money; they indicate you're smarter," said an obviously pleased Rod. The bus bench and billboard campaign, incidentally, was largely thanks to the presence on Rod's campaign team of Gene Filipski, former Stampeders footballer and by then owner of Tioga Signs with close to a monopoly over these facilities in Calgary.

The press had to contort themselves to say anything positive about Rod's win. "We would be dishonest if we said we were delighted," wrote *Albertan* editorial writer Peter Hepher. "Mr. Sykes' victory must be attributed not only to an aggressive and professional campaign, but to skillful employment of the political opportunities of his first term in office." He noted that Johns had started out the campaign as a virtual unknown. The fact that all the incumbent aldermen running had also won was further sign Calgary voters were not ready for change.[17]

The new term was off to a good start when Rod went to Edmonton for his first meeting with the shiny, polished, just-installed Premier Lougheed. He returned "buoyant," according to one description,[18] with all kinds of job-creation good news, including a promise from the Province to contribute $42 million for housing through its Alberta Housing Corporation. Other money from Calgary's share could go to seniors' and veterans' housing, airport construction, transit improvements, and the New Life for Old Neighbourhoods program, which all fit in well with Rod's agenda.

A fascinating detour was Rod's appointment as Finnish consul in Calgary and the official representative of the Finnish government in the city. Asked by the Finnish ambassador to Canada to assume the position, Rod called it a "particular honour since I am not a Finnish national."[19] He was still familiarizing himself with the duties and official protocol involved. In general, he explained, he would represent Finland in Calgary, looking after the interests of Finnish nationals in the area, and fostering social and commercial ties between Finland and Calgary.

Rod professed to an abiding interest in and respect for Finland. "The Finns put on an extraordinary performance during the last war [World War Two] when they defended their country single-handedly," he said. "That admiration has always stayed with me." As confirmation of these ties, Rod sixteen months later appointed Nalle Sumelius, a native Finn from Helsinki and the son of the Finnish ambassador to Canada, as his executive assistant to replace the departed Tom Yarmon. Fluent in English, holding a degree in regional economics, and by then an assistant lecturer in that subject in the Swedish School of Economics, the twenty-six-year-old Sumelius had just completed three months in Ottawa working on his thesis on regional development.[20] His skills, plus a quiet charm and ease with people, seemed well suited to his new job.

Rod had previously known his father, Holger Sumelius, and met Nalle during a visit to Finland. Rod and Holger had, during an inspired evening, discussed the Finnish word *Sisu*, which Rod came to understand referred to a quality of not counting the costs when going to war. Rod certainly appreciated that attribute in Finns; they reflected well his own sensibilities. After Rod assumed his consulate duties, Holger Sumelius instructed Rod on required protocols. As part of his lessons, Rod had clear memories of eating reindeer tongues. Holger also taught him a toast in Finnish. "What does it mean in English?" he asked. "You could say 'Up your kilt,' " Holger replied. To indicate his prowess with Finnish ways, Rod later used the toast at a Finnish banquet. Hearing nervous titters among his audience, Rod afterwards asked another Finn what the toast really meant. "A good deal further than up your kilt," replied his jovial translator. Rod was careful not to toast that way again, at least not in public.

Back to more sober but important affairs at City Hall, Rod continued pushing his public and seniors' housing agenda. A good example of his success was Bridgeland Place, a seventeen-storey high-rise at 736 Memorial Drive Northeast with four hundred tenants. At the official opening, Rod described the project as one of the best examples of social housing.[21] It was built by a private developer, Paragon Properties, with government funds; in other words, a public-private partnership. The president of the company was Charlie Smith, a Sykes backer whom Rod appointed to the planning commission, and later other boards, prompting bitter criticism of Rod for promoting his cronies. Originally, Paragon wanted to build an upscale building at that location, but Rod managed to nudge the company along a different path.

The idealism of Rod's comments at the Bridgeland Place opening still sparkle. "If developers concentrate on trying to maximize their profits from buildings designed strictly for private rentals, then the people who need shelter won't get it," he said. "The free enterprise system can expand its benefits. Developers have to work on projects like this that are not so highly profitable, but which do bring a bread and butter return—and everybody's entitled to that."[22] Rod realized the city would need an increasing inventory of affordable housing. "I knew we were going to attract growth," he said years later.

With some urgency, Rod was the major force behind a new zoning bylaw by the end of 1972. A zoning bylaw would offer orderly development, he said. The city had been operating under a system of development control resulting in considerable uncertainty to residents about what could be built in their neighbourhoods. The bylaw's restoration of planning certainty was a positive move.

Despite Rod's successes, disillusionment was apparent in a *Canadian Press* interview with Rod that ran across Canada. "I don't like politics and I've never made any secret of that," he said. "I think it's a dirty business, there have to be better ways to earn a living ... I can't afford what I'm doing. I'm earning less money than I ever did in recent years here, and I have far, far less security and a far less pleasant life. You've got to be crazy to be here." At the time, he earned $27,000 a year and had resisted any attempts by council to increase pay.

The headline, "Council rises against Mayor,"[23] did not augur well, either. The election the previous fall had resulted in five new aldermen. Reporter Jim Dau suggested Rod "has apparently lost majority support of council." The issue came to light in the annual appointment process for the City's forty committees, boards, and commissions. Rod's choices were rejected by a consistent 8-4 vote. Council named all new members to the police commission, and shockingly, Rod was excluded from the Stampede Board. Dau described the four-hour meeting filled with "hot debate and shows of temper."

Columnist Fred Kennedy gloated. "It is not necessary for Calgary citizens to light bonfires on the hills ... to herald the first concrete move by members of the City Council against the 'Tammany Hall type of domination' by Rod Sykes at City Hall," he wrote. He described the refusal of council to accept Rod's appointment wishes as a palace revolution. "The revolution now is well under way. The aldermen have made the first move to stand up to the acid tongue."[24]

Despite charges that Rod knew only how to respond with verbal overkill to opposition or disagreement, he knew and occasionally practiced the arts of quiet diplomacy and conciliation too. A scourge for Rod in his second and third terms was Alderman Ed Oman. An ordained minister with a Master of Divinity degree, Oman officiated at Calgary's Covenant Church for seventeen years. He was director of the church choir for thirteen years. But relations with Rod were not harmonious, especially when Oman openly declared he would run for mayor in 1977. After failing badly in that race, he was elected to the Provincial Legislature in 1979 as the Conservative MLA for Calgary North Hill. In council, he often came across as confused, without a good grasp of municipal issues. Despite Oman's rather bland persona, Rod believed he harboured less benign intentions.

Still, when Oman wrote to Rod well into his second term to express his concerns over the divisions within council and the negative impacts on civic business, Rod responded openly and at great length.[25] "There are times when I have been very irritated with council," said Rod. "You must have noticed that I am almost continually the target of one alderman or another … I am only human, and you must not be surprised if there are times when I become very impatient indeed. I do not dispute that there are times, also, when I may instigate some conflict. Do you know any one of us who is without fault?" That represents a relatively rare confession, combined with a non-too-subtle biblical reference to Jesus' admonitions about the man without fault casting the first stones at the condemned criminal.

More qualified contrition followed. "I am sorry that you think that I have been downgrading council efforts," said Rod. "Certainly, I am frequently disappointed with the results of council's efforts and I do not think that it helps any of us … to have a council so thoroughly divided and so frequently engaged in petty squabbling and name calling as we have." Later in the letter he continued, "I think you are quite correct in saying that we must rise above our personal prejudices." Most important, Rod added, is for council to realize "that their personal feelings have nothing to do with their duty. They are bound to work together." He then outlined other practical, procedural changes to improve co-operation in council chambers. He thanked Oman for his "sincere and constructive" letter. That certainly came across as helpful language, but icy winds from predictable directions soon extinguished this flicker of hope.

Before Christmas, at the height of the good will season, Alderman Don Hartman came unglued again, this time with a torrent of criticism of Rod's attendance record at City Hall.[26] The mayor had missed a portion of six out of the seven last council meetings, Hartman charged. Also, "we shouldn't be criticized later in the press for action at meetings he didn't attend." Hartman added the ominous-sounding warning: "Some action must be taken." The issue bounced back three months later with *The Herald's* publication of Rod's attendance record in the previous twelve months. It showed he'd been at only 36 of 131 major City policy committee and commission meetings, prompting the comment from Hartman to fellow aldermen: "Any time you're ready to cut his salary, I'm ready."

On the question of salary, the mayor and council had already caught public flack for meeting in camera to discuss pay raises for themselves. The result was a motion in council in early 1973 to boost the mayor's pay to $30,000 a year, and the aldermen's to $9,000, approved in a 7-4 vote. The recommendations for the increases came from consultants Kate Peate Marwick and represented the first raise in over three years since Rod was first elected. That didn't stop Fred Kennedy. "There was something extremely hypocritical and even vulgar after the action of the mayor and council voting themselves a money grab behind closed doors."[27]

Next came *The Herald's* Don Whitely, suggesting Rod rivaled former U.S. Secretary of State and globe-trotting diplomat Dr. Henry Kissinger as the most-travelled man in North America.[28] Since 1969, Rod Sykes had journeyed to Australia, Britain, France, and Italy. Now it appeared, Whitely said, he was off to Finland and Scandinavia for two weeks, partly in his capacity as Finnish consul, just as budget time was approaching. "He is abandoning taxpayers at a time when they really need him." Although that was hardly a lot of travelling for a big-city mayor, Whitely called on Rod to "surrender his wages" for that period.

True to previous form, Rod left behind a five-page letter of guidance for the budget deliberations he would miss while away. Eight of the aldermen rose up in rage. Petrasuk said the letter contained "accusations by innuendo and inference." Hartman called it a poison-pen letter filled with character assassinations. Ayer said Rod Sykes "feels he's touched by the hand of God and can be mayor in absentia." Council then voted 8-3 to "regret" that the mayor did not see fit to bring his comments in person to council.

What got their blood boiling? Rod was again practising his red-cape routine with the raging bull. In his letter, he had expanded membership in what he called the "big spenders club" to find a place for Petrasuk and Hartman, alongside Musgreave and Berry. Petrasuk, by now quite actively considering an entry into the 1974 mayoralty race, promptly challenged Rod to compare their voting records on expenditures.

Rod was often asked during and after his time as mayor whether, in retrospect, he might have accomplished more with aldermen and city commissioners if he had been less abrasive in his tactics. His usual observation was, "When things get difficult, you can't always mollify or conciliate. There are times when you must come out kicking. Harmony is desirable, but sometimes it doesn't get things done, whereas the shock treatment may succeed."

The media gloom turned murkier. Under the heading, "Mayor's Grip on Council Weakens," Gary Park stated in his regular column, "The past week may have been the worst of Rod Sykes' three-and-a-half-year occupancy of the mayor's office. And the mayor has only himself to blame for the ridicule, scorn, and anger that have been heaped upon him." Reviving the issue of Rod's travel spending, Park asked, "Why did he feel it necessary to attack reporters with such force?" Park questioned Rod's blast at the sniping from two members of City Hall media whom Rod refused to identify. "It was a curious position for the mayor to take after three and a half years of constantly chiding reporters for failing to pursue the truth," he said. "In this case, the truth involved public money, and it's well known that Mayor Sykes is the self-proclaimed, single responsible guardian of the public purse on council. He has harped without let-up on the need to spend other peoples' money with prudence. The feeling now is that Mayor Sykes is interested in the truth only when others are on the receiving end." Ouch. Then more harsh words from the normally sanguine New Zealand-born journalist: "It's about time he learned to take his lumps with better grace."[29]

Despite the media nay-saying, Rod still possessed an aura of invincibility. "I will go where I think it's necessary, in my discretion, and I'll answer for it to the people of Calgary, and not to some aldermen who have got ambitions of their own." To further drive his point home, he confirmed he would be a candidate in the October 1974 election. "In case there's any doubt about that ... I will be there." A council censure motion on his travels lost when it was tabled *sine die*, which meant indefinitely. Rod had once more dispatched his enemies, and he had demonstrated in this case they were a minority of council.

Positive things were happening too. During early 1973, Rod named five citizens to head up his personal initiative to open up City Hall to regular folk. Lawyer Dick Armitage, teacher and Victoria Park activist Rebecca Aizenman, University of Calgary political science professor John Woods, and house-wives (as they were then called) Betty Thomas and Pat Donnelly were the big wheels for the Citizens Open Government Study (COGS). Holding open workshops around the city, COGS later produced positive ideas for broadening the opportunities for more people to participate in the affairs of their local government, and determine ways citizen input could be incorporated into policy-making.[30] Pat Donnelly went on to successfully run in 1974 as an alderman.

Rod also pursued in 1973 a long-held ambition to force developers to make a percentage of their serviced house lots available to smaller builders. In a motion he took to council, he said he wanted to prevent major developers from hoarding land and to create healthy competition among the various builders. This wasn't his first or last effort to bring a greater supply of competitively-priced housing on the market for Calgarians. The previous year he had pushed for a land study to ensure that an adequate supply of residential land was available for development at reasonable prices.[31]

In a momentary diversion from the drudgery of everyday responsibilities, Rod pricked the hide of a moose of a Manitoba MLA called Joe Borowski. Rod accused Borowski of making "foolish, ignorant, and irresponsible" remarks about Quebec politicians at a Calgary student forum and said he was investigating the possibility of laying charges under appropriate human rights legislation for his intemperate language. During his talk to the students, Borowski, then an independent politician after quitting the Manitoba NDP caucus, had intimated the people of Quebec deserved to suffer because they had elected "morons" who were also "corrupt". Rod called the remarks insulting to all French Canadians. These were times, of course, when sensitivities between Quebec and the rest of Canada were on edge. When Borowski heard of Rod's reaction, he branded him a "headline rustler" who "would walk naked down the street to get into the newspapers."[32] He also said he would write to council asking for an apology. "I hope the council will deal with his outburst. I'll ask them to put a lasso on that big, fat tongue of his." He even sent Rod a short letter of response on his MLA stationary that read, "Dear Mayor Sykes (Headline Rustler): In reply to your letter of May 1, 1973, I would like to make the following comments – YAWN King-size YAWN. Kindest regards, etc."

A report in the spring of 1973 by auditors Arthur Andersen & Company offered intimations of hanky-panky in the City's library operations. But the company dismissed the accusations against the library as "groundless or relatively unimportant."[33] Its final report also said it had been unable to check many of the allegations made. For Rod and for others, this was another exercise in sweeping corruption under the rug. He had instigated the review of library operations when a library board member, Dr. M. Mackie, approached him with a list of complaints she was unable to find answers to. The thirteen allegations investigated included the operation of a loan business to employees operated by a high official; the conduct of a catering business in the library by an employee's relative; the case of a new refrigerator bought for the library but ending up in a private residence and substituted in the library by a used fridge; the burning of files after a board meeting where these questions were raised; a system of weekend employment at overtime pay for officials' relatives; and predictably given this litany of troublesome activities, low staff morale. Although this mystery story was never fully resolved, the auditors found that three relatives of senior library officials did work at the library. A principal recommendation was for the library to hire a business-oriented person to be responsible for internal operations. While the revealed scandals were not on a grand scale, this was hardly reassuring.

By early 1974, Rod had more questions for City Solicitor Brian Scott regarding various conflict of interest scenarios affecting council members. The land registry rules council introduced for itself in 1972, requiring the mayor and aldermen to list all their properties within the city, now appeared inadequate, Rod said. He then asked about other activities that he felt contravened the spirit of those rules. He questioned the legality of aldermen offering their personal, well-paid services in certain fields, such as charity fundraising, planning consulting, or public relations, for which they had no prior training or experience. He wondered about aldermen serving, without declaring their

interests, on City committees dealing with specific actions or policies affecting their private-business clients. Rod also raised the issue of aldermen with
interests in apartment holdings, yet voting on matters that might affect their
investments. Should they not abstain from discussing and voting on matters
that put the public interest in conflict with their private financial interests?[34]

"We may need a change of rules," Rod told Scott. This effort to limit wrongdoing is as valid today as it was then. The reality was, most elected officials
were not interested and continue to lack an appetite for this kind of openness
in their affairs.

A clear boost to Rod came when *MacLean's Magazine* declared him the
best mayor in Canada after a reader survey. "Sykes, say the Calgarians who
sing his praises, is concerned, intelligent, active, outspoken and 'really cares
about people,' " wrote Walter Stewart.[35] "There are some naysayers, a handful
of Calgarians who find Sykes overbearing and cantankerous," Stewart added.
One reader suggested, "He is the only man in Canada who knows anything;
if you don't believe it, ask him." The *MacLean's* poll received 339 letters from
across Canada. The recognition came as a welcome surprise. Obviously, the
poll was not scientific, but *The Herald* and other local media ignored the
story entirely.

Rod's friendship with federal Urban Affairs Minister Ron Basford was a
big factor behind the granting in 1973 of $3 million in federal funds under
the Neighbourhood Improvement Program (NIP) to Calgary and Edmonton.
The working-class Inglewood-Ramsay district in east Calgary was the first
neighbourhood to benefit from the program, designed to provide residents
with low-interest home improvement loans.[36] This was an important part of
Rod's push for competitively-priced housing. He believed that the residential
rehabilitation encouraged by NIP would allow families to remain in older
neighbourhoods. It would also help home owners to maintain reasonable
safety and health standards for suites, whether legal or otherwise. Rod took
the position that illegal suites, if safe and conforming to health standards,
should be allowed. They obviously provided important, lower-cost accommodation, as well as giving owners additional income to remain in their
homes. The end goal was good, safe, affordable housing for Calgary's rapidly
growing population.

That's the reason he was so opposed in the summer of 1973 to City plans
for the annexation of 2,400 acres in northwest Calgary for high-end housing.
The planning commission approved the annexation after a "long and heated"
debate.[37] Rod promised he would do everything in his power to halt the
proposal, in which Carma Developers would be the primary beneficiary. He
called it "the most destructive and damaging thing ever done to prospective
homeowners in Calgary." He sought instead a balanced annexation covering

all areas surrounding the city where far more lots in the medium and low price range would be available.

So resistant was Rod to the annexation plan, he attacked it nine months later at a Local Authorities Board hearing. He described Carma's plans for the northwest as "horrible little environments ... a reversion to caveman urbanism." The plans called for village-style subdivisions grouped around a central core. He lost that battle, and those village-style subdivisions subsequently became common in Calgary and most other North American cities.

His push for a reliable stream of affordable housing never abated; ten per cent below the Edmonton market price for starter homes was a specific target. Because of his good relationship with the people concerned, he was able early on in his tenure to encourage the creation of a tri-level partnership, with then federal Housing Minister Ron Basford and provincial premier, Harry Strom, as the other two partners. "We worked well together to build an experimental housing program," Rod recalled later. The main role of the Feds was to ensure availability of mortgage funds. Down payments were to remain low, and the purchase costs were to be controlled.

Because bureaucratic delays in the conventional subdivision approval processes were a deterrent for builders to become involved in such projects, the tri-level partnership established an approval process that would give the mayor astounding and fast approval powers. "I was the cook, the deck hand, the navigator, the captain," said Rod. If the planning and engineering departments were slow approving projects, Rod was able to let developers proceed on his own say-so. "The administration was thunderstruck; they couldn't stop the mayor actually overriding their rules."

Contacting builders he was familiar with from his Marathon days, Rod persuaded many to collaborate. His message to them was, "I want you to have a ten-per-cent profit, use your unused land within the city limits and keep your skilled builders working through the winter." Initially, the program worked well. Rod estimated three thousand homes were built this way in his first term. However, when he spoke to an international symposium in Montreal in the spring of 1974, Rod was less enthusiastic about Calgary's housing prospects than he was when he, Basford, and Strom worked out their unique deal four years before. The power struggle among governments was crippling housing efforts in Canada, he told the symposium.[38] "There is no credible social housing policy in any level of government," he said. Senior governments had abandoned responsibility for housing. The federal successes in 1970-72 came from their dealing directly with cities, but that roused resentment in provincial governments because they sought exclusive constitutional authority over cities. "Many provincial governments are hostile to their cities," said Rod. That was a sharp slap at Alberta's Lougheed Tories.

He then added a point as valid today as it was then: Inadequate housing was reflected in the crime rate, broken marriages, mental illness, and increased costs for social services. Adequate, low-cost housing today still languishes in inter-jurisdictional disputes and doesn't get built.

The winds of an approaching election were now blowing through our prairie city. Rod had to gird himself for more battles.

8
ONE MORE ROUND

Through ubiquitous sources offering him a constant trickle of intelligence about the intrigues of City Hall, Rod learned that Aldermen Ross Alger and Peter Petrasuk had worked out a deal that both would express an interest in running for mayor in the October 1974 civic election. When it became apparent that one candidacy was more popular than the other, the candidate with the lesser support would withdraw, and they would combine their forces. That was the plan, at least. The idea was to avoid splitting the vote and letting Rod come up the middle to victory.

So, it came as a surprise when Alger announced his candidacy just before the July Stampede during the height of summer in the election year. Alger was forced to acknowledge that most of his campaign committee members were out of town at the time, and he hadn't yet discussed campaign details with them.[1] Had he jumped the starter's pistol to gain a step on Petrasuk? It's hard to know, although the odd timing of the announcement prevented Alger from getting off to the strongest of launches. Slamming Rod's leadership during the previous five years, Alger said he was basing his candidacy on a "peace-making platform." The main issue, he said, was determining what kind of man Calgarians want to lead the city. Rod Sykes was not interested in leadership, but "in doing things on his own." Alger, in supposed contrast, promised a "level-headed government that will make sense, not headlines."

Alger conceded that he was originally going to wait longer to make the announcement, but "the city's poor performance on setting the mill rate crystallized my thinking today." He went on to insist he would not "denigrate, insult, and harass" senior civil servants the way he claimed the incumbent had done during the previous two terms. "The list of senior civil servants who have left because their life became unbearable is long and distinguished, and very sad for the city," he bemoaned. Oddly, he announced he would push for full-time aldermen and favoured their need to "do a great deal of their work out of the glare of Council Chambers." In other words, farewell open government. The patrician accountant was revealing his true colours.

For media consumption, Rod welcomed the announcement from "my most credible opponent in the mayoralty campaign." With Ed Dooley already a declared candidate, he also knew that a stiffly proud and competitive Peter Petrasuk was waiting in the wings to inform Calgary about his mayoralty intentions and would bristle at his remarks.

Less than a month later, Calgary's worst-kept secret finally became public knowledge. Nattily dressed in blazer and light slacks, two-tone shoes, and a flower in his lapel, Petrasuk used a party in the back garden of his comfortable northwest Calgary home to break the news. The forty-seven-year-old lawyer, born in humbler circumstances in Ukraine, was looking forward to being a "player" on the Calgary political scene.[2] He had a BSc. in electrical engineering from the University of Alberta and a law degree from the University of British Columbia. After articling in Calgary, he had set up his own firm here.

Taking the obligatory swipe at Rod, he declared, "It is my firm intention to restore respect, along with honesty, integrity, and a commitment to public service at City Hall." Too bad, of course, that he didn't quite fulfill that promise—seven years later, he offered a guilty plea to charges of theft and breach of trust after having stolen a million dollars from clients of his law practice, including his mother. For that indiscretion, he was sentenced to ten years in the federal penitentiary at Bowden in central Alberta. Yet, at his candidacy announcement, he was able to say, "These qualities [honesty and integrity] have been on a measurable decline for the past five years. Today they are almost non-existent ... I think I can do a much better job than Sykes." Now there were two candidates saying they would play nicely with the City commissioners. Alger and Petrasuk shared the same platform of administrative appeasement. Asked how he would assess the current mayor's performance, Petrasuk huffed: "What can I say? He's so seldom in town." Petrasuk said his goal was to create a city for people, not for developers.

While many citizens were still away at the cabin, the race was on. From Rod's perspective, then and later in life, Alger was seeking to be a figurehead mayor as a way of capping off his career. Petrasuk, on the other hand, while dour and humourless, did demonstrate a competence and understanding of civic government. In mid-August, reporter Frank Dabbs scooped his competitors with a story that "an active corps of City Hall administrators is fostering an anti-Sykes political movement to tilt the mayor from his throne."[3] They were studying the City manual to find a loophole to the no-politics rules governing civil servants. They were determined to be active in the October 16 election and back Petrasuk, according to Dabbs. Asked to comment on a story that he may have helped fabricate himself, Petrasuk blamed Rod for bringing this situation on his own head. "Mayor Sykes will never be able to repair his relations with senior staff," he said with a thrust of the dagger. The more clueless and politically naive Alger could only stammer he was unaware that those at City Hall upset with Rod "had jelled into a Petrasuk group."[4]

At the same time, the *Globe and Mail's* Suzanne Zwarun made public a report by Clive Chalkley, manager of the Calgary Manpower Department, that was, in Rod's words, "devastating" in its indictment of the planning department. The report revealed that nine city planners, almost a third of the senior group, had quit in the past year. "Employees blame the mayor for ridiculing their efforts and resent his references to them as faceless bureaucrats," the report said.[5] Rod's immediate reaction was that more should be fired.

Even though he was virtually blind, columnist Fred Kennedy was still able to discern the unfolding mayoralty race drama the most realistically. "With four candidates vying for the anti-Sykes vote [a plumber's helper called John Mason, whose later bizarre behaviour prompted consternation over his mental health, had entered the race on nomination day], the present incumbent will be a galloping winner on October 16," said a clearly embittered Kennedy. "Even if there is tremendous revulsion against the Sykes regime, it is inconceivable that the protest vote would be large enough to split four ways and still ensure the mayor's defeat."[6]

With less than three weeks to the election, wily reporter Frank Dabbs wrote a prescient analysis of the upcoming vote. "River flows to the heart of the race," said the headline.[7] Ed Dooley had been campaigning since January, but Dabbs quoted Rod's dismissal of him as a clown. Dabbs' analysis went this way: As a boy, Peter Petrasuk had lived north of the Bow River in the Bridgeland-Riverside neighbourhood. Ironically, in view of his later tangle with the law, Petrasuk recalled light-heartedly most of his friends either went into the police or into jail. With his extensive circle of friends, he felt confident he could take the north. In the meantime, he hoped Alger would "chip away" at potential Sykes voters in more waspish south Calgary. In fact, Dabbs pointed out, both Petrasuk and Alger, who had broken their mutual agreement to concede to whomever seemed more likely to win, believed they could win on their respective side of the river and have the "other fellow erode Sykes support on the opposite bank."

Rod, meanwhile, was quoted as being confident of loyalty from working families and varied ethnic constituencies throughout the city. "People vote for me because they can trust me—they know where I stand," was his well-used turn of phrase. He also contended that Petrasuk's much-touted ethnic bloc didn't exist. Minorities were insulted because Petrasuk lumped them into a bloc and implied they were in his hip pocket, Rod said. With that in mind, Rod predicted a third place for his long-time rival.

Much of the pre-election chatter was predictably directed at Rod. The perception he had treated City Hall administrators too harshly featured strongly in the attacks. Release by commissioners during the campaign of a report on concentration of land ownership in Calgary in the hands of a few notable developers was supposed to provide a whiff of scandal and hurt Rod, but it was then Chief Commissioner Geoff Hamilton who initiated the report, without consulting Rod or his fellow commissioners. There was little fall-out on Rod's campaign. In fact, the report showed that Rod had acted above board in his efforts to bring as much developable land on stream as possible in a competitive environment.

For Rod, the issue of land ownership concentration struck him as significant from the time he first took office. "The City had land control locked in with Carma and Nu-West," he said. "This was an intolerable position for my housing ambitions." That's why he invited companies like BACM, Genstar, Daon, and Melcor to become active in the Calgary housing market. Previously, they had felt excluded by Carma and Nu-West, but if the City opened up more land for housing, then they agreed to become involved. Rod enlisted co-operation from those he called the "better members of council" to back his wooing of other companies to develop land. These matters were discussed in camera, that is, in secret.

Jack Poole, self-made building magnate who had co-created Daon Development Corporation almost a decade earlier, was one of the people Rod approached to work with him on his affordable housing ambitions. As a result of Rod's contact, Poole optioned a large amount of land and, in Rod's words, "met every commitment he made ... he was going to carry out policies I wanted." Daon went on to become a great Canadian rags-to-riches story, building tens of thousands of homes in North America until soaring interest rates during the 1980s brought about a spectacular crash of Poole's company into bankruptcy. Poole clawed his way back to success through his British Columbia-based construction company and died in 2009, just before he could enjoy the fruits of his labour as chairman of the Vancouver Organizing Committee in the 2010 Winter Olympics there. His was quite a story for a man who grew up in Saskatchewan during the Depression with no indoor plumbing, running water, or electricity.[8]

Other developers were involved too. Rod acknowledged he couldn't have succeeded in lining up the necessary support for his housing plans if they had not made common sense. A key in the success of his end-around the normal approval processes was Rod's strong background in property development. That's why federal Housing Minister Basford and Alberta Premier Strom let Rod have such extraordinary powers in the tri-level arrangement alluded to earlier that enabled fast-track approvals for housing developments.

In the meantime, Rod was busy seeking voter approval for his third election. He attracted a disparate group of people to his campaign team. These included pot-smoking hippies, young people, stay-at-home housewives, working people, folks with a myriad of ethnic backgrounds, rabbis, priests, professionals, community association leaders, and a number of business people with good reasons for maintaining as friendly ties as possible with the City and its mayor. Community activists Harvey Cohen and Rebecca Aizenmann rubbed shoulders in the campaign room with Rabbi Lewis Ginsberg, once a professional wrestler who also went on to help the Salvation Army with their winter appeals for funds, or Father Greg Hildebrand, who lived downtown and ministered to street people. The professionals and business people included accountant Bill Friedman, architects Shelly Chandler and Martin Cohos, developer and lawyer Charlie Smith, development lawyer Bruce Green, developer Al Bell, and lawyers Darryl Raymaker and Vic Burstall. It was certainly an interesting assortment, and some of them harboured ambitions of their own. The idiosyncratic Larry Ryder, with family links to the prominent Belzberg family and then owner-operator of the Trade Winds Motel on Macleod Trail, was another trusted supporter, and part of the Jewish contingent that made up three-quarters of Rod's campaign team.

Green was among a group of people who, over three decades, found their way into the campaign headquarters of front-running mayoralty candidates. Green was close to Rod during the 1969 and 1971 elections, and there he was again in 1974, positioning himself, with Rod's approval, as one of the campaign's key fundraisers. Campaign chair was Rosemary McBain, wife of labour lawyer Ross McBain. She presented a reassuring and friendly front for the campaign. Close observers believed, however, that it was people like Green and Bell who really pulled the strings. Familiar names appear in the later campaigns of Ralph Klein, Al Duerr, and Dave Bronconnier. Many of the subsequent City committee appointments were familiar names too. Green, for example, was either a member of the planning commission or the development appeal board for varying terms through much of three decades. As a lawyer, he sold his services to developers and landowners seeking to negotiate through the City's regulatory maze. As a result, he had to walk a fine line between his professional responsibilities and his duties as a dedicated civic volunteer.

A week before the 1974 election, some of the trusted team became conspicuous by their absence. Doubts were apparent regarding Rod's electability. Some supporters were nowhere to be seen in campaign headquarters as the first polls showed Alger enjoying a slight lead. Only when it became clearer that Rod would eke out a third consecutive win did they re-appear, letting everyone know what a good job they had done in the campaign.

Even Alger was surprised how close he came to winning in 1974. Rod received forty-two per cent of the vote, just 2,600 ballots ahead of Alger.[9] "I hope he [Rod] will see the writing on the wall and at least realize a lot of people support the thing I'm working for," Alger said. Electors backed seven incumbent aldermen. Because two incumbents had run for mayor and two had retired, this meant only one lost.

Assuring the news media the bitterness and pettiness that marked the previous council would now be avoided, a somewhat chastened Rod declared, "I'm prepared to work with a different set of individuals." The previous council, he explained, fragmented their power with their anti-mayor antics. "This one, I hope, will turn the tide against the dukedoms that are growing up in some city departments." In other words, let's focus on the force we're supposed to be keeping our eyes on—the administration. One of his most immediate goals was to place labour relations at City Hall back on an even keel, "to create a commitment to a good labour relations climate."[10] The same day he was saying this, workers marched on City Hall to seek a cost-of-living hike in its present contract. These were years, after all, of soaring inflation.

As had occurred in his two previous elections, the media across Canada followed the results closely and lined up to interview Rod. "Five hot years as mayor of Calgary have not cooled Rod Sykes' passions very much," stated a *Southam News Service* piece by Nick Hills. "He is still the Muhammad Ali of City Hall, the champion mighty-mouth of Canadian municipal politics." That was a reference to the famous heavyweight boxer still strutting the rings of the world at that time.[11]

Analyzing his recent close election, Rod told Hills, "I practice the purest form of deception. I tell the truth when I am not expected to, and this is what gets you the reputation of being a manipulator … the ultimate insult to the political system is the maverick who gets in for a while and says 'I can play that game too.' " Rod obviously considered himself the ultimate maverick. Hills explained Rod had relied on the so-called little people for his constituency; that is, the middle and lower-income citizens. "I don't bother with the others, they can look after themselves," said Rod.

Astutely, Hills then noted the apparent incongruity of this former businessman, "sitting squarely to the left side of the Liberal Party, while he swats away almost endlessly at generations of Calgarians whom he regards as the quick-rich group." He outlined Rod's premise that "Calgary is a smug town made up of three groups: the immigrants, the pioneers, and the 'post-war, smart, young businessmen on the make who made money fast and who think they're sitting on God's right hand.' " In Rod's eyes, this third group of professionals and entrepreneurs had taken over the city's clubs and institutions, including the Chamber of Commerce, against which Rod continued to hold a grudge because of perceived insults to Gisele, his French Canadian wife. "They think they are better than others," Hills quoted Rod about them.

"I work for public housing and killing expressways. I work for the elderly, all those people who don't have a voice," said Rod. Hills was able to identify the beam-from-a-lighthouse idealism that emanated from Rod from time to time throughout his three terms. Sykes read like a cliché, said Hills. Yet, the reporter could still hear the intuitive phrases and the instant thoughts "that sound so outrageous, they automatically attract new converts." His article thus captured the quality that Rod displayed only occasionally but that drew people to him throughout his political career. He ran for a third time, he explained to Hills, because "I wasn't going to let the bastards have it. They [Alger, Petrasuk, and Dooley] wanted it for the wrong reasons." With an eye on his legacy, Rod added, "I want to see someone succeed me who is socially responsible." His hopes were ultimately dashed, of course, by the ascension in 1977 of Ross Alger to the mayor's chair. It will also become apparent Rod's support for the unprivileged later flagged as his political leanings veered to the right.

For the purposes of this interview, he offered a final justification for the vexatious public role he had chosen that all candidates for municipal office could inwardly digest. "City Hall has the inside track on property. It is where fortunes can be made very quickly. I will not be involved in real estate development in Calgary as long as I'm mayor," he said. He kept his promise. "I am just a pilgrim passing through ... to do something in a few, short years for those people who do not have a voice of their own. I don't want to reform the world. I just want to do my part."

Those were, without doubt, heartfelt motivations revealed in a moment of clarity; an understated *cri de coeur* to express the genuine origins of his cause. Not that some didn't view such expressions with cynicism and disdain, and not that pursuing such an idealized cause excluded other characteristics that radiated anger, moral outrage, and cynicism. His unorthodox childhood, his early relationships, and his other experiences of life, including his attachment to the commitment of standing up with conviction for perceived truth no matter how confrontational or daunting the process, clearly shaped these contradictory impulses.

His lack of rapport with Premier Peter Lougheed has been alluded to. Soon after his third election victory, while attending a banquet to honour retired popular Medicine Hat mayor, Harry Veiner, Rod used the occasion to publicly reprimand the provincial leader. "The government has not been responsive to the needs of Calgary or Edmonton for more diversified secondary industry," he said in his speech.[12] At issue was the Lougheed Conservatives' policy of offering direct subsidies to manufacturers to locate in smaller communities.

These "ill-conceived industrial development policies," as Rod called them, are just a way of currying favour with smaller communities, he said. The result was that Alberta as a whole lost potential economic benefits, because many industries were only interested in the broader person-power base that larger metropolitan areas offered and had, therefore, settled in places like Vancouver or Winnipeg instead.

Informed about provincial proposals to hold hearings on establishing what Lougheed called Restricted Development Areas—or green belts—around the metropolitan areas of Calgary and Edmonton, Rod was infuriated. "The chief commissioner told me about the most disturbing project being undertaken by the department of environment," he told Lougheed. "If you read the terms of reference you will find that they are so emotional and couched in such extreme and negative terms as virtually to amount to an attack on the cities where three quarters of the people live."[13] He called the hearing a kangaroo court, pre-determined by the terms of reference. Rod's main objection was the limit the green belts placed on Calgary's growth. In his mind, developable land would become sterilized. His peremptory strike worked. Plans for the green belts were dropped, but Lougheed never abandoned his goal of spreading the growth across the province and capitalizing "on the potential of the smaller centers."[14] A common refrain of Lougheed's was, "Better to have four Red Deers than everyone living in Edmonton and Calgary."

Less than four months after this flare-up, Rod expressed "grave doubts" about Lougheed's ability to govern effectively. "You have government by whim and ignorance, which, when you have a huge majority as well, destroys the parliamentary system of checks and balances," he said.[15] He made this comment seven weeks after the Lougheed Conservatives had taken Alberta by storm in a provincial election, winning sixty-nine of seventy-five seats and knocking the once-dominating Socreds down to four seats. Rod criticized the appointment of first-time MLA Dick Johnstone from Lethbridge as minister of municipal affairs. Lougheed and Rod were on a clear collision course over growth issues again. With a growing treasury of petro-dollars at his disposal, Lougheed was using direct economic subsidy policies to manipulate where industries settled, earning Rod's contempt as the leader of one of the most interventionist provincial governments on record.

Shortly before Christmas, Frank Dabbs of *The Albertan* scooped other media with the revelation that Rod had formed a private company with former staffer Tom Yarmon and Chris Graeffe from Edmonton called Community Properties Research Ltd.. It had secured a contract with CN Rail to help prepare the master plan for the redevelopment for CN's eighty-two-acre rail yard in the heart of Edmonton.[16] The redevelopment would ultimately be a two to three billion dollar project. In view of Rod's successful involvement in development around Calgary's rail line, CN's hiring of him made sense. Rod told Dabbs he still stood firmly behind the full disclosure of any real estate dealings in Calgary by its elected representatives, but this requirement clearly didn't apply to his new business in Edmonton.

Several aldermen expressed resentment that Rod was going to be spending considerable time and energy outside Calgary. Defeated mayoralty candidate Ross Alger went as far as publicly speculating that, such was the scale of the project, Rod would retire half-way though his third term. After the 1975 Calgary Centennial landmark year, his fascination for the Mayor's job would fade, said Alger.

Rod's Christmas message that year was sombre. "As we approach our Centenary [1975]. I believe we are facing one of the most difficult years in our city's history. A critical shortage of adequate housing at a reasonable price, rising costs, and the prospect of a worsening unemployment are among my particular concerns."[16] These were hectic times globally and across Canada, but was self-doubt colouring his calculations too? In his year-end piece on City Hall, Frank Dabbs captured again some of this disjunction. The just-past election was a "confusing and contradictory verdict on City Council," Dabbs said, because it threw in some new reform-minded faces, but kept all the old conservative-minded bodies. He grandly referred to the assessment that Rod had become "the plaster colossus of a small-time city with big-time dreams." Dabbs added, "No individual has ever so completely dominated the city's political life, mesmerizing foes and charming friends." You might wonder who could be entrusted with the larger-than-life statue commission. But then he brought things back to earth with his view of Rod's dilemma: "Despite his command of city politics, the future of Sykes' leadership is shaky, depending as it does … on the consent and co-operation of the City administration and the aldermen."[17]

Early in 1975 convention centre allegations pre-occupied Rod, prompting him to eventually demand that the Province call for an inquiry into the matters raised. As I describe later, the inquiry cleared Rod's name. During this period, Rod also grappled with the prospect of a twenty-three-per-cent tax hike, forcing him to double-down on his spendthrift council. The accumulation of more than five years of unrelenting tension and combat were taking their toll, though. The public perception of the mayor was evolving too. Whether the following public comments by one of Rod's close supporters from 1969 reflected the public mood or not is disputable, but they could influence how people regarded him.

In an interview with *Albertan* reporter Eric Denhoff, Gordon Plowman recalled the heady days in 1969 when Rod's campaign team, including Plowman, met for bacon and eggs in a downtown restaurant and prepared for the fight against the Jack Leslie juggernaut. "He was a most humble man and he was the nicest man I ever had an opportunity to work with," Plowman said of Rod. "Sykes was going to try to change the system. He was lined up against the power structure of the day and he was working for the public, in the public interest, to protect the little guy against a small group of men who were running the city."

Then the twist of the knife: "He's not the same kind of guy now. I don't think he has done too much wrong in the sense of what he was trying to accomplish, but he has alienated so many people and he seemed to fall into the same kind of system he was out to change at first. I think politics ate him up, in a way. He tried to change the system but he became a part of that system." Plowman referred to Rod's millionaire friends. "He was trying to change the power structure in the city, but maybe they changed him."[18]

If, as Ross Alger suggested, Rod was fixated on relishing his mayoral role in the city's centenary festivities of 1975, it turned out differently than how Alger envisioned it. See how he dealt with Century Calgary, the citizens' committee set up by council to co-ordinate the city's celebrations. Rod was aghast at ongoing irregularities in the committee's spending of public funds. After ordering the City to conduct an audit of the committee's business, he grew even angrier over his view that some of the centennial volunteers were feathering their nests. He cited the example of the book printer on the committee who seemed to be awarded most of the contracts to produce centennial books.

An exasperated Rod eventually told Century Calgary chairman Tom Walsh,

I have no choice ... but to take whatever action I can to dissociate myself from an operation that is not in my opinion capable of handling public funds in a manner in which I can approve. Please take this letter as indicating my firm decision to cut any official ties that exist between my office and that of Century Calgary. I would like you to obliterate my name from all your stationery, to cease to refer to me as Honorary President and to make it clear whenever my name comes up that I have no connection whatever with Century Calgary, that I do not endorse its opinions in any way.[19]

An image of bridges burned, as depicted by *The Albertan*,[20] did some justice to that bitter break-up, although Rod added his note of understandable regret: "Since I was instrumental in setting up Century Calgary, you will appreciate that this decision is not an easy one to make." Rod had little regard for Walsh, then a Queen's Counsel and operating his own law firm specializing in real estate. Loud, bombastic, and inattentive to detail was a less kind way of describing him than the panegyric composed for him when he received the Alberta Order of Excellence in 2008. "Tom Walsh has long served as a dedicated and caring member of the community of leaders and volunteers who make Alberta a great province. His influence can be seen in programs that have become essential components of the quality of life enjoyed by his fellow Calgarians," said the biography accompanying his award.[21] Rod had a different view.

It's easy to see a consistent pattern of Rod's sense of effrontery regarding insiders' attempts to skim the system or waste public money. No one escaped censure if he suspected corruption. He could be hard-hitting, sarcastic, and humorous all at the same time. Take his letter to Paul Godfrey, head of the Canadian Federation of Mayors and Municipalities (CFMM) that had chosen Calgary as the site for the next federation executive meeting if the City would help cover expenses. "Our gratitude is somewhat tempered ... by the suggestion that you will meet here during Grey Cup week as long as we provide you with hotel accommodation and tickets to the game. It makes us feel like the shy, young heiress facing her suitor. Is it us or our money you're after? I would suggest that at this stage it might be difficult to make the arrangements you would like ... I would further suggest that if the CFMM is interested in getting some work done at an executive meeting, it will not choose Grey Cup week in Calgary as the time and place to hold such a meeting."[22] Rod knew how to deflate a party.

When Rod announced his plans for a trip to Germany in the fall, the usual media sniping erupted. "City Hall's embattled boss headed for four weeks in Germany," wrote reporter Frank Dabbs.[23] Two weeks would be as a guest of the German government, and two as holiday. Rod defended his travelling as part of his mayoral duties. Calgary in the 1970s was becoming more multi-cultural, and he considered it appropriate to visit the homelands of some of the larger cultural groups. Besides, such visits could open up business opportunities. Many in the media thought otherwise. "Sykes is stepping aside from the local political fray tired, disillusioned, angry, and somewhat depressed, according to his friends," Dabbs said in his article. His enemies claimed he was ducking out of the committee appointment process scheduled for that time and not a happy experience for Rod in previous years when council had blocked him and his appointment recommendations. The article raised further speculation on Rod's future as mayor by quoting an anonymous senior administrator lamenting Rod was no longer as heavily involved in City matters as he used to be. There was a sense, even among those most loyal to him, that his heart was not in the affairs of the City as it had been. He would occasionally disappear for long periods during the day, making himself unavailable.

Life was not without its lighter moments, though. At a Calgary Ad and Sales Club roast of Rod, lawyer and local wit Chris Evans declared, "He's participated in broomball in Calgary, both as a broomstick and as a referee. He wanted to take up cross-country skiing, but he was afraid he'd get lost with all the other twigs." Rod's response: "There's 140 pounds of me." As so many found out, he may have been light in weight, but he packed a hefty wallop. Thin power, indeed.

Another challenge was tackling what Rod branded as bribery by big city developers in their relationships with community associations. Alderman Gordon Shrake blithely confirmed to the media that several associations had accepted sizeable gifts and cash donations from developers.[24] He himself had solicited some of this graft on behalf of community groups. An example was a $10,000 cash and materials donation from Qualico to build the foundation for a community hall; Daon also constructed a $100,000 community hall. The genial Shrake said he didn't see these donations as bribes. They made him "feel a little kinder toward the developer … but you won't switch your vote for it."

Rod demanded Municipal Affairs Minister Dick Johnstone look into the matter. "The introduction of bribes and pay-offs or inducements of any kind in connection with development applications or any other kind of public business is disgraceful," he said. "They destroy integrity in public service and public confidence in the institutions of government."[25]

After Johnstone sloughed off Rod's demand, suggesting council should deal with the matter themselves, Rod stepped up the rhetoric. "Because council is involved, it won't investigate itself," Rod told Johnstone. "The only alternative is to refer the matter to the minister, which I have done." Johnstone's refusal to get involved, Rod charged, indicated he either failed to understand the significance of these practices, or he condoned them. You might think this would leave Johnstone little wiggle room, but his evasions persisted. Rod kept up the pressure, though. "The swapping of votes and the peddling of influence seem to have become the normal way of doing business in this council … the whole practice represents the utter and complete collapse of morality in government."[26] His strong words were still ignored.

During 1976, Rod showed no fear of wading into the muddy waters of Aboriginal rights. He slammed the barrage of Native claims at the Thomas Berger inquiry into the proposed Mackenzie Valley Pipeline to bring natural gas from the North. When he declared the inquiry was an ill-conceived exercise giving a platform for "troublemakers" threatening the energy supplies of all Canadians and setting up claims that some Canadians had more rights than others, he drew "boos, jeers, and a few cheers."[27] Jack Gallagher, founder and head of Dome Petroleum, was among the cheerleaders. "I wish to commend you on your recent statement at the Berger Hearings … it is unfortunate that the native people are being misled by the socialist leanings of their advisors," he wrote.[28]

When the Berger Report was released a year later with recommendations for a ten-year delay of the pipeline (it was never built, in fact), Rod again made his views clear in a letter to Gallagher. "It is a political document devoted to ... native pressure groups to the detriment of all Canadians and Canada's economic future," he said. "The Berger Report is one man's opinion ... it is not justification for the formulation of policy ... If we were to put the preservation of the barren lands as barren lands and nothing more ahead of the welfare of all Canada and all Canadians, we would literally be programming a reduction in living standards and increasing unemployment for the foreseeable future ."[29] With oil and gas pipeline construction still a divisive issue in Canada, expressing those sentiments today would create a bigger political storm than it did then. Still, there was no mistaking where Rod stood.

With his propensity to embroil himself in political matters outside Alberta, Rod used an appearance on Calgary Community Cablevision in 1977 to suggest that the recently elected Parti Quebecois in Quebec comprised "saboteurs, gangsters, and murderers." He had just returned from attending the Winter Carnival in Quebec City. He called the PQ a left-wing socialist elite "who had lied to win the election." Some Calgary aldermen, whom Rod called the usual suspects—Don Hartman, Ed Oman, Barbara Scott, John Ayer, and Patrick Ryan—reacted with horror at his remarks and signed a petition disassociating themselves from them. This infuriated Rod. "They dissociate themselves from the personal opinions I expressed! Since when were they ever associated with my personal opinions?" he asked with obvious passion. "What is the purpose of their statement? Is it petty spite? Is it publicity seeking? ... What I condemned was the FLQ [Front de Libération du Québec], the terrorist revolutionary organization which could have destroyed Canada only a few years ago. What I condemned was the tactics of intimidation, violence, terrorism, and bloodshed for political purposes. These aldermen disagree with me! ... I think that any good Canadian should be concerned. Apparently, these aldermen are not!"[30]

Copies of this passionate missive went to the Royal Canadian Legion, other veteran groups, unions, and the news media. This was clearly an outburst of pent-up emotion and testimony to his strong connection to events in Quebec. As was often the case, Rod couldn't resist metaphorically grabbing an offender by the neck and wiping his nose in his own mess. Some may interpret that what Rod did in this episode was what he condemned in a Manitoba MLA a few years previously; that is, heap scorn on an elected government in Quebec. He felt that the fact that the new PQ government was hell-bent on the break-up of Canada justified his passion. Also, let it be noted, the target of his anger was the government of Quebec, not its people, as in the Joe Borowski anecdote recounted earlier.

Then it was back to more mundane development issues in Calgary. By an 8-3 vote, council adopted a twenty-year growth plan for the city. By preparing for the accommodation of another 300,000 people in Calgary, it was the final step in what was billed as the biggest single planning exercise ever undertaken by council to that date.[31] The plan objective was to cope with a rapidly expanding population in the least disruptive way, while getting the best uses out of public and private investment. By nudging the city toward higher housing densities, assuring long-term land supplies and through limited annexation, a specific aim much favoured and successfully guided by Rod, was to keep house prices down.

After the perceived downturn in his political trajectory the previous year, 1977 was turning out better. The usually insightful reporter, Frank Dabbs, quoted campaign supporters confident that Rod could be re-elected in the fall "without spending a campaign nickel." A standing ovation for Rod at a banquet for the city's transit workers helped confirm this hubris. "He's been cutting ribbons and attending social functions, particularly in the ethnic clubs in town. He's taking back control of affairs," said Dabbs.[32] Even his bitter foe, Alderman Don Hartman, glumly conjectured, "When you put all the moves together, Sykes looks like he could be mayor for a long, long time."

However, by spring, Rod told a reporter that he still disliked politics and found it "sordid and frustrating."[33] Later that summer, Brian Scott, former City solicitor and friendly with Rod, declared he would run for mayor in the October election, prompting Fred Kennedy to speculate about the "happy ending" for Rod now that Scott was in the race. "Unless there is a totally unexpected about-face, Mayor Sykes will leave office," Kennedy wrote.[34]

Rod had one more important piece of business to take care of, however, which was to give Calgary's light rail transit system the green light. Despite attempts by declared mayoralty candidate Ross Alger to derail the project, council voted to spend $21.8 million for twenty-seven LRT cars to operate on a twelve-kilometre route from the downtown to the south. "It was a satisfying moment for many of the aldermen and also for Mayor Rod Sykes, who lauded council for facing up to its responsibilities," said one report.[35] The *Globe and Mail* was also able to report, "The commitment [to LRT] has been made."

Early August in 1977, Rod announced what most people had speculated. He wasn't going to run in the fall. *The Herald* reacted with little grace. "The city could certainly use a breathing space from incessant controversy and an excess of name-calling," said an editorial. They called him the mayor with the fastest tongue in the West. They added, though, "He has excelled as a news-maker, the master of the cutting barb, the cruel put-down. It's questionable how much of his high profile in civic affairs has been due to showmanship and how much due to solid accomplishment. And that's a pity. At his best,

Sykes can be effective, energetic, and persuasive."[36] This was grudging praise from a relentless foe.

"I'm going to spend more time with my family and earn a living," he told *The North Hill News*.[37] He also noted that, at age forty-eight, he was going to be out of work. "There's always welfare," he joked as he continued to promote the candidacy of Brian Scott and didn't rule out provincial politics for himself. He listed some of his achievements as: Opening up City Hall, avoiding any labour strikes during his eight years, surviving the hippie era without a riot, and being God's gift to cartoonists.

You couldn't argue against any of those points, and yet, in the four decades since, he has received little credit for any of them. There were other highly significant legacies, but the public, City Hall, and the news media have mostly ignored them in their historical reviews. Did his sometimes imperious manner, biting tongue, and pursuit of those he believed had sinned scar so many that any residue of good will after he left dried up like a prairie slough after a hot summer? Perhaps there were just too many sore toes in big boots. Rod faced criticism that he was not as consistent in his positions as he portrayed himself to be and that he regularly misrepresented what other people had said. Some critics charged that, in his final years, he was not as visible a leader as he was in the initial years. Was his occasional insistence on becoming embroiled in peripheral issues draining the reservoir of public magnanimity?

The *Saint John's Calgary Report*, under editor Ted Byfield, described Rod in his final months as "relaxed, almost jovial, as he sat on a desk in his office ... to reveal his intentions." Rod made it clear he was not leaving his post because he feared defeat at the polls. "I have never been so sure of winning an election," he was quoted as saying triumphantly, "but this is the time to quit; I can exit laughing."[38]

Rod's desire to earn a regular living again was apparent in several of the letters he wrote in his final two months. "The fact is that I cannot enter federal politics because it is impossible to live a normal family life when your job is (at least in part) 2,000 miles from home," he responded to one letter urging he run as an MP. "I have certainly had all the inducements that could reasonably be offered, but I have come to the conclusion that my family comes first ... I have been totally unable to look after my own financial future, which means security for my family, and indeed to spend any reasonable amount of time with my family."[39]

A *Herald* poll on Rod's performance as mayor showed five per cent of respondents thought he had done an excellent job; twenty-two per cent good; thirty-four per cent fair; and twenty-eight per cent poor. It's hard to judge the validity of the poll, especially considering the source. Rod dominated City Hall "with political skill, a quick wit and the kind of incendiary personality

which could start a blaze in a fire extinguisher factory," said *Herald* columnist Jim Stott. "One thing can be predicted with certainty: [City Hall] will
almost certainly be a quieter and duller place … There is scarcely a group
in this city which has not at one time or another felt the bite of the mayor's
acidic tongue."[40]

In a letter to Brigadier Shaver, head of the Salvation Army in Calgary, Rod
unloaded more of his burden. "I must say that I find this office increasingly
difficult, not because there are so many challenges before me, but because
most of the challenges have been met and dealt with," he wrote. He referred
again to his worries about providing adequately for his growing family. "After
all, if your job in life ends automatically every three years, and you enter into
some kind of lottery to see whether you will keep it for another three years,
and if you have no pension and no security whatever—well, is that a way for
a family to live? That's the political vulnerability facing all who run for public
office." But, he can't quite let go. "If I can combine my work with family life
and some political activity, then that would be ideal."[41]

Rod's last archived letter on file was to Chief Commissioner Denis Cole.
"Now I must move on to other things. First of all, I must earn a living and
lead a reasonably normal family life … beyond that, I would like to take an
active role in politics at the provincial level for the Social Credit Party if that is
possible," he said. "However, my priorities have to be income and family first,
and I hope my experience in real estate development in the past will serve me
in good stead in the future. We'll see."[42] Again, you can spot this dichotomy of
ambitions for doing well in business and playing a political role.

Despite the fact Brian Scott had backed out of his commitment to run for
mayor, Rod showed no regrets over his decision. When he said he was ready
to move on, he meant it. He had virtually no involvement with the civic election, which Ross Alger won in a landslide against Ed Oman. Of the vote totals
in the fourteen wards then in effect for the electorate, Alger came out ahead
in thirteen. He was fifteen thousand votes ahead of his nearest rival.

On his last day, Rod was still in his office at six o'clock doing a final cleaning out. He was cheerful, without apparent regret that his years in the City
Hall spotlight were over. Chief Commissioner Denis Cole accompanied him
out of the sandstone building where their offices were located. They chatted at
the bottom of the steps. As they turned to shake hands, Cole wished Rod well.
"Your regime will be hard to match," said Cole, eyes beaming. "I wonder who
will be running City Hall now?" Because Alger was a clear favourite, this was
a mischievous question. Rod articulated what they both were thinking: "You
will." Cole's quiet response, according to Rod, was, "Yes, sir. I will."

They both knew instinctively there'd never be another mayor like Rod
Sykes. Most of the subsequent mayors preferred being official greeter to

riding herd over the administration and standing up for ordinary citizens. By the time Dave Bronconnier wielded mayoral power, the Province had emasculated the position. As they parted, Rod and Cole knew well that Alger would be easy meat for the City Hall civil servants. After all, Alger had run on a platform of appeasement and, as City Hall found out, he had to have time for his golf. He lasted just one term, losing in 1980 to Ralph Klein in a three-way race that included Peter Petrasuk again.

Before detailing the chronology of Rod's life after City Hall, it's time to look more closely at specific achievements from his time as mayor. They represent significant themes characterizing his mayoralty and warrant separate focus. They are part of the Sykes legacy, and stand as important sign-posts along the mayoralty journey. Many of the pre-occupations described in the next eight chapters overlapped. In chapter 18, I will revert to an account of Rod's pursuit of other interests in his later years.

Glenbow Archives NA-2864-5926
Rod as bartender at Theatre Calgary auction. (April 8, 1970)

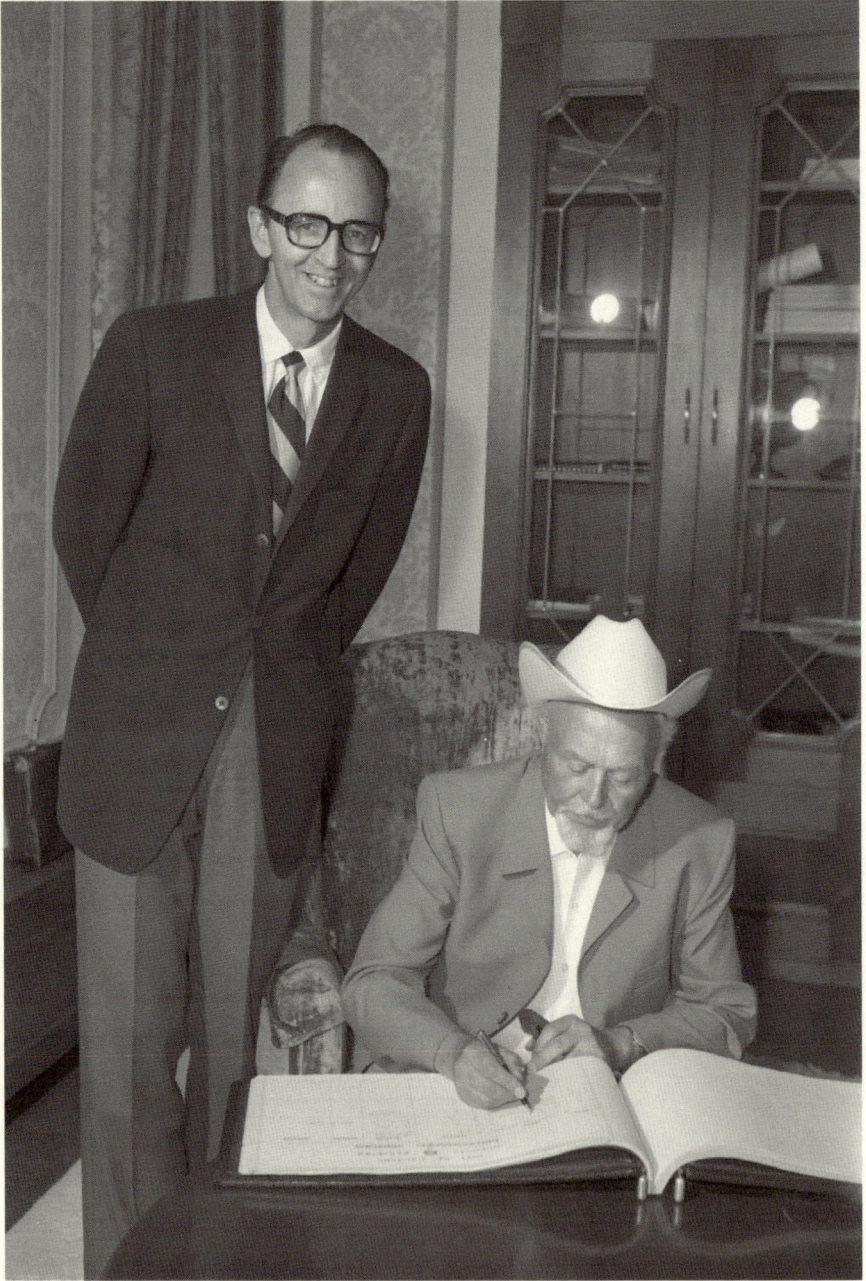

Glenbow Archives NA-4476-638
Rod with dignitary signing guest book at City Hall. (July 1973)

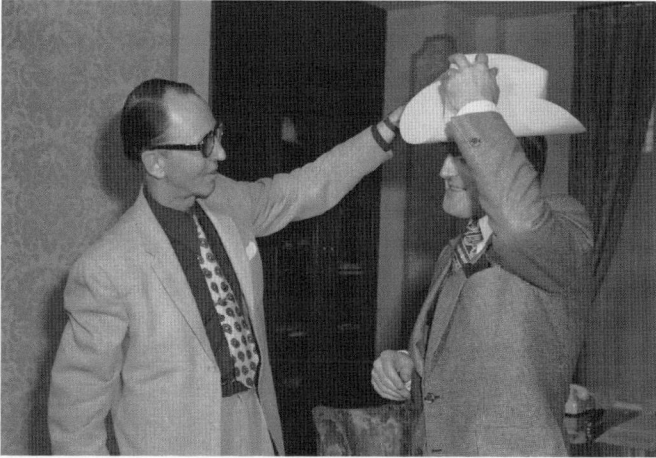

Glenbow Archives NA 4476-668
Rod presents Brian Mulroney with a white hat. (November 1975)

Glenbow Archives M-8787-16
Rod has a bunch of ripe issues to deal with. (Feb. 21, 1973)

Glenbow Archives M-8787-18
"This town ain't big enough for both of us."
Council denies Rod a position on the Stampede board. (April 1973)

Glenbow Archives M-8787-42
"Who are you calling a a … hic … drunk?"
Rod accused of spending too much. (Feb. 23, 1974)

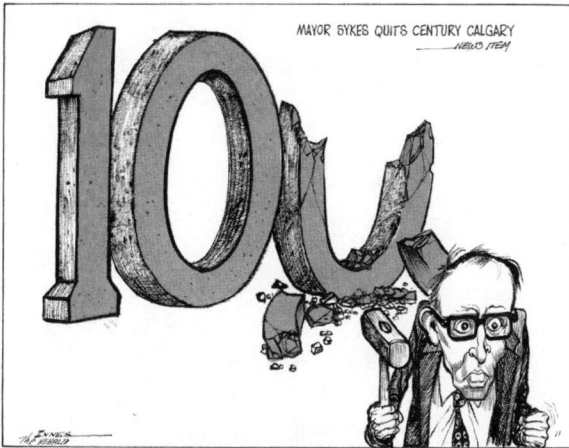

Glenbow Archives M-8787-237
Rod quits Century Calgary after bitter break-up. (Aug. 23, 1975)

Glenbow Archives M-8000-130
"The job I wanted to do has been done."
Rod Sykes prepares to leave City Hall and his battered council. (Aug. 6, 1977)

9
UNION AND HARMONY

The desire to clean up what he called the closed-club atmosphere at City
Hall was prime among Rod's reasons for serving in public office. Integral
to this was an obsession with bringing those outside the fence into the game.
Whether it was inborn or absorbed through his reading and contact with
others, a practical and pragmatic view of justice motivated Rod throughout
his adult life. Born into a world of declining privilege in English Victoria, he
developed a strong sense for rebalancing inequity and helping the downtrod-
den. Supporting the afflicted and afflicting the comfortable were constant
refrains. He retained a life-long affinity for the working class, especially those
struggling with dignity to shelter and feed their families. He spoke of seeing
many poor people during the Depression years of the 1930s having to beg to
survive. He campaigned for a safety net for the poor and needy, particularly
the elderly.

Whenever I witnessed this, I could imagine Rod as a paid-up member of
the New Democratic Party. Incongruously, his political leanings, particularly
in his later years, veered heavily toward right-wing parties such as Alberta's
Wildrose Alliance. These espoused philosophies of pulling oneself up by the
bootstraps, survival of the fittest, and limiting government intervention. He
continued to take a hard line, though, against those he believed exploited
the disaffected and the indigent. A favourite target were those who assumed
privilege or who enjoyed access to power without accountability. He also
bore an instinctive disregard for bearded, bare-feet-and-sandaled academics
with their theoretical views on social justice. Social workers and other social
engineers met with his disdain. It was an odd combination of impulses. He
liked to boast of his NDP friends, but devoted energy toward strongly right of
centre politicians and their causes.

Grappling with this apparent dichotomy, I recall Rod's strong champion-
ing of Aboriginals and hippie youth against bullying and harassment by the
police. Then I remember his anger for those involved in the illegal occupation
for Aboriginal causes of federal offices. His distaste for lawlessness in this case
trumped any sympathy he had for the occupying forces. He blasted what he
called the Native pressure groups, the left-wingers, and the "hangers-on" who
sought to stir up public opposition to the building of the Mackenzie Valley
pipeline during the Thomas Berger Hearings in the mid-1970s. Where some
saw righteous defence of Aboriginal rights, he saw professional agitators and

a self-interested attack on broader community benefits. Rod's disparaging comments about gays, lesbians, and feminists were also discomforting.

Rod's practical and pragmatic perception of fair play took many twists and turns during his years as mayor. One significant and far-reaching aspect was his support for unions, particularly those that did the dirty work—that is, the down-to-earth labourers who worked with their hands and bodies. He understood and appreciated the power they had and the significance of the work they did to get projects done. As a successful developer, Rod knew he had to have these people with him and not against him. Like the wise battle commander, he learned to value his front-line troops. Examples can be drawn from his Marathon days, when he had major jobs to complete, of his non-doctrinaire, constructive approach to dealing with unions.

That approach led to prolonged labour peace during his years at City Hall. In a year-end message ten months before he left office to the commissioners, department heads, unions, and the Calgary Chamber of Commerce, he was able to declare with justifiable pride, "The people of Calgary have benefited for the last few years from the best labour relations of any city in Canada anywhere near our size, and we all have a record to be proud of."[1] He could say that with certainty because the City did not lose a single day to an official strike during all his eight years there. He was careful to spread the credit. "Our proud record is due to our people, and not just the leadership … I've tried to build trust in fair and honest bargaining while I've been here, and I'm pleased with the results. Let's keep it that way." He singled out for particular praise those who delivered "the services of civilization" no matter what the weather—that is, the outside workers and the transit system employees.

During his first term, the union challenges came early. The outside workers, represented by the Canadian Union of Public Employees, Local 37, were not a happy lot when he was elected. Years of neglect and hostility from out-of-touch managers had built up bitterness, distrust, and resentment among the ranks. It was common for contracts to remain unresolved years after their expiry dates. The members felt they were at the bottom of the pecking order, deprived of the privileges and benefits they saw their bosses and inside workers enjoy. Rod had been particularly struck by the cavalier treatment of the three hundred or more temporary workers, hired on when needed but unceremoniously dumped as soon as they became eligible for full-time employment and benefits. Although it took him a couple of years to fully resolve that situation, he signalled his determination early to do so. Rod's persistence paid off. By 1975, the regular seasonal workers got their full-time status and their pensions. He called the earlier City practice a "cynical old game of breaking employment just before a man qualified for permanency."

With the union holding a positive and strong strike vote in their pocket, two intense days of bargaining in May 1970 averted a dreaded walkout. Both sides agreed to a contract that would give Local 37 members a nineteen per cent pay hike over two years.[2] Annual inflation in the early 1970s was rising above six per cent, soon to reach double figures. "The contract is not quite as good as we wanted," said Local 37 president Ron Brown, "but it's better to accept this than jeopardize the citizens of Calgary with a strike ... it's the best contract we've ever signed for a temporary worker." The agreement marked the beginning of a long relationship between Brown and Rod.

Gruff, heavy-set, and ready with disarming cuss words, Brown looked the part of the union leader. Starting out with the City in 1951 as a heavy-equipment operator, he was quite confident in his physical abilities. He became local vice-president in 1952 and president in 1953, a post he held until retirement in 1982. He did not suffer fools gladly, and there were few he was afraid of standing up to. Intimidation of those opposed to him was among his tools of trade. Some of his own members even complained of his rough and sexist treatment. A reputation for even harassing his own members followed him. He enjoyed his station in life, though. "I never backed down for no one," he said in 2011. That's probably why he got along with Rod. "He carried himself pretty good," was Brown's assessment of the mayor.

It should be noted that during the 1980s Brown was convicted of impropriety in the handling of union expense accounts, and spent six months behind bars. Such was his relationship with the bosses at City Hall that they then rehired him, placing him on the payroll for several more years—much to the dismay of some former colleagues, who still regarded him with fear and disgust. None of this bothered Rod. He and Brown remained friends into old age.

The two met a couple of days after the 1969 election. Rod was sitting in the downtown office of prominent Calgary labour lawyer Ross McBain, who had represented Local 37 in various cases. Ross's wife, Rosemary, was a member of Rod's first campaign team. Ross called Brown up, telling him he'd like to introduce Rod to him. Before meeting him, Brown's impression of this brash new mayor was of a "hard-nosed guy who would wreck unions." Their first chat lasted a long time, with Rod getting an earful over how the City was dragging its feet in negotiations. Rod's response was to promise immediate action. "We hit it off. We both wanted better relations with the City," Brown said. Rod's gesture of having an outside door removed from his office as a sign of his open policy impressed Brown. A key to the labour peace that followed was Brown's understanding he was always welcome in the mayor's office. He was also impressed that Rod early on joined in with union volunteer activities such as helping homeless people. "He attended functions, handing out presents and that sort of thing," said Brown.

However, to Rod's horror, the day the first agreement with Local 37 was announced, a report became public that the City's senior administrators were to receive twenty per cent raises. Adding to the consternation were comments by Chief Commissioner Ivor Strong that these weren't raises but deferred benefits.[3] Rod called it an "intolerable situation," and at his direction, the City's finance committee proceeded to temporarily cut salaries for the brass back to 1968 levels.

The next union crisis broke two months later. A delay in issuing back pay won in their contract with the City provoked a predictable stir among the workers. When he found out, an irate Rod demanded an explanation. "We made a deal with the union when a contract was settled in June, and it should have been honoured promptly ... I don't know how we are expected to build confidence and trust when we don't honour our commitments."

In the meantime, Rod knew he walked a tight-rope between satisfying the unions and keeping a lid on the municipal tax bill. While speaking to federal senate committee hearings on poverty, he didn't shrink from swiping at organized labour for "excessive wage demands which push management into operating efficiencies which can result in manpower reductions." He suggested labour leaders should prefer to have more workers employed for reasonable wages than have fewer people earning higher wages."[4] That kind of statement was part of his balancing act between the various interests he felt responsible for.

His major concern at that time, however, was inflation and its impact on working people and the elderly. Rod was a constant advocate for seniors and those least able to defend themselves against the ravages of rising prices. "Inflation is robbery, plain and simple," he reminded the senate committee. Inflation was created mainly by governments, he said. The federal government, therefore, had to accept its full responsibility and, among other actions, "assure retired people ... those hardest hit by inflation, the right to live without reductions in their standards of living."

Around this time, welfare recipients in the city hit a post-war peak of almost 1,500 cases. [5] When council heard City Social Services had already spent its total budget with three-and-a-half months to go in the financial year, Rod's commitment to the afflicted helped guide council's response. Aware of more than $5 million of unallocated reserves in City coffers, he called for this money to be accessed to meet the soaring welfare costs. "I don't feel we are facing any kind of financial crisis. Rather, it's a social crisis. It's a very disturbing situation to have so many people who are unable to pay their way in what is a time of prosperity in Alberta." His financial stewardship instincts also kicked in. He made sure an adequate checking system was in place to prevent anyone taking advantage of the program.[6]

Then the turn came for the one thousand inside workers in CUPE Local 38 to enjoy inflation-adjusted pay hikes of twenty-two per cent over two years and the creation of a thirty-five-hour work week. This deal, overwhelmingly backed by the membership, came after two weeks of intensive bargaining. Rod had been pushing the idea of consolidating bargaining into an uninterrupted block of days, rather than spreading it out. The Local 38 settlement was also the first to conform to a City policy, encouraged again by Rod, of signing agreements before the previous contract expired.[7]

Rod reinforced that principle when the City faced the expiry of six union contracts at the end of the year. The unions were CUPE 38, the inside staff; the International Brotherhood of Electrical Workers (IBEW) Local 254; the electrical workers in CUPE 182; the Alberta Transit Union members in City transit: CUPE 1169 employees in the libraries; and public health nurses belonging to the Alberta Association of Registered Nurses employed in the City's public health department. In a year-end labour statement,[8]Rod was pleased to announce the fast resolution of all these disparate negotiations. "I did not want our people negotiating after contracts had expired," was his order to administration. Employees had to know by contract expiry where they stood, he said. At his insistence in the previous fall, the City had scheduled periods for negotiation of two weeks each for the larger unions, and one week for the smaller ones. "Concentrated bargaining," was the term used. It enabled the City to bargain in "earnest" from the start, Rod said. All except one set of negotiations were completed in the allotted time. The sixth wrapped up successfully within a month. This was a first for the City. "We've shown our people we know how to bargain honestly, in faith," he said.

Rod had shown his ability to set broad parameters for important negotiations when they needed that kind of guidance, but he quite rightly didn't get involved in the details. It was a delicate balance, and he wasn't afraid of using the media, special statements, letters, or personal contact with negotiators to put his points across. He sought a role in labour negotiations with broad boundaries. Some aldermen considered this gross meddling, but Rod insisted he was just doing his job.

"I may discuss policy with the commissioners and make suggestions and recommendations but … I do not become directly involved in negotiations and … I play no actual role until negotiations break down when I have to intervene directly with the parties … Normally I wait until things break down and I recognize it or I am asked to intervene and get us over a difficult spot," he explained.[9] "This is the role of the chief executive. That is the role I have played throughout."

This represents a subtle definition of his powers. It let him stay out of the fray, only to descend from on high, as it were, and intervene when things went wrong. Defining responsibilities this way was part of his cunning. He sought as much flexibility with his powers as he could. His goal, as always, was to secure positive, practical results. This approach harked back to his extensive powers with CPR. Do what you need to do, just get things done.

To see this modus operandi in action again, let's cut to the fall of 1973, when critical negotiations with the City's unions had broken down. Rod heard this news directly from union leaders, rather than from the commissioners. Ron Brown, the CUPE 37 boss, had told Rod the City's main negotiator—the down-to-earth, no-nonsense Angus MacDonald—did not seem to have full negotiating authority. He was also being called away for other work, thus disrupting proper continuity of the negotiations. "I am not prepared to tolerate this kind of nonsense," was Rod's angry response. [10] "This is not labour negotiations in good faith." He promised to take the matter up with the commissioners and get talks back on the rails. In the meantime, Rod wanted to let Brown know, contrary to stories in circulation, he was not against a dental plan or shorter work week for members "providing these matters can be phased in on a proper basis over a reasonable period of time." Observers might interpret this as Rod becoming directly involved in the details of the talks, but these were also important conciliatory steps toward achieving a contract and avoiding a strike.

To that end, he launched a barrage of pointed questions at then Chief Commissioner Geoff Hamilton. [11] His intention was to place blame on the administration for the break-down in the negotiations and put forward his view it was the City and not the union that was bargaining in bad faith. In a final blast, he said the commissioners were mishandling the talks.

"Name-calling is not negotiation. Even if the union were unreasonable, that would not justify the City being equally unreasonable." Rod then informed the commissioners he had requested all the parties to get back to the bargaining table. Rod copied the media on the memo. This action demonstrated once more his bold ability to take the initiative in controversial circumstances.

Seven aldermen were furious, or claimed to be, over his questions. Comments ranged from "irresponsible and immature" to "unjustified and unprecedented." [12] Peter Petrasuk said he was aghast at the mayor's involvement and the public release of his questions. Don Hartman's response was, "Labour negotiations are difficult at the best of times without having this kind of interference." For Eric Musgreave, "the best thing a mayor can do is stay out of this." Rod's sentiments were again apparent three days later when he opposed a motion to boost pay for commissioners by 9.5 per cent over two years. "I don't care what personal antagonism I cause if it is in the public interest," he said. "This measure will have an adverse effect on labour relations currently being negotiated with the City's outside workers."[13]

Rod's public criticism of Hamilton relating to the CUPE 37 talks was the last straw for the chief commissioner. He responded publicly to Rod's barbs with his own. "Mr. Mayor, the information then available would have been provided to you had you not risen in sudden anger and strode out of that board of commissioners meeting," he was quoted as saying.[14] That wasn't the first time Rod stormed out of a commissioners' meeting when he felt nothing tangible was being resolved. *The Herald* predictably piled on with its scorn. "Mayor Sykes appears to have a deep-rooted, ineradicable suspicion and mistrust of the city's civil servants, which makes it almost impossible for him to judge their actions with any degree of impartiality," said an editorial.[15] "The mayor's quick temper has gotten him into hot water many times during his four years in office … It is undoubtedly unpleasant for Mr. Hamilton to defend himself and his commissioners in the pages of the press." The editorial noted its pleasure that "at least seven aldermen have since deplored the mayor's interference in the ticklish area of labour negotiations." *The Herald* apparently had the party line down pat too.

Was Hamilton wise to have backed himself into defending himself in the press? That depends on your perspective. Rod accepted the union's version of events that did not coincide with the chief commissioner's. What surely mattered was that Rod's intervention kick-started talks that had, from at least one party's view, broken off or stalled. The result was a quick resolution to the talks, and acceptance by the members. "Talks would have broken down if Rod Sykes had not become involved," Brown said thirty-eight years later.

Just a week or so after that contract settlement, other significant and welcome changes were agreed on, affecting the pension plans for five thousand City workers. When *The Herald* reported on that outcome, there was no credit for Rod. The story merely said the deal had been worked out in highly complex negotiations with the city's union representatives.[16] The principal change in the new deal involved the transfer of employee benefits under the existing City pension plan to one operated by the provincial government called the Local Authorities Pension Plan (LAPP). This not only placed employees' pension plans on a stronger footing, but gave City workers the rights to a pension surplus the plan had built up over the years. "That money rightfully belonged to the people who earned it," Rod explained. Ultimately, the transfer to the provincial plan would mean better benefits to city workers.

Hamilton soon after announced his intention to resign, and council named Denis Cole the new chief commissioner. *The Herald* added a customary sour note. "[Hamilton] joins a lengthy list of City Hall administrators and senior civil servants who simply wouldn't or couldn't put up with it any longer," said an editorial. "And when the word 'it' is used, there is no point in equivocating or tip-toeing around the bush. 'It' means only one thing … the intolerable atmosphere created in City Hall by Mayor Rodney Sykes."

The editorial continued, "It is a wonder that Mr. Hamilton, and others before him, displayed the fortitude and forbearance to stick around the place as long as they did … the mayor demonstrably has either never learned, or has rejected, one of the basic premises of modern management, that to attain goals one must get along with other people, especially those with whom one works … Nobody with any self-respect has to put up with this kind of treatment indefinitely, and a lot of them, now culminating in the resignation of this city's chief commissioner, have come to the end of the road … Why in the world would anybody deliberately choose to work in a hall of horrors if anything else was available?"[17]

That represented another predictable take on events by *The Herald*: Everyone has to be nice and get along. Anyone who rocks the boat—that is, upsets the establishment, even if it leads to tangible, positive achievement—is a villain and a cad. Hamilton's new job, incidentally, was president of the Glenbow Foundation, operating the Glenbow Museum. That job lasted until CPR chairman Buck Crump, a member of the foundation board, had him fired, according to Rod. As a result, Hamilton found himself deep in debt. Personal challenges and his involvement with an unsuccessful attempt to create an Alberta movie industry through Tri-Media Studio of Calgary added to his woes. He remained in private consulting work and moved to Edmonton, operating as a consultant to the provincial government in the early 1980s. After a job fell through as executive director of the Regional Utilities Commission, he died under troubling circumstances in 1984 at age sixty-two.

To place the horror story of employee defections, as described in *The Herald*, in another context, personnel director Peter Thompson reported staff turnover in Rod's first two years in office, through resignations and dismissals, was half the rate of the mid-1960s. In 1971, it was 6.28%, while in the mid-1960s the figure averaged 15% annually. The figures were high compared with federal and provincial government statistics, but lower than the private sector, Thompson said in his report.[18] This buried story confounded many of the criticisms against Rod. It was likely, however, that turnover of senior staff was relatively high, but Rod clearly was demanding an accountability that many had not had to face before. It's also worth noting that Hamilton's replacement, Denis Cole, managed his portfolio and his relationship with Rod professionally and with aplomb.

Settlements with the outside and the inside workers during the 1970s raised hackles then and still seem excessive today. The two-year deal for a 17.5% hike for CUPE 37 in 1972 was seen as particularly generous. Rod's defence was, "This settlement is more than we would like, but considerably less than was demanded [15% for one year]."[19] During that period of runaway inflation, it was not far from the norm.

These settlements obviously strained City resources, though. That situation prompted a clear request from Rod for provincially-imposed wage guidelines with teeth to limit the size of future wage awards. "I think the government has a responsibility to assert strong moral leadership in this matter," Rod said. "We must do something about the inflationary spiral that is having a detrimental effect on older people and families."[20]

Upcoming compulsory arbitration with the police and firemen couldn't be effective without guidelines, Rod said. Average provincial settlements of 6% compared with 9.4% for the City's outside workers so far in the 1970s. Defending his members, Ron Brown said there was ample room for cuts—but only in the area of department heads. "Aldermen always want to cut back on labour staff, but not on department heads," he said. During budget discussions, Aldermen Peter Petrasuk and Adrian Berry placed the blame squarely on Rod, the commissioners, and the finance committee (with Chairman Alderman John Kushner) for soaring wages. Berry lamented council had capitulated to the mayor over the increases.

What Rod knew then and what local governments were well aware of before and since were the shortcomings of the property tax system. The budgetary black hole that gaped open before the City vividly demonstrated the property tax base had outlived its sufficiency as a source of revenue. "Raising property taxes may defer the evil day, but it doesn't solve anything. You can't go on raising taxes indefinitely," Rod said. One obvious solution lay in the Province's ability to create an additional revenue source. "I know of no other revenue source than a sales tax, but I'm perfectly willing to let the government make its own decision. I've made my point."[21] The response from the Peter Lougheed Conservatives was as predictable then as it's been ever since with subsequent Conservative administrations, just as subsequent independent groups, including business organizations, have kept on promoting the concept of provincial sales taxes. Dave Russell, Minister of Municipal Affairs, curtly replied, "Mayor Sykes knows better than to foist a sales tax on the province when the Tory administration is opposed to such a levy."

Rod's approach to welfare took another twist after two and a half years in office, when he became a convert to the work of the City's social services department. He paid a glowing tribute to the efforts of department head Sam Blakely and his number two Al Hagan for their tough-minded performances. When Rod was first elected in 1969, he confessed he had a businessman's dislike for people on welfare who couldn't stand on their own feet. "I was totally wrong. I've since seen a need that can't be met in any other way. I have seen Mr. Blakely and Mr. Hagan try to get value for money. I have seen them stand up to government and private agencies and be tough-minded when they have to be ... In their job, it's much easier to say 'yes' because they're dealing with other people's money." However, he'd found they could and did say 'no' when conditions warranted. Consequently, Rod was a strong ally as he helped the department win approval for its budget from council. His relations with Blakely and Hagan remained positive throughout his mayoralty.

In view of increasingly more challenging economic times, the decision by council in early 1973 by a 7-4 vote to increase the mayor's salary by thirty-seven per cent to $30,000, their own by fifty per cent to $9,000 was controversial. Even worse for the public and unions was that it was done in camera. In 1976, council again voted themselves and the mayor a twenty per cent hike, even though the original recommendation was for a thirty-three per cent jump for the mayor. That prompted Rod, agreeing with the motion, to remind council, "Think of the office, not the person."

The media predictably made the 1976 pay hike a personal issue. A cartoon by *The Albertan's* Rodewalt had Rod looking at himself reflected in a pool of water, with the caption, "Hello, beautiful. Want a thirty-three per cent raise?" Discussing these raises in retirement, Rod said these were the only two increases during his eight years in office. Spread over that period, they represented annual increases less than what most workers in Canada received. Remember, the 1970s were economically volatile years. To have these matters go to public debate would have resulted in grandstanding and confusion, said Rod. A year and a half before his retirement, he wanted to make sure his successors received reasonable remuneration. That, at least, was his justification for the 1976 pay boost.

Six months after that first council raise, Rod was embroiled in trying to prevent a strike at the Calgary General Hospital. After meeting with CUPE and hospital officials, he said, "We are on the verge of a strike in Calgary, with all that will mean for thousands of people, and the legacy of bad feeling that strikes of this kind can produce." He added, "I am proud of our hospital and its record of service, and I ask the CUPE negotiators, the eight hundred hospital workers, and the management to continue their negotiations in good faith to settle the dispute in a fair and sensible way."[22] He told Premier Lougheed and board chairman George Cloakey he intended to personally become fully informed on the facts of the dispute. "The future of our hospital and the fair treatment for its workers, who do some of the hardest and lowest-paid work in our community, are both important to me." With fairness and balance, he was boldly entering a mine field. This was not the bull in a china shop approach that some accused him of, though.

Christmas and year-end often induced in Rod a tendency to see the city in a Dickensian and *Hard Times* context. In his 1973 Christmas greetings to a city school, he served up a strong social justice message. "You will probably sing carols promoting concepts of peace and good will," he told the students. "As you sing them, there will be people in Calgary sitting in lonely rooms, wondering where their next meal is coming from. There will be people living in squalor because they don't know any better … there will be people confused and alienated by the injustice and insensitivity of the world that goes on around them." Moreover, these scenes won't only play out at Christmas. "They will be there the rest of the year. All of us have a responsibility toward people less fortunate than ourselves … have fun but do not forget your concern for others less fortunate than you. Resolve to show this concern actively throughout all seasons."

In a similar vein, his year-end letter to city policemen concluded by reminding all officers "of our prime duty to help and serve those around us with compassion and good will, especially those who are less fortunate than ourselves. Let's remember that no matter how little of the world's goods a man may have – or a boy, for that matter – he has a right to human dignity. Let's never forget that."

Securing a four-day week for outside workers that actually saved the City money was another priority that Rod diligently pursued. Although the union asked for it in 1973, they didn't get it incorporated into a contract for another two years. When it was first broached for a trial period, the City appointed a committee of senior managers and union representatives to review it. According to Brown, the City's personnel manager Peter Thompson said, "There was no goddam way he was going to allow a four-day work week on a permanent basis." Rod called a meeting with the commissioners and Thompson, and as a result, Thompson soon after left the City, adding to the statistics of departed employees.

Another Dickensian message at the end of 1974 sought to dampen the expectations of unions and others. "My New Year's Message is not a particularly happy one," Rod said. "As we approach our centenary, I believe we are facing one of the most difficult years in our city's history. A critical shortage of adequate housing at a reasonable price, rising costs, and the prospect of a worsening unemployment are among my particular concerns." Some gloom, even self-doubt, was apparent in the message. It was certainly an unusual greeting letter, with no sugar-coating of realities.

In the next year, 1975, came yet another attempt to tamp down ambitious hopes. "The New Year will be a difficult one for many. People suffering hardship already will undoubtedly suffer more. Even for governments, including our own in City Hall, the gravy train is coming to an end," Rod said. "If you need housing in the coming year, you're in trouble. It will be harder to find, and more expensive. If you have a good apartment, don't leave it. If you have a good home, don't sell it. If you have a good job, keep it, for there will be many Canadians worse off than you next year." This letter represented an unusual call to arms for restraint, with a lot of practical if not gloomy advice. Again, there was not much feel-good about this.

The lower-your-sights message was quite a habit by the time the next year-end came around. "I told the administration last year that 1975 would be one of the toughest years in our city's history. I am sorry to say that I believe that 1976 will be far more difficult," he said. "Our problem with the federal wage controls, for that is what they are, is simply credibility. It looks to our labour unions as if the little man always bears the brunt of cutbacks and deferments, and he is supposed to make all the sacrifices this time too ... We have to earn their confidence, and we can do that only by proving that the sacrifices are going to be shared fairly."

That was certainly a message of fairness and equity that makes sense today as much as it did then. "I believe that in our desire to serve people well, we have built a government at administrative levels that is too expensive for us to continue to support with automatic expansion and automatic salary increases. In fact, I think we're top-heavy, and the place to economize is not necessarily the fellow on the wrong end of a shovel, or the man driving a truck or a bus. We've got to deliver the services at their level, but what about the departmental administrations? ... To put it simply, I believe that we have more government than we can afford at all three levels." This wasn't an anti-government tirade, but rather a thought-out and rational response to economic realities of the day.

He went on to offer some practical solutions, not the kind that municipal mayors often propose. He called for a freezing of salaries over $25,000 [$112,000 in 2015 dollars], a moratorium on hiring, and a stricter review process for job reclassifications. Staff may wonder "why I would choose to put bad news into my Christmas letter," he said. "The reason is a simple one: I believe in plain talk and I detest hypocrisy. How could I write you a bland, conventional Christmas letter this week, and then hit you behind your back with my austerity request next week?" In his usual style, Rod didn't avoid tough news. He concluded, "Let me thank the many public servants who do their job conscientiously ... and let me wish you good health, happiness, and income stability in 1976." Wishes of "income stability" must have been a first, but there was no mistaking his intentions. We wish in vain for such straightforwardness from other politicians and those responsible for the public purse.

Incredibly, Rod was at it again the following year, restraining contract wishful thinking, and feeling unsurprisingly self-conscious about it. "I am beginning to feel like a prophet of doom. Each year I warn you that things are going to be more difficult next year, and sure enough, I'm right," he said. "This year is no exception, although there are some bright spots. For example, I believe that the federal government's anti-inflation program is having a measure of success."

Rod continued with some homespun lecturing and an old-fashioned scolding. "There's nothing wrong with working and saving and doing without—at least, that's what I tell my wife," he said. "It is also a world in which Canada's economic position is deteriorating. Our costs are too high and our production is too low ... We aren't competing effectively ... It's not nice to be greedy, but if you're both greedy and lazy, you're going to get hurt. Canadians are, and Canadians will."

Rod then returned his attention to City Hall. "We're in good financial condition, provided we handle our business responsibly," he announced. "Now, City Hall isn't here just to give you and me a warm place in which to spend our days ... improvement has to start at home and I'm not happy with our performance in some areas." Now he was venturing where few political leaders ever go. "I'm talking about a small number of people only, but any is too many ... I don't like to see so many people in the cafeteria who should be at work. Have your coffee and read the paper at home. Talk to your friends when the work is done, and on Friday take only one hour for lunch, stay with us until the offices close, and then drop into your friendly neighbourhood tavern." He couldn't resist a final shot at planners. "Finally, there's one department that I'll try to have time-clocks put into," he said.

He concluded this unprecedented pitch for better productivity with this promise that would surely draw attention outside City Hall. "If you do your share, and council does its duty, there needn't be a municipal property tax increase this year." This kind of link was likely never delivered so clearly before or since Rod's tenure.

In early 1976, Rod presided over the acceptance by CUPE 37 outside workers of a one-year contract, even though the members had earlier rejected a similar deal and had voted to apply for a strike vote.[23] The deal provided a 10.2% raise for the employees and a thirty-eight hour work week. Union leader Ron Brown had been talking publicly about the ability of the union to cripple the City, or "shut 'er down," as the delightful union idiom described it. The reason for the change of heart was the agreement by the City to make the new work week hours a permanent arrangement, rather than a one year test. It is possible to see Rod's hand behind this conciliatory adjustment and his ability to avoid another walk-out threat.

If people believed, as some aldermen claimed, that Rod was a patsy for the unions and didn't stand up to them, they hadn't studied the record. Look at the carefully but sharply worded message Rod sent to all City Hall's seven thousand employees in October 1976, when the City unions planned to participate in a national day of protest across Canada against the Trudeau government's wage and price controls, introduced the year before. "You're entitled to plain talk, and that's what you've had from me … Plain talk is what I'm giving you now about October fourteenth and the National Strike. It's not a 'day of protest.' That's just wishy-washy words to cover up the fact that it's really still what the leaders called it in the beginning—a national strike." The action would not hurt the federal government, Rod said. Neither would it hurt City Hall, because the City would save about $400,000 in wages it wouldn't pay to those who walked out. The elderly, the poor, and the sick might suffer from the withdrawal of essential services, but the real victims would be the strikers themselves foregoing a day's pay.

"Some strike!" Rod exclaimed. "My wife says that if I don't go to work on October fourteenth, there's no reason why she and the kids should show me more consideration than I show them, so she won't be cooking or house cleaning for me that day. Instead, they'll go shopping with charge accounts, and I'll end up working harder to pay the bills … As for the unions' call to kids to stay out of school and defy their parents and teachers, as long as my children live at home, they'll listen to father and they'll get all the education they can. I remember history, and I don't like the kind of people who try to exploit kids for political purposes and turn them against their parents. I don't think people will stand for it—not parents, and not kids."

The proposed strike was illegal, Rod pointed out, "and if one party can ignore its commitments and tear up its contract today, so can the other party tomorrow. The contract is the only thing that protects the working man and his family … Use your best judgment on October fourteenth, but I'm asking you to do what I often have to do: live with things you don't like until you can change them the right way—not by force and by threat, but by reason and within the law."

An estimated million people across Canada participated in this day of protest, including a number of children. In Calgary, numbers were low. "It wasn't a full-blown walkout," said Ron Brown. There were compromises, he said, and no one lost any pay from that day's action. It's hard to argue against Rod delivering some theatrical rhetoric. Its evocation of housewives taking their own actions in the home injected a dated feel, but this was still another example of Rod tackling an issue head-on, but leaving himself room for a peaceful resolution.

This insistence by Rod on fighting for the underdog was not confined to the benefit of unions, seniors, and welfare recipients. Rod took up causes for a wide and disparate range of people while he was mayor and during his whole life. A corollary of that, of course, was a tendency to resist those in positions of privilege, especially when they sought further benefits and advantages. We'll see in the next chapter how this worked out.

10
JUST CAUSES

B ecause of its apparently inconsequential nature, an incident in 1974 toward the end of Rod's second term illustrated well the extent of his efforts on behalf of citizens to be fair and considerate no matter how humble their need. A young girl who lost a quarter while seeking to buy an item from a City vending machine and who was unable to collect a refund felt motivated enough to contact the mayor's office and relate her plight. One of dozens of complaints, letters, and calls that came to the mayor's office every day, it would have been easy to cast aside as Rod grappled with multimillion dollar budgets, rampant land speculation, and a hostile council.

Sensitive to the fact that more than two bits were at stake here, Rod took the trouble himself to write to the recently appointed Chief Commissioner Denis Cole about the matter. "Anything that causes small children to lose their money without an immediate refund is wrong," he said[1] He knew this incident could influence a young girl's future relationship with her local government. He empathized with her dilemma.

Too cute, you may say. But that little girl probably never forgot the trouble he took to return her quarter and make sure similar refusals to refund such losses were minimized in future. Reminded of the incident in later life, Rod asked, "How could a child learn to trust an institution that stole her fortune?" A pleasant aspect about being mayor, he added, was the ability to remedy injustice and bureaucratic pettiness.

He remembered talking to the City law department about the large number of women who complained about catching and tearing their stockings on bus seats or other City property. The department was aghast at the notion of paying out any compensation. "The City fought this tooth and nail. There was, in effect, a conspiracy to resist every claim," he said. Applying his full powers as mayor, he told the department that trivial claims should be paid and not contested. The meanness of City Hall today and its determination to resist any minor claims never cease to amaze him. The costs of reasonable compensation don't come close to matching the ill will engendered by bull-headed bureaucratic responses. The costs would generally be infinitely less than the hourly salary of zealous law department employees sticking to petty principles.

However modest their issue, Rod held out a hand of welcome to almost any citizen approaching his office. Take the young boy who wrote him a note offering suggestions for improving public business in City Hall. So struck was Rod by the boy's earnest maturity, he invited him for a visit. Sure enough, the boy showed up not long after with his mother in tow. Mother seemed embarrassed by her son's temerity. Rod assured her there was nothing to apologise for, and had her wait in the reception area with a cup of tea while he chatted with the boy alone. The boy seemed delighted at this opportunity and probably told many people about his personal audience with the mayor.

Rod's determination to help people in trouble stayed with him throughout his life, far beyond his years in the mayor's office. Whether there was any political calculation in getting a quarter refund for a girl, or spending twenty minutes with a bright young boy is not really the issue. The fact is, Rod helped an enormous range of people, and much of that help occurred in private without public recognition.

In his eighties and infirm, he still liked to offer a hand. "I've tried to help people all my life, but I didn't seek glory. How can it have merit if you're looking for self-advertisement? I was always nice and polite to the little people. They put me where I was, why crap on them?" He knew many in public life and in business who ignored those precepts, though. Rod's approach had a practical angle too. "The best way of getting something from the boss is being nice to the secretary. I went out of my way to speak to CP workers on the tracks—they're the boat we floated on," he said.

There is irony, of course, in his insistence that blowing his own trumpet was not his modus operandi. Still, he believed that doing things "behind the scenes is the most effective way to help people." That approach brings other practical advantages too. For example, it gives people causing trouble the opportunity to change their position and resolve clashes with no loss of face. This is a different Rod Sykes that most of the public didn't see or appreciate.

Preventing the threatened closure of Canadian Forces Base Calgary was an ongoing issue for much of his mayoralty, to which he applied these principles through his dealings with the federal government. The result of his efforts was to delay the closure and let the city enjoy the many benefits of the base for another twenty years. Trudeau announced in April 1976 that the base would remain open, even as others across Canada were closed as part of cost-saving measures. "Trudeau based his decision on the economic, political, and social aspects," said *The Herald*.[2]

That gave no credit to Rod, of course, who had done much of the behind-the-scenes work. With up to 2,400 servicemen stationed there, plus a civilian force of 480, the base payroll was $33.5 million a year. With its annual $8 million budget for outside services, the base was vital to Calgary's economy.[3]

Rod's friendship with Prime Minister Trudeau was clearly a major influence in the final positive decision. But at the time, the prospects were in doubt, prompting Calgary Conservative MP Eldon Woolliams to ride his high horse and rail against the Trudeau government for the base's demise. He charged Trudeau with favouring Quebec against the West. Rod sent Woolliams a telegram. "If you want the Calgary base closed, please go on talking." Two weeks later, he dropped the sarcasm. "I feel more optimistic about the future of the base," Rod told the MP. "I'm trying to keep politics out of the debate ... the less said about it politically for the time being, the better."[4] This was Rod Sykes diplomacy at the forefront. "This wouldn't have worked with publicity," he said.

As chairman of the City's board of health, Rod undertook interventions that saved the careers of employees. They remained grateful throughout their lives. Approaching ninety, George Kurdydyk could still recall in detail the part Rod played in backing him when his position as laboratory supervisor was threatened. "I could always count on him." The source of Kurdydyk's problems was then Medical Officer of Health Agnes O'Neil. Slim, prim, and bespectacled, she projected a sensitive, strangled look. Her managerial style sparked anxiety throughout the department.

Dr. John Willey, director of City dental services, recalled his own issues with O'Neil. Rod intervened on behalf of both men and ordered O'Neil to cease interfering with the employees' security or peace of mind. Even the health board chairperson, Nancy Maguire, a nurse by profession, grappled with what could only be called harassment from O'Neil. Years later, Maguire sent a note suggesting Rod, through his interventions, had saved Maguire's career at a critical time as well. "Women's bullying is usually more thoughtful and calculating," Rod mused when recalling this period. The upshot of his interventions was that O'Neil was soon gone from the City. Many may have said good riddance. Kurdydyk stayed on, and Willey remained as a loyal and dedicated chief dentist until his retirement.

It's instructive to view some of Rod's actions on behalf of embattled community groups too. For more than a year and a half in the early 1970s, the proposed development by the Alberta Livestock Co-operative of a $2.5-million slaughterhouse and animal processing facility called Agrimart close to residential homes in northeast Calgary captured an almost endless stream of media headlines in Calgary and even nationally. The working-class residents of the Mayland, Vista Heights, and Belfast neighbourhoods were fighting the prospect of odours emanating from the facility and the creation of a bird hazard to aircraft approaching Calgary International Airport, thus causing a drop in the value of their homes.

With the help of well-known Calgary lawyer Milt Harradence, the residents had fought the development through the planning processes at City Hall and in the Alberta Supreme Court. Although the citizens, led by a determined John Schmal, later to become one of the longest-serving aldermen in the city's history, had been so far unsuccessful in halting the project, they insisted they hadn't lost the war.[5] They raised their own stink with demonstrations flaunting signs such as "The Whole Thing is a Lot of Bull." Later in the fall, a hundred or so descended one Sunday on Rod's Elbow Park home to protest. Rod had been sympathetic from the beginning, but had been unable to persuade others in City Hall there were valid enough reasons to reject the project. He also maintained close contact with Harradence and Jack Major, the lawyers for the so-called 24-25 Council. Those numbers represented the legal sections of the affected communities. Incidentally, Major later represented Rod in the Supreme Court of Canada appeal on the Fortieth Avenue lawsuit. Capping his career, Major went on to be a Supreme Court judge.

Following behind the scenes maneuvering, plans emerged for the proposed Agrimart to move to another site north of the original location at Thirty-Second Avenue N.E. and Barlow Trail. With Rod's encouragement, council voted 10-2 to purchase land in this industrial area for Agrimart's new location. Members also amended approval conditions to prevent animal-parts processing on the site. At first, there was relief a compromise had been made, but the deal fell through when Alberta Livestock refused the land offer, and the City decided anyway the land price was "out of sight," as Rod put it.[6]

In a wearying process for all concerned, Agrimart eventually settled on another site at Nineteenth Street N.E. and McKnight Boulevard. Whether the reason was declining cattle markets or other factors, the Agrimart did not last long and closed its doors after a few years, ending a chapter of bitter citizen involvement in City planning.

The citizen leader and later alderman, John Schmal, described the dispute as a sparkplug for greater citizen input in City Hall planning matters, a process Rod had already signalled he was willing to promote. "Rod Sykes was a different kind of politician who believed people do have the right of access to planning matters. We saw eye to eye on that," said Schmal. He noted Rod was always ready to help when needed, and his rapport with Harradence benefited the process too. Rod appeared before the City's development appeal board to oppose the City's approval of the project—an unusual action for a mayor to take. Rod also had a lead role in persuading commissioners that City funds be used for some of the 25-24 Council's legal costs. The group didn't have much money to pay for Harradence. At meetings, they'd pass the hat and give Harradence all the contents for the many hours he toiled on their behalf. "Whatever you collect, that's what I get," Harradence told them. "That's good enough for me."

Schmal said he respected Rod and his determined stand on issues. "His door was always open," he said with appreciation almost four decades later. They've stayed in touch, although they've disagreed on issues, including whether the City should proceed with the airport tunnel road project that Schmal favoured. A recent conversation on that issue ended with Rod hoping that Schmal could sleep at night after taking the stand he did, a remark Schmal said he objected to but tried to put behind him. Needling even his friends remained a life-long habit for Rod.

Another community issue of justice and fair play that Rod became deeply involved in was Victoria Park and the expansion plans by the Exhibition and Stampede Board into the old residential area. This was a top-of-mind issue from the beginning and a source of great frustration. One of the residents leading the fight to preserve Victoria Park as a viable neighbourhood, and a frequent visitor to the mayor's office, was Rebecca Aizenman. She lived and owned property there, and was utterly committed to the cause of justice in her neighbourhood. But the campaign by the big Stampede guns against the "little" people was as debilitating as anything Rod took on. He was up against the core of Calgary's establishment.

Toward the end of Rod's first term, hopes were higher for Victoria Park residents than they'd been for a while under the threat of Stampede expansion. Instead of bulldozing north, the Stampede board was being urged to consider expansion south.[7] A new area sector plan for the residential neighbourhood talked of a stronger emphasis on people. "It will be interesting to see what happens," wrote *Albertan* reporter Stephani Kerr. Four months later, with a new mandate under Rod's belt, *The Albertan* quoted him as saying, "I think within a month or so we'll resolve the whole Stampede problem."[8] However, the response from Stampede board president George Crawford to southern expansion began to assume ominous overtones. The land in question was "too remote and not acceptable to us," said Crawford.[9] The battle lines were being drawn.

Writing to federal Minister of Public Works Ron Basford, Rod summed up his frustrations with Victoria Park. He referred specifically to a $10-million grant the Stampede board sought from the Feds for its expansion plans to the north into the existing residential neighbourhood that he was intent on preserving. He criticized what he considered Basford's department's view of Victoria Park as an old, rundown residential area that wasn't worth saving against racetrack expansion and other Stampede projects.[10]

Rod noted the City agreement from the 1960s letting the Stampede acquire up to half of Victoria Park for expansion. This occurred, he said, without prior planning or sociological studies, and without consultation with the affected residents. "They were sentenced to death without a hearing, in absentia as it were." He concluded with a sarcastic shot at City administration attitudes. "The houses are old, the people are poor, and they are mostly tenants anyway—they don't count! Well, they *do* count. These are the people I work for, the ones who don't have a voice of their own."

After making sure the Victoria Park studies were completed, Rod interpreted their conclusions as confirmation "that destruction of this neighbourhood would be a disaster ... the Stampede board has shown an utter and complete disregard for the welfare of the residential neighbourhood." He also questioned the Stampede board's ability to act with such impunity. "It is certainly destructive to the public interest and it apparently violates the rights to justice of a good many people. It is unworkable," he said.[11]

Normally, it would be inappropriate for the City to involve itself in grant requests from an autonomous group like the Stampede board. But, in his letter to federal minister Basford, Rod declared, "The granting of such a loan would mean destruction of a viable residential neighbourhood and the creation of a most serious and most traumatic housing problem ... any government that gets involved in such a scheme has been inadequately informed." Despite Rod's call for a meeting to discuss the matter further, his entreaties were ignored. The Feds and the Province continued to allow the demolition of Victoria Park.

In 1974, Rod was angered to learn the Stampede board had ordered demolition of six properties in Victoria Park, without City approval. It was done, he said, "in total disregard for the 1969 agreement for the extension of the Stampede area."[12] That agreement specified the board should not undertake demolition of any dwelling which it acquired, unless occupants were offered alternative accommodation at "reasonable" rates. "Once again, it would appear that the City and the Stampede Board are making a mockery of commitments made to the people of Victoria Park," Rod said. He was doing his best, but the odds were unfavourable. With the popularity of the Stampede on the rise, the board was clearly set on expanding the scope of the outdoor show and accommodating even more visitors.

Rod saw clearly for whose benefit the Calgary Stampede primarily operated. The directors often conducted their affairs "with a relative lack of concern for the community as a whole," he was quoted as saying in a book of essays, *Stampede City, Power and Politics in the West.*[13] "Sykes has convincingly cited several cases of the Stampede's insensitivity and determination to have its own way." Rod was particularly derogatory about the role the board's general manager, Bill Pratt, played in this and other issues. A man with ruth-less tenacity who helped build several major projects in and around Calgary, including McMahon Stadium and the Saddledome, Pratt led the Stampede expansion efforts during the 1970s. He later worked as project manager, president and chief executive officer of the 1988 Winter Olympics in Calgary. He died in 1999, and Rod despised him to the end.

Stampede City further characterized the board this way. "Residents and former residents of the Victoria Park community … are adamant in main-taining that the Calgary Exhibition and Stampede is a private company domi-nated by a core elite of commercial and agricultural businessmen. They are convinced that the Stampede board, while espousing a civic-minded philoso-phy, is a self-perpetuating group who uses the Stampede and its reputation to accumulate money for the Alberta corporate sector and at the same time uses the Stampede's themes and celebrations to legitimize themselves."[14] For some Calgarians, these comments were heresy; for others, a bitter truth. For Rod, Victoria Park's demise was a dark chapter in Calgary's history, and the board's role was "wicked and immoral." However, when you see the high-rise condominiums, rather than expanded race tracks and other Stampede facili-ties, taking over Victoria Park today, it's impossible to imagine the original residential area would ever have survived redevelopment pressures.

Rod didn't offer all causes a warm reception. Consider his response to an invitation from the Women's Canadian Club to speak to members on the topic of "Integration with Aboriginals." He said he could not accept the invitation "because I know very little about the subject of integration of one society with another. I have had a good deal of contact with Indians in our area and, generally, I believe a good working relationship over the years has been established." He added, "My attitude has been that the Indian is entitled to exactly the same treatment as any other kind of Canadian, no more no less … I am sick and tired of the do-gooders, the sociologists both amateur and professional, and all the people who meddle in the lives of others without being invited. I don't think the Indians need them and I don't think anyone else does. I think they've helped to create a very difficult situation of expecta-tions and dependence, but I have no solution for that."[15]

This stand didn't endear Rod to groups he viewed as elitist dilettantes, fid-dling on the fringes of social action. He believed the Women's Canadian Club and other women's groups consisted of mostly white, privileged, middle-class women who could look after themselves. He considered them part of the establishment. There was, in his view, no more genteel way of saying no to them. If he held an unjustifiably contemptuous and reactionary view of the rising feminist movement, at least he was consistent.

Maybe they reminded him of the English socialites in Victoria he sought to escape from as a boy. As you can see, he brushed them off dismissively. His disregard was disturbing to many, including me, and unnecessarily alienated him from what should have been a significant segment of his constituency.

With his Catholic grounding, it wasn't surprising Rod opposed abortion. See how he responded to a Calgary Birth Control Association request for funding for its counselling and other activities. "Counselling is … certainly valuable as long as it remains educational counselling designed to inform people who can use information intelligently … What concerns me is that there are a number of fanatically pro-abortion people within its ranks, and the most aggressive ones do seem to take over all these voluntary organizations. Further, some people apparently associated with the group seem to be part of a pipeline to abortion which has become the principal operation and even industry of half a dozen doctors in this city." There was no fudging on his position apparent here. "Abortion is not an acceptable substitution for birth control." But then this important proviso: "I cannot take a hard and fast position on the issue of abortion itself, because I believe that if it is medically necessary for the physical health of the mother, there is little choice."[16]

In his final year as mayor, Rod publicly clarified his position on abortion following a suggestion from Alderman Pat Donnelly that council better be behind the local board of health birth control counselling program. "I am personally opposed to abortion on demand, to abortion as a substitute for responsibility, to the use of public funds to promote private irresponsibility," he said. "At the same time, it is my duty to support the law as it stands, and that I do. Therefore, I am prepared to see that women who need counselling by qualified medical practitioners according to the terms of the criminal code receive what is their right under the law."[17] By this time, of course, access to abortion was a right under Canadian law. In reality, he could not use his office to oppose the law, but his response revealed some pragmatism.

The provision of guaranteed access for all people with disabilities was another topic that Rod didn't fear tackling head-on. Answering a request for more consideration for handicapped people in the planning of the Light Rail Transit system, he said, "The problem is that it is very clear that a mass transit system which can only attract passengers away from the private automobile by providing speed and efficiency in somewhat crowded conditions cannot possibly afford the loss of space, the real hazards to personal safety, and the delays involved in handling the handicapped. So far as we can determine, there is not a system in the world that does this, and the comment in city after city in Europe was that it would be cheaper to provide a personal, private service as, in fact, we do through the handi-bus system."[18]

He denied, though, that the City was ignoring the needs of the handi-capped. "In a city where great numbers of people in a hurry want to get to and from work quickly, there is no opportunity for the very personal assistance that the handicapped need. To say that their disability must be imposed on every other person seems to me to be unfair and unreasonable," he said. "The answer obviously lies in separate facilities designed for their special needs." Today, this position comes across as backward, particularly in view of the gains people with disabilities have won in the years since. Rod did not hide behind political correctness, and one usually knew where he stood on con-tentious issues like this.

On the topic of appropriate responses, Canadians across the country may recall the notorious bumper stickers that first appeared during the interna-tional oil crisis of 1973 and given prominence during the National Energy Program hostilities of the late 1970s and early 1980s. "Let Those Eastern Bastards Freeze in the Dark," they said. Calgary oilman James H. Gray first publicly quoted this delightful gem of Alberta friendliness in *The Toronto Sun* on December 15, 1973. According to Rod, Alberta Social Services Minister Helen Hunley took some stickers to Toronto with Alberta Premier Peter Lougheed. The premier would later disavow the attribution, said Rod, but he knowingly allowed Hunley to distribute the stickers at a function. She wouldn't have done it if he had tried to prevent her, Rod noted. The slogan originated with Calgary oilman John Frey, who created it more as a prank than a dark political message. Frey was a former chief geologist at CP Oil and Gas. Invited to speak to a Toronto service club not long after that, Rod took his own stickers that read: "That Eastern Bastard is My Brother," prompt-ing an entry in *Colombo's All Time Great Canadian Quotations*. "Rod Sykes, Mayor of Calgary, was appalled and responded with his own bumper sticker," said the popular book.

This chapter closes with the George Abouna affair, another tale of injustice that captured Calgary headlines for years during Rod's tenure, and that placed Premier Peter Lougheed in a dismal light. Born in Chaldea in Iraq, mentioned in the Old Testament and later one of the first Christian communities, George Mansour Abouna was raised as a Christian Arab. According to a biography,[19] he rose from deep poverty to become a pioneer in modern medicine. He met and conquered many adversities in his pursuit of a better living and his goal of becoming a physician. His chosen path briefly took a different direction when he was granted a full scholarship to study engineering in the United Kingdom, but he eventually returned to a successful career in medicine, becoming a leader in organ transplantation. "Unfortunately, he became the victim of his own success when his achievements created animosity among colleagues, who waged a political war and booted him to another country thousands of miles away."

The source of that animosity, to Calgary's lasting shame, was the University of Calgary and the faculty of medicine, which invited Abouna to join its kidney transplant team practising in the Foothills Hospital in the early 1970s. Later court findings assessed the transplant results at the Foothills before his arrival were "substantially below the North American rate." The results with Dr. Abouna "were approximately equal to the North American rate."[20]

Abouna held the highest standards, and like many outstanding people, had little room for compromises. He wanted the transplants done his way. He formed his own team of highly loyal healthcare professionals. After an operation, he would often stay with patients, sleeping in the hospital to deal with any complications. The rest of the team, meanwhile, felt threatened by this demanding man who had come from the outside and who was telling other surgeons how to do things, worked independently, and was devoting extra hours to hospital care. On top of that, he was an Iraqi Arab.

In a shocking move, the hospital suspended the kidney transplant team. Following months of internal intrigue, Abouna was fired on October 15, 1975. He also lost his position as assistant professor of surgery at the university's faculty of medicine. There followed two horrific years for the perfectionist surgeon under attack from the university, the faculty, and the Foothills Hospital. "It was the crudest form of discrimination against an Arab person I'd ever seen," said Rod. Used to hardship and practised in personal discipline, Abouna wouldn't go quietly, however. As court proceedings later confirmed and as Rod related, he found no support for his case inside the establishment and, consequently, went outside it. He approached the news media and enlisted then television reporter Ralph Klein, as well as Rod, to back his efforts for a fair hearing. Rod's reputation as a fighter for the underdog was undoubtedly a persuasive factor in Abouna's decision to take his case to the mayor.

It proved impossible, however, to get a fair hearing, taking into account the cozy relationship between medical leaders and the Lougheed Conservatives. The courts were the only alternative, and so Abouna hired one of the outstanding lawyers of his time, Ross McBain, later appointed an Alberta judge. Although the legal process took years of anxiety and costs, Abouna won hands down and was awarded damages of $100,000 in a decision that clearly recognized the wrongs done to him and that roundly condemned the behaviour of the university and the medical staff involved.

Although Abouna had been fired on the recommendation of the hospital's medical advisory committee, he had received no notice of the committee meeting or of the proposal to fire him, according to court testimony.[21] Justice

Hugh John MacDonald found that the rule of natural justice required a notice of the complaint against Abouna, a notice of the hearing, and an opportunity to answer the charges. Far more damning was MacDonald's finding the unfavourable charts submitted against Abouna by the hospital board were "obviously false" and "inaccurate." The court finding that medical records had been falsified was humiliating, said Rod. "It should have been crushing in any system devoted to the ethical practice of medicine."

Abouna also won his suit against Dr. Tait McPhedran, Foothills director of surgery and a faculty of medicine professor, who had told the university medical surgery staff Abouna had published incorrect or incomplete data. Ordered to issue an apology, McPhedran quickly acknowledged, "the information upon which my statements were based was not correct." The written apology was hardly fulsome in that he pointed his finger at colleagues, Dr. Gordon Dixon and Dr. R.B. Church, as people who had supplied the information on which he based his remarks.

Still, McPhedran apologised "for this error on my part and for any damage to your professional reputation and standing which such statements may have caused." He went on, "I personally regard you as having integrity as a research scientist, and as a competent academic surgeon." McPhedran agreed to circulate and repeat the apology, and "I have no objection to you making use of this letter in any manner which you consider necessary to further exonerate your good reputation and standing as an academic surgeon." Court evidence had revealed Abouna applied unsuccessfully for positions at seven Alberta hospitals, seven in other provinces, thirteen in the U.S., and three in the U.K. The U of C had allowed Abouna's appointment at the medical school to lapse in 1976. This "shy, modest man from humble beginnings," as *The Herald* described him,[22] had also been stripped of all hospital privileges.

"I am delighted to hear of your success [court victory]," Rod wrote to Abouna.[23] "I am shocked at the findings of the judge that the charts and statistics presented were fabricated to produce a result other than the truth ... the minister of health [then Gordon Miniely] must take some action in connection with the hospital board and with those members of the medical advisory committee involved ... I do hope that you will not remember Calgary solely in the light of your sad experience, but rather in the light of your triumph which is a triumph of justice."

Rod followed up with a stern letter to Miniely. "The MacDonald judgment clearly places the responsibility for acting on your shoulders, and I would like to know why Dr. Abouna has not been fully reinstated in all his hospital privileges." To his credit, Miniely acted on Rod's letter. The reward for his efforts was demotion by Lougheed from cabinet. This proved to be not only the end of his political career, but Miniely died soon after his firing. Predictably, no admission came from the Lougheed government that any wrong had been done. McPhedran, in the meantime, kept all his positions and healthy salaries. Alberta cabinet minister Roy Farran later referred to the case of "the brilliant transplant surgeon." He said, "his shafting by the establishment made me more ashamed than anything else that has ever happened in public life." [24]

The Abouna affair inflicted harm on the university too. It refused to re-instate Abouna, despite the clarity of his lawsuit victory. As a result, the Canadian Association of University Teachers (CAUT) blacklisted the university in 1980. It also put the U of C board of governors under a procedure called the "third stage of censure" for its handling of Abouna's case. "Under this stage, CAUT recommends that faculty members not accept appointments at the university ... the seriousness of the case warranted the strongest sanction which the association can impose," CAUT said in a letter to board of governors chairman P.A. Mackimmie. [25] Following the blacklisting, the transplant program folded. Only at Abouna's request was the blacklisting lifted in the 1990s.

To no one's surprise, Abouna quit Calgary for the U.S. "In his voluntary exile, he refused to be defeated and ultimately emerged stronger than ever," said his biography." In the U.S., he continued his mission as a surgical innovator and pioneer. Among his many accomplishments, according to an award citation, was his invention of an artificial liver support system for the treatment of patients, thus saving "hundreds of lives" and making a "significant impact on the science and practice of transplantation throughout the world." He had by then received fifteen formal and international honours from universities and societies.

At the time of writing this book, Rod still received a regular Christmas card from Abouna. At seventy-six, Abouna was still lecturing and teaching in Pennsylvania. He was also travelling a lot and enjoying his grandchildren. "I don't know how you could rate a city that did this to a man of that calibre," said Rod. "As for me, with my small part in helping George Abouna get what passes for justice in our part of the world, I can feel privileged to have known him. I only hope that the purgatory he passed through in Alberta contributed in some positive way to his great achievements of later years."

11
COPS AND KIDS

After former Calgary Police Chief Duke Kent died in the spring of 1994, media stories focussed on his three years of crossing swords with Rod, as much as on other aspects of his career that saw his thirty-two year rise through the force's ranks. "Kent's rocky relationship with the mayor became an enduring part of city lore," wrote reporter David Climenhaga.[1] Police veterans said Kent, promoted to chief in 1968, one year before Rod became mayor, was crusty and unafraid to fight City Hall if he felt the interests of his force were threatened. After retirement, the Calgary-born Kent complained in reference to Rod, "the man simply wouldn't let me do the job." Kent, nicknamed Duke, considered himself a "hard-nosed cop" who backed strong laws for the protection of society and tough penalties for criminals; you could call him old school.

Rod had a different and less complimentary view of supposedly straight-shooter Kent, a stocky man with fleshy nose and jowls, a slab of hair, and bulging eyes. Rod also had an ambivalent attitude toward the police generally. Sykes forefathers had links with the armed forces, and he held an inherent respect for the military and for quasi-military organizations like the police. He adhered to law and order principles that his upbringing and background instilled in him. At the same time, though, his sense of justice, his antipathy toward bullying or abuse of power, a streak of rebelliousness, and his insistence on accountability from all publicly-funded institutions put him in conflict with the police. He later became enraged at what he considered police targeting of two particular groups in Calgary society: aboriginal people and kids. Chasms with the police were then inevitable.

What also got the relationship off to a bad start was that, within days of becoming mayor, Rod found out how serious the epidemic of thefts from the transit and cashiers' departments really were. He was appalled that City management had been so lax in pursuing prosecutions for the thefts—a sentiment justified publicly through the inquiry by Mr. Justice W.G. Morrow of Yellowknife, requested by Rod and ordered by the Alberta Attorney General within nine months of Rod's swearing-in. Rod was convinced the administration, in cahoots with the police, had made an effort to keep the thefts under wraps until after the 1969 election so that incumbents weren't implicated. Although Morrow didn't specifically make that link, he did excoriate the authorities in his final report released in May 1971. "A complete abdication by the persons who should be in charge" was among blunt condemnations.

Rod's rocky relationship with Kent didn't preclude being on good terms with other policemen, though. He was a frequent visitor to the shooting range, and early in his first term, many officers viewed him as a breath of fresh air. One aspect of Kent to remember is that he didn't have much education outside the force and had spent most of his life in Calgary. City personnel manager of the day, Peter Thompson, noticed the discrepancy between the education levels of some constables and that of senior officers like Kent, who had left school far short of his Grade 12 diploma. Many of the lower ranks had higher qualifications than the brass. He therefore introduced into the files of the senior officers changes that, while misguided, struck Rod with their fiendish cleverness. With Kent's help, he invented what he called a "life experience equivalent." So, a senior officer who had put in thirty years could claim a life experience equivalent that would grade him the same as a university graduate. Their thirty years went on the record with a note they were the equivalent of a degree. "I couldn't believe my ears when he explained that to me," said Rod. The life experience equivalent scheme collapsed amidst ridicule the moment it became public. But it showed how desperate Kent and other senior officers were to prevent an outsider becoming chief.

Efforts by Rod to encourage more female police candidates hit a wall. "They'll just be a nuisance," was Kent's response, according to Rod. In the past thirty years, the number of women constables has gone from less than 5% to 20%, according to Statistics Canada. Medical fitness standards also became an issue, particularly when Rod heard of an officer who had collapsed in Elbow Park after chasing a couple of youngsters involved in some minor mischief. Little to no physical training or physical testing occurred then. Since those days, challenging physical testing and ongoing evaluation have become an important condition of employment.

Former city policeman Chris Murphy confirmed the view that police at the time had little formal training. When he became a Calgary first class constable in the 1960s, Murphy had received just seven weeks' classroom instruction. After several years on the beat and in patrol cars, he went on to become one of the two first beneficiaries of a city police sponsorship program to attend university and graduate. He later created and taught leadership courses and a criminal justice program at what was then still called Mount Royal College. That all came after Kent retired, but interestingly, Murphy kept a soft spot for Kent, in part because Kent made an effort to improve working conditions.

From Rod's perspective, though, Kent retained a kick-ass approach to people on the street. Once, when a young, long-haired hippie-type complained to Rod the police had beaten him up and he had the bruises to prove it, Kent cynically asserted the kid's hair was over his eyes and that caused an accidental fall down the stairs at the station.

Obscene phone calls to the Sykes home traced to a police sergeant further undermined relations with the department. "Go back to Quebec, you French Canadian whore," was among foul-mouthed outbursts heard directly or on the recording device Rod had installed. The discovery of the police sergeant resulted from Alberta Government Telephones (AGT, then Calgary's major phone company) putting a tracer on the Sykes phone. AGT agreed to prosecute the suspect, but Rod then learned the incriminating tapes had been lost. They had been in police custody and had disappeared while being taken to the courthouse. Years later, while Rod was chatting with lawyer Milt Harradence, who also represented the Calgary Police Association, Harradence let it be known he couldn't elucidate further because of lawyer-client confidentiality rules, but that someone had suggested those tapes "better be lost." Rod often teased the showman Harradence with the slogan, "If you're guilty, call on Milty." The Sykes family went through inexcusable suffering from the nasty calls. The only conviction on record was a $100 fine against Kenneth Henry Stromberg, fifty-nine, for making harassing phone calls over a two and a half month period.[2]

The first major crisis between Rod and the police erupted out of the rock 'n roll extravaganza at McMahon Stadium on July 5 and 6, 1970, called Festival Express. This was the brainchild of Toronto promoter Ken Walker. So thrilling was this event for the backwater city that people who were around at the time still recalled the event and the participation of some of North America's top bands four decades later. So violently did it shake the city's conservative police force and create disharmony between senior officers and the mayor's office that the Morrow Inquiry, originally set up to look at City Hall thefts, was expanded to examine charges of obstruction and improper interference of the police by City Hall during the festival.

To put the event in context, this was the era when promoters across North America organized two-day or longer concerts with several top-line bands and lured tens of thousands of young people to urban stadiums. The youth counter-culture revolution that began in the 1960s with so-called free love, drugs, and rock 'n roll was still in vogue. Activism by young people against the Vietnam War, or for civil rights, feminism and other hot-button issues was pandemic. People over thirty and formal authority were viewed with suspicion. The result was a titanic clash of values between newly empowered young people and their fuddy-duddy parents and other authority figures. Sexual abandon and drug experimentation were among perceived youthful manifestations of this divide.

The hedonistic music festival culture of these times provided a dramatic expression for this youthful exuberance. It was also a chance for aspiring impresarios to appropriate this exuberance for considerable profit. In the summer of 1970, it became Calgary's turn to host one of these musical spectacles. The mayor's office received a copy of a memo in the March before from then Medical Officer of Health Dr. Leslie Allan warning, "These music love-in festivals are generally only attended by hippies and the oddballs of society and create nothing but serious problems … to say nothing of crime and general disorder. Everyone is certainly resolved to discourage any plans for such an event in this region."[3] Rod's response was a quick, verbal slap. "I do not believe that it is advisable to circulate a letter expressing such views … In no way does this administration support the expression of only negative, destructive, contemptuous, and antagonistic attitudes toward any group of people in this community. All have the same rights, and those rights will be respected." He then specified what the response had to be, leaving no room for ambiguity. "Any inquiries respecting folk music festivals or similar undertakings must be treated with complete courtesy and the fullest co-operation."[4]

The prospect of Festival Express at McMahon may not have thrilled him, but he left no doubt that the public policy should be to licence the event. That made sense, since these events are difficult to stop, but it also reflected his consistent view of young people's place in society. He went out of his way to defend the rights of youth and value their presence and contributions. That likely resulted from his own experiences as a rebellious young person struggling to find his way, and an affinity with his own children, two of whom were by then in their teens. Executive assistant Mike Horsey, then twenty-eight, also helped influence how Rod approached the Festival Express. Horsey saw the festival as a way of putting Calgary on a broader cultural map, and shedding its hick town image.

The result was a collision with the police brass. Deputy Chief Gordon Gilkes distributed a memo from a meeting of senior officers saying, "It was agreed that we should take steps to try and stop this thing from happening."[5] When Rod made clear the festival would proceed, however, senior police discussed plans to have the militia ready for the marauding hordes. Rod said no and insisted the police must handle the affair themselves, creating further anxiety in the force. According to Rod, the police, in their zeal, even approached the commander of Canadian Forces Base Calgary, asking him to be ready to declare a state of emergency when the drug-addled masses arrived.

Former policeman Murphy noted over forty years later the police department in 1970 had little training in crowd control. Officers were aghast at the prospect of widespread lawlessness. The department consulted with other police services across Canada and even brought in a special RCMP riot squad, as relations with the mayor's office became more adversarial. Local residents became fearful too. Tension and excitement were in the air as the Festival Express rolled into town after its cross-country railway tour.

The Grateful Dead, The Band, Ian and Sylvia, New Riders of the Purple Sage, Tom Rush, Buddy Guy, Eric Andersen, Mountain, Ten Years After, Traffic, Seatrain, James and the Good Brothers, Cat Mashmakan, and The Modern Rock Quartet were just some of the awe-inspiring names playing Calgary that happy weekend. Four decades later, the Boomers who were there still turn giddy over recalling the line-up. A former *Herald* photographer could still visualize in exquisite detail the startling moment the Friday night before the festival when singer Janice Joplin, drinking in a local bar, raised her T-shirt to reveal tattooed breasts and screamed, "Take a picture of these." The Canadian documentary, *Festival Express*, directed by Bob Smeaton and released at the 2003 Toronto Film Fest, captured those heady days. Aficionados may recall the Grateful Dead song about their Festival Express trip:

Never had such a good time in my life before,
I'd like to have it one time more.
One good ride from start to end,
I'd like to take that ride again.[6]

And what a ride it was for the locals. Glorious summer weather helped lure 22,000 people to McMahon Stadium and create an event *The South Side Mirror* described as a "beautiful experience."[7] A photo of a broadly smiling Rod in a short-sleeved, button-down shirt and with thick, horn-rimmed spectacles, sitting amidst a sea of long-locked, lounging youth offered an idiosyncratic commentary of the affair and Rod's involvement with it. "Calgary Rocked but Didn't Tumble," said *The Albertan* headline after the festival. "Calgary has just spent two days as the rock music capital of Canada," said a swaggering piece by *Herald* reporter Jacques Hamilton in the paper's lead front-page story on the Sunday. "Despite scuffles between gate-chargers and police, Festival Express was every bit as cool an event as optimists had hoped during the tense weeks that preceded the show." Most of the credit has to go to Calgary police, who spent their time inside McMahon Stadium bouncing babies instead of teens and looking the other way at some open use of alcohol and drugs, he wrote.[8] The impression was that police had been told before the concert to ignore minor offences and only make drug arrests outside the show's perimeter

However, in his weekly CHQR broadcast a week later, Rod branded as lies reports the police had turned a blind eye to crime at the festival. He vehemently denied reports that turf at McMahon had been destroyed, or that trees were cut and boats burned at Prince's Island, where a free alternative concert took place for those unable to pay the high admittance to the McMahon event. He said the police were not under orders to ignore crimes, and congratulated them for their "good judgment" and those attending for their "reasonable behaviour." The reason people concocted such lies, he concluded, was that they must be "sick with fury and frustration that their predictions of tragedy didn't work out."

In his inquiry report, Judge Morrow agreed no riot or general disturbance took place, and few serious breaches of the law were reported. "True," he added, "liquor and drug offences became the rule of the day ... Nudity and other breaches of what might be termed rules of morality were prevalent."[9] What the public didn't know until the release of testimony from the inquiry three and a half months later were the details of a full-blown confrontation between Rod and Festival Express promoter Ken Walker that had at least one of them swinging his fists, and both exchanging insults and having to be physically separated by senior officers a few hours before the concert finished.

Rod had broached the idea of the young people gathered peacefully outside the stadium being allowed in free for the concert's final hours. Organizers even told him he could make the announcement—until Walker came on the scene and nixed the idea out of hand. In his testimony, Rod said Walker was in a highly agitated state. "I looked upon him as an animal in the condition he was, because I am not tolerant of drunkenness in public or drug-taking or whatever." Rod acknowledged that he too was under considerable strain by this time, and lost his temper. According to testimony, Rod charged Walker with having set out to "skin us ... make a quick killing, to try to make a fast buck having exposed the whole community to the risks of violence."

The Festival Express had drawn sixteen thousand people in Toronto and just four thousand in Winnipeg. Maybe the financial picture was deteriorating by the time it hit Calgary. To warranted snickering, Walker testified his doctor, in attendance throughout the festival, had given him sedatives for his troubled nerves. To let unpaid people in might have created an insurance liability problem, he said, prompting a torrent of abuse from the mayor. "We were eastern scum and I was a son of a bitch," Walker told the inquiry. Voice levels escalated, attracting attention from other people near the stadium passageway where this took place. When Deputy Chief Gilkes stepped between them, Rod told him to handcuff Walker. "Arrest him. This is an order," Rod shouted. Gilkes' response was, "I don't take orders from you." Rod testified that the deputy's tone was disrespectful. Meanwhile, Walker's solicitor joined the throng crying, "Yes, yes, go ahead. Take him [Walker] away, then we'll sue." Gilkes and an RCMP officer, Staff Sgt. Michael Collins, tried to separate the two warring parties. Collins described Rod as still "very agitated and very loud and very abusive to Mr. Walker and shaking his finger in his face." He feared the argument would end in a physical fight. Walker was so mad he took a swing at Rod, missed, and hit a garbage can.

In his report, Morrow offered the opinion, "it was wrong for the mayor to use his position as he did." Walker hardly emerged from this contretemps with dignity either. It had been a long, hot weekend for everyone, and Walker did not present himself well. The media had fun with the whole episode, of course, but it surely didn't warrant the time it took at the inquiry. There are justifiable suspicions it was part of the police campaign to put Rod in as negative a light as possible. Rod wanted to let in young people who couldn't afford the high entrance fee, while the businessman Walker had a clear eye on his bottom line and the high expenses of the concert.

George Kemp, serving as field commander at the concert, described the report he wrote on the rock festival and the goings-on that weekend as one "I am ashamed to put in." Former policeman Murphy's unofficial view was, "Under-trained officers assigned to the event seem to have exaggerated both the extent and the nature of the stadium goings-on."

What Morrow really got his teeth into, however, was the conduct of the Calgary Police Commission, at that time still with local control as set out in the Police Act, and with the mayor automatically chairperson. On becoming mayor in 1969, Rod established as a priority the opening up of City Hall boards and committees to public scrutiny. That included the police commission which, under his encouragement, began to vet police budgets and hear complaints in public from citizens about police misconduct. Three aldermen and two citizens joined Rod on the commission. Because of police and provincial government pressure, Morrow expanded his inquiry to hear police discontent with this new accountability and oversight. There was an obvious campaign to curtail the influence Rod was exerting on the police commission.

Police Chief Kent testified the commission was predominantly political, with "less dignity and less understanding" of police perspectives. He felt the majority of commission members were too inclined to take the side of the complainant, and the force thought it was being "thrown to the wolves." From Rod's viewpoint, the commission was only interested in misconduct and breaches of discipline, and it held its hearings in the open "to inspire public confidence."

At one commission hearing into a complaint from a youth that police had beaten him up while in custody, Rod agreed, "this young man got a mouthful of fists," prompting police anxiety that Rod was overly friendly to the complainant. Rod mocked the police evidence that they'd found a copy of Karl Marx's diatribe against capitalism, *Das Kapital*, in the youth's room, which further incensed them. Meetings were "charged with suspicion and tension," Morrow said, noting that policemen were "sensitive people."[10]

He concluded there had been obstruction of the police. "No doubt ... Mayor Sykes and some of the other commission members are earnest in their desire to see justice done," but they must take care that "a loyal and honest body of men with exceptional esprit de corps does not become discredited in the process." He recommended full-scale police commission hearings be discouraged, leaving breaches of discipline to the chief, while the commission should discuss only matters of general policy. In other words, it should abandon its role of meaningful oversight. That was indeed the direction the Morrow inquiry deliberately initiated, with a wink and a nod from the provincial government, Rod felt.

Civilian oversight of the police was at the heart of this discussion. A hot issue then, it remains so today. Within two years of the Morrow Report release, an amended Alberta Police Act, introduced by Attorney-General Merv Leitch of the recently elected Peter Lougheed government, eliminated the mayor's automatic membership on the commission, and took away municipal control over the commission. The 1973 changes to the act ended the commission's ability to give direction to the police. The changes also introduced a new system of dealing with complaints about police conduct. Such complaints would first go to the police chief, then to a Law Enforcement Review Board established by the Province.

"Sykes bypassed by A.G. Leitch," said one headline.[11] With the council complicit in the scheme, a new commission was appointed, excluding the mayor and adding a legal partner of lawyer Leitch, as well as radio reporter Ralph Klein, which was a blatant case of conflict. Before introducing the new legislation, Leitch visited Rod in his office to inform him of his intentions. When Rod reminded him about the consultation process he was required by law to follow, Leitch replied, "This is the consultation process." The two clashed on other occasions. "Leitch was a nasty piece of work," said Rod.

There's little doubt these changes were directed specifically at Rod by a provincial government that, although wildly victorious in the 1971 election, felt threatened by the mayor and his critical views of the police. The Province, with direct police encouragement, ensured no mayor could ever again do what Rod did. Rod said many police association members campaigned for the Conservatives in the 1971 election campaign and enjoyed a direct line to the government. Thus, the police were able to use their considerable clout to put the mayor in his place. Former policeman Murphy said many police officers interpreted the new provincial legislation as proof they had gained real political muscle. In the years since, they have never hesitated to speak out publicly when they felt threatened. From Rod's perspective, "the inquiry was bastardized and twisted to get me."

The changes to the police commission legislation diluted the chain of accountability of the police to the public. Rod was without allies in this battle and was the target of opprobrium on many sides for trying throughout his mayoralty to exercise civilian restraint over the police. They didn't want to or couldn't see the broader principles at play. While Rod was mostly able to aggressively grasp the reins of mayoral authority, in this case, the horse clearly got away on him.

Another matter that dropped into the Morrow grab-bag of "sensitive" issues related to a speech Rod made to University of Calgary students on political liberty, law, and anarchy. In it, he stated that police treated Indians differently than they did other people. He also re-emphasized his commitment for the right of any youth to congregate on the downtown mall. A recent attempt to snatch this right away was "disgracefully contrary to democratic principles," he said. [12] Just a few days earlier, he had blocked a request from the Downtown Business Association for a bylaw giving police the authority to move people they thought might be in conflict with other pedestrians. Of the proposed legislation, he told council, "I can only say it must have been brought back from Moscow." It could "prohibit freedom of assembly and freedom of speech on a public street. It would turn a public street into private property belonging to merchants." Others on council had not seen these implications, and the bylaw was voted down.

In his U of C speech, Rod also raised the issue of riot sticks for police that Vancouver had purchased and that he assured the students would not be used in Calgary. "Riot sticks are associated with repression, and they're not needed here." Besides, if riot sticks were purchased, police would be tempted to use them. "Police are like children. When they get a new toy, they want to try it out." He also referred to the low level of education of most city policemen. This was all fair commentary, but hardly designed to make him a police hero. Many policemen subsequently saw Rod as a traitor who went out of his way to characterize them as dumb, uneducated brutes.

During his inquiry, Morrow delved into another more light-hearted issue that fell into his lap: The John Kushner apple tree incident. Even Morrow admitted the facts took on all the facets of a comedy. Alderman Kushner had been charged with having a fifteen-foot apple tree removed from an urban renewal site and taken on a city truck to the front lawn of his son's Calgary home, and did so with a police escort. Calgary author Brian Brennan dug nicely to the core of John Kushner in his book, *Scoundrels and Scallywags*. [13] He described Kushner as a "wily rogue" who, during almost thirty years in public life as an alderman, school trustee, MLA, and Member of Parliament, "scored some dramatic political victories followed by humiliating failures and more than a few moments of controversy." He was the master of malapropisms and fractured syntax, wrote Brennan, and said things like "off the cuff of my head," or "I don't want the information, I just want the facts." Reporters gleefully kept note of these gems from the Polish-born man whose father was Austrian-Ukrainian. Brennan described him as a big, unpolished, raw-boned man with hands like meat cleavers and the mutton-chop sideburns of a river boat gambler. Despite his verbal mangling, he claimed to be fluent in five languages. "You quietly made your points loud and clear," he once told a fellow alderman. Reporters called him "dumb like a fox."

Although Kushner may have been more liability than asset, Rod took him under his wing after his election and covered his hefty backside for as long as Kushner was an alderman. Rod appointed him chairman of the finance committee, earning the ire of other jealous aldermen. In his report, Judge Morrow noted that Alderman Ed Dooley in particular seemed to have "constituted himself as a one-man watchdog over Alderman Kushner." Although Dooley had requested a complete police investigation into the apple tree affair, the conclusion was "no justification for criminal charges." Rod's comment to Dooley was, "The entire incident is bordering on the ludicrous, and it is about time some of our elected representatives got down to the serious business of running our city rather than playing petty politics with the press. To my knowledge, this is the only apple tree which has produced a lot of nuts."[14]

What motivated Rod in his dealings with the police was a desire for justice, plus a concern about police abusing their authority. He was furious about actions he considered discriminatory against young people or Aboriginals. His own family had felt the sting of police persecution too. The RCMP, for example, tried to trump up charges against his older son, James, for skinny dipping in the Elbow River, and his second son, Henry, for smashing beer bottles while at a campground west of Calgary—charges that defence lawyer Milt Harradence said were based on fraudulent evidence. CFCN-TV reporter Ralph Klein later told Rod that city police had contacted him to be ready with a cameraman as they "discovered" a bag of marijuana planted on his son Henry's Volkswagen.

These sorts of things understandably angered Rod. Because he largely acted alone, his response was to hit hard enough verbally to put his adversaries off-balance. That was a conscious tactic he acknowledged when reminiscing about his CPR experiences. He was convinced that too many people equivocate when trying to defend a public position. Waffling may not leave sore toes, but it doesn't change the course of events either. "There are times when you must come out kicking," he said. "Harmony is desirable, but sometimes it doesn't get things done, whereas the shock treatment may succeed."

Rod had varying success in forcing effective reform, but he had a surprising number of accomplishments, despite the prickly style. Thin power did have its upsides.

His sense of fairness came to the fore when he became aware of police protecting prominent Calgarians caught breaking the law. Well-known judge Justice Harold Riley was a notorious imbibing driver the police would pick up and then take home without charges. His problems with alcohol were the subject of much chatter among the Calgary establishment, said Rod. However, he still judged him to be a bright, fair-minded, decent man—a future Chief Justice, in fact. A common public comment was, "I'd rather have Harold Riley drunk than any other judge sober."

After one incident Rod heard about in which Riley was excused a breath-alyser test, he contacted police commission chairman Jack Prothroe. "The law applies to rich and poor alike," Rod said. "Preferred treatment for promi-nent persons cannot be tolerated, and it is now time this was made clear to the police department. It is time to take a stand."[15] Not long after, Riley was indeed charged with drunk driving; he was caught not far from Rod's Elbow Park home driving from the Ranchmen's Club. The police told Riley he could thank the mayor for his arrest. Naturally, the charge made the news, and Riley resigned from the Bench. Rod described it as a sad end to a distin-guished career.

When Riley visited Rod in the mayor's office after his resignation, Rod expressed regret over how things had transpired. Riley demurred, however. "What you did was absolutely right. I am here to thank you for it," Rod remembered Riley saying. "I knew I had a problem, but the system allowed me to avoid dealing with it … I know I would have killed someone sooner or later, and thanks to you, that won't happen now." Rod noted there were plenty of others the police could have nabbed too.

Rod himself was charged just before he retired with driving over the legal limit and lost his licence for twenty-four hours. The story had the heading, "No special treatment for Sykes."[16] Rod often believed he was frequently tailed by the police trying to catch him in compromising situations. Former police-man Murphy said he had spoken with a detective who claimed he had been involved in that operation. Ralph Klein also tipped Rod off that *The Herald* had hired a detective to follow him.

Rod regularly challenged police estimates during budget discussions. He noted the police department's manpower demands seemed to increase at six to ten per cent every year, but the population was only growing at three to four per cent. Yet, "every year we hear that our police programs have, in fact, failed to produce any decreased crime."[17] That didn't earn him any more love from the local cops.

A source of shame to the police department during Rod's time as mayor that he had nothing to do with but could only observe with bemusement was the case of Sgt. Harvey Grieves. Within a short time of the Calgary Board of Education naming Grieves Calgary's Policeman of the Year, and he doing the rounds of city schools as part of the resulting public recognition, Grieves faced charges of major theft and participating in a Canada-wide stolen goods ring. "That Grieves was able to function for some time before his arrest, and then only after information from another police department [Saskatoon], reflected very badly on the force," said former policeman Murphy. "This came as a complete shock to the rank and file." The ring operated by selling goods, particularly jewellery and electrical items, stolen from homes and businesses. Grieves' elevation to top cop probably resulted from his involvement with the school patrol program, but his conviction was certainly a major embarrassment to police.

Of greater shame, from Rod's perspective and that of many others in Calgary at the time, was the torpedoing of the appointment of Charles Gain from Oakland, California, as police chief after Kent's 1972 retirement. Quite within its powers, the police commission hired Kates Peate Marwick to conduct a search and make their recommendations. In the end, Gain, who had a reputation as a tough but fair manager of change in Oakland's police department, turned out as the commission's unanimous choice. As Murphy pointed out, though, chiefs had been appointed from within from as far back as people could remember. As soon as the Gain appointment hit the headlines, he was portrayed by many within the Calgary department as an outsider and a threat to the way chiefs had until then been appointed.

Several aldermen undermined the appointment from the beginning with their plans to refer the matter to Alberta Attorney General Merv Leitch. They also sought to have the police commission disbanded. When Gain's appointment came to council on August 2, 1972, the city was already deeply divided. An unruly crowd filled council chamber as Rod ruled out of order a motion from Peter Petrasuk that only a Canadian could be named to the post. Instead, Rod insisted the only motion would be whether to welcome Chief Gain to his new position or not. After an acrimonious two-hour debate, with some audience members derisively singing the *Star Spangled Banner*, members voted 6-5 to welcome Gain to Calgary. But the bitterness and hostility toward the American chief were palpable.

A week later, council passed a motion to ask the Province to make it mandatory for a police chief in Alberta to be Canadian, a proposal the Province enacted with the 1973 Police Act. [The act contains no such requirement today] An hour after the motion, police commission chairman Prothroe announced Gain had withdrawn his candidacy "because of the intense nationalistic feelings he had experienced at our hands." In a statement, Prothroe added, "This day will long endure in infamy ... I am ashamed."[18] Rod said Chief Gain "was not only the best man, but an honest and decent man and a great loss to Calgary ... we invited a man into our house and then hit him on the head and kicked him out." In a speech to the International Institute of Municipal Clerks a week later, with ninety per cent of attendees from the U.S., he called the Gain affair a "tragic controversy." He explained that Canada and Calgary had been built from many different backgrounds and that the aftermath of the Gain affair was unpleasant for Calgary. "The simple message sifting around this part of the world is that Calgary is anti-American. That is not true."

The opposition's strident anti-Americanism seems so out of place more than forty years later. It is unimaginable that such antagonism would rise against an equivalent appointment today. But at the time, parochial narrow-mindedness was still prevalent in Calgary, particularly among some aldermen and their supporters. To them, Gain was not one of us.

In retrospect, it became clear that many policemen in Calgary mobilized themselves and their friends to fight the appointment. Significantly, Murphy said the Calgary Police Association leadership took unprecedented steps when Gain's appointment was first announced. They used association funds to pay for a group of officers to fly to Oakland and mix with police who came to their hotel room and told them their view of Gain. Booze apparently flowed freely. The officers they met seemed almost unanimous in their opposition to Gain because, Murphy believed, of his stringent attempts to clean up operations in Oakland. The Calgary contingent obviously feared what he might do in Calgary. Publicly, they based their opposition on Gain's lack of Canadian citizenship. But that made no sense, said Murphy, because planeloads of British officers were being hired around that time to fill police vacancies in the city. Clearly, he said, the police association went to Oakland looking for dirt, and they got it from less-than-sober officers, each with their own axe to grind. Murphy was shunned by fellow officers for objecting to the way the association conducted its review. The whole Gain affair was indeed a shameful event in Calgary's history.

Less controversially, the police commission ended up hiring Brian Sawyer as chief. Sawyer, an RCMP superintendent in Victoria when hired who had been more involved in administration than hard-nosed investigative work, was considered a safe choice after Gain. He was likely the only person available who would accept the job. His specific mandate was to bring zone or neighbourhood policing to Calgary. The system he introduced during his nine years as chief is still in place today. Although his reputation was not that of a "real" policeman, Sawyer presented himself positively, and knew the art of kissing the hands that fed him. Some called him a "master manipulator," but he certainly smoothed relations with the police commission. An early victory was to subtly persuade several hide-bound, senior officers they should take their pensions and retire.

Initially, Rod got along with Sawyer reasonably well, maybe not so surprisingly since they both had spent time in east Montreal. After a divorce, however, Sawyer gained a reputation as a ladies' man, and he and commission chairman Prothroe raised eyebrows once with a trip to Las Vegas together. Relations between Rod and Sawyer soured considerably, however, during sharp disagreement over police handling of an aboriginal occupation incident and a hostage-taking later in Rod's term.

During 1974, Canadian Aboriginal groups, encouraged by the militant American Indian Movement (AIM), began to intensify rhetoric over land claims issues, Native poverty, and other pressing matters. Feelings boiled up in Calgary on November 28 when several aboriginal people evicted staff and occupied offices in the city's downtown Federal Building. It was part of a pattern of forcible occupation across North America. Although threats were reported and weapons displayed, nobody was hurt. The action continued into the next day, resulting in a stand-off between police and the occupiers.

At this point, Rod was exasperated at police doing nothing more than negotiate with the occupation leaders. "This incident is clearly an act of violence ... and it should have been dealt with at once by the authorities," he said after meeting with Chief Sawyer.[19] Sawyer, however, preferred to wait the occupiers out. It was a political action, he argued, that negotiation would best handle. Rod countered, "Negotiation with lawbreakers under threat of violence weakens and eventually destroys respect for law." Branding the occupation group hijackers, a charged word in the heydays of aircraft hijacking, Rod warned Sawyer's strategy would lead to escalated violence. He called on Sawyer to arrest and charge the occupiers without delay.

The same day, Rod contacted Alberta's Solicitor General Helen Hunley to oppose Sawyer's strategy, which he said included a failure to discuss police tactics with him or the police commission. Rod called Hunley's response weak, if not an abandonment of her responsibilities. She could not intervene, she said, unless Sawyer asked her to. Rod received a better response from Federal Minister of Indian and Northern Affairs Judd Buchanan. Rod knew the fed's reaction would be more robust. After all, Trudeau had shown his mettle during the FLQ crisis with his declaration of a state of emergency. Buchanan said he was "appalled that more vigorous action was not taken by Calgary City Police," and Rod could quote him on that. Buchanan added, however, he would meet with Treaty 7 chiefs once the offices were cleared and the occupiers charged. The occupation did indeed end peaceably, but without charges laid. Rod seethed over what he saw as police "playing politics" rather than applying the law.

Less than sixteen months later, a far more serious event grabbed public attention when a policeman was shot while responding to a bank hold-up call. The two gunmen and their girlfriends fled to a private house where they took two hostages. Police provided drugs to the killers as part of their negotiation tactics. After forty-five hours, the ordeal ended, with one gunman dead from an overdose and the other seriously ill. Again, all this occurred under Sawyer's watch.

Rod wrote a scathing, nine-page letter to then Attorney General Jim Foster regarding police handling of the incident.[20] He said the matter raised issues of civil control of police, accountability, training, and tactics, which were all responsibilities of the attorney general. He criticized specific aspects of the event, such as the delivery of narcotics by the police to the hostage-takers in the bargaining process. This action, Rod said, showed the police trafficking in drugs and negotiating the law with criminals, thus encouraging criminals to seek the hostage-blackmail route in future conflicts. Police hints of immunity from prosecution for the hostage-takers heightened impressions justice can be sold and even suspended by police. The failure of the police to consult any civic authority also sparked his anger. "What should be the police responsibility to advise and inform the civil authority at the local government level?" Rod asked.

"[Police] do not accept their accountability to the public," Rod continued. The solicitor general, the police commission, senior administration, and the mayor had no jurisdiction in police operations. Taxpayers just paid the bills and had no say either. In short, Rod said, "Police believe they have no accountability to civil authority."

These were urgent questions for Rod then, and they remain significant today as we see the lack of clarity at the federal level regarding civilian control over the RCMP, for example. Some critics called Rod shrill and unbalanced in his response. Most aldermen dismissed his position as grandstanding. As with other initiatives Rod undertook, his position was discounted, with no informed response. In fact, council, in a superficial attempt to embarrass him, debated a motion to censure the mayor for his remarks. While it lost on a tied vote, council got its message across by passing another motion supporting the police action during the siege. One alderman who opposed the censure motion contended the mayor "has the perfect right to put his own foot in his own mouth."[21] In this way, council ducked a debate on a serious issue. There was an argument, though, that Rod's excessive rhetoric during this incident could have handcuffed his efforts to limit police powers.

12
UNCONVENTIONAL SUCCESSES

When Rod retired as mayor in 1977, journalists inevitably asked him what projects he was proudest of. The Calgary Convention Centre, light rail transit, and the new airport were usually on the list. Let's look at those tangible achievements. Of them all, the building of the Calgary Convention Centre, on time and within budget, was surely the most worthy of recognition. The City danced around the idea for such a facility for a long time before Rod hauled the project on his boney back through the sloughs of indecision and incompetence.

To have squeezed within the timelines and the costs alone was significant. To complete this advance for urban renewal in an area where urban blight had prevailed for decades was also a great achievement. Then, acknowledge the year-round economic significance for the whole downtown, indeed the whole city, of a major convention facility, and you see how important the venture was. Major conventions bring in hundreds of thousands of visitors into the city over a year, adding multi-millions of revenue dollars to local businesses, and, indirectly, to City coffers.

The public efforts to undermine the project were apparent before even the formal approval by council in June 1972. Alderman Tom Priddle, a lightweight who had clashed with Rod when the latter wanted to run against him as an alderman in 1969, was the first to raise the issue of a provincial public inquiry. Priddle wrote to Premier Peter Lougheed asking for the Province to examine whether the location of the centre, opposite Palliser Square, was specifically chosen to benefit Canadian Pacific Railway [Rod's former employer]; to investigate relationships among the Convention Centre Authority, landowners on the site, and political campaign workers for elected officials [meaning Rod's campaign workers]; and look at the relationship between the mayor's executive assistant Tom Yarmon and the developers of the complex; plus some other matters, including determining whether the proposed expenditures were a judicious expenditure of tax dollars. Rod said Priddle, through "vicious innuendoes," had cast a "contemptible slur on many fine people who had worked for this project."[1] Priddle's motion for an inquiry was defeated.

At the official construction start in the fall of 1972, Rod apparently enjoyed himself by assuming controls of a huge tractor and showing, according to one report, he could "handle heavy machinery as well as a gavel" at the project site between Eighth and Ninth Avenues and Centre and First Street S.E.[2] The project included an 184,300-square-foot convention centre; a twenty storey, four hundred room hotel; and a museum-gallery facility called the Glenbow Museum. A particular point of pride for Rod was that more private investment dollars were behind this project than public money.[3]

However, after the centre was opened in 1974, and deeply frustrated by continuing media nitpicking about it, Rod was eventually driven to demand, not ask, Attorney-General Merv Leitch to authorize a judicial inquiry into the centre and the Calgary news media. Among Rod's media complaints was the bugging of a private convention centre meeting by CFCN-TV reporter Ralph Klein, later mayor for two terms and Alberta premier for three. "Several members of the news media have waged an intensive smear campaign against the Calgary Convention Centre," Rod said. "Despite this massive propaganda, not a single clear piece of evidence of misconduct on the part of anyone has been brought out. On the contrary, some members of the news media are themselves guilty of criminal conduct," which referred to the bugging incident. He also said the public should know whether any person improperly benefited from the project. "I am confident the convention centre will come through with a clean bill of health. My own conscience is clear."[4]

Rod had been elected four months earlier for a third term as mayor, albeit by a smaller than hoped for margin, and the centre was up and running. His demand for an inquiry was a bold move to quash the ceaseless sniping surrounding the project. Steer's inquiry, which failed to address his concerns about the media, was a drain on his energy for the year it took to complete. Matters such as campaign donations of $5,000 from Four Seasons Hotels Ltd., partners in the centre consortium, and Rod's long-time friendship with Elliot Yarmon, came under intense public scrutiny, but in the end, Rod was cleared of wrongdoing. Tom Yarmon, Elliot's son, who took over Mike Horsey's role as the mayor's executive assistant in 1971, also came out of the inquiry unscathed. Evidence showed he stayed out and was kept out of matters relating to the convention centre.

When Leitch announced the inquiry and named Steer to head it up in March 1975, the mandate was to examine the circumstances surrounding the acquisition, construction, and operation of the centre. It was also to determine whether anyone in City Hall "has been guilty of malfeasance, breach of trust, or other misconduct." Then he added the catch-all condition that the judge inquire into "such matters as may be deemed relevant ... to ensure a fair and full inquiry."

While hardly a torrid page-turner, the resulting 112-page report, with its sworn testimony from participants, offered the best historical record of what actually happened. The benefits that would accrue to the city from a major convention centre facility had been on the public agenda since the 1960s, and yet getting the centre built was a convoluted process, the report said. A 1967 economic study demonstrated the obvious benefits would include higher visitor spending resulting in a positive multiplier effect on the economy. Also important was "the encouragement of complementary downtown development and stimulus to the downtown urban renewal scheme."[5]

Back then, the blocks east of The Bay in Calgary's downtown "could only be classed as being in a condition of urban obsolescence."[6] In plainer words, the place was a dump. Rod remembered back to 1962 when then mayor Harry Hays talked up the potential for a convention centre in that area. A consensus grew that the only way to find the money was through the federal urban renewal program, with contributions from the Feds (50%), the Province (30%), and the City (20%). So, the Urban Renewal Co-ordinating Committee was set up. Rod suspected, however, several members were involved in irregular land dealings on their own account.

By the time a convention centre committee was formed in 1967, various plans had been considered, but nothing concrete achieved. Rod, through his position with Marathon Realty and its extensive renewal development along the CPR property in the form of Palliser Square, had signaled his company's eagerness to help rejuvenate this part of Calgary. Around 1968 while still with Marathon, Rod approached his friend Elliot Yarmon of Toronto-based Tankoos-Yarmon, a privately held Canadian real estate investment and development company formed in 1955, to consider the project. Rod first met Yarmon in Montreal in 1956. After Rod settled in Calgary, the two discussed several projects together and enjoyed a close friendship.

Five other companies also responded to a call for renewal proposals for that area of Calgary. However, because of federal doubts over the feasibility of the plans, the minister in charge of federal urban renewal, Paul Hellyer (later to become well known for his Canadian Armed Forces reunification plans), announced he was cutting off urban renewal funds for Calgary.[7]

Soon after, Hellyer resigned from that portfolio, and Bob Andras took over. The City tried unsuccessfully to secure the federal contribution critical to the centre's feasibility. After his election, Rod hit it off with Andras. "We trusted each other and worked well together," he said. Thus, as mayor, he managed to obtain federal commitment for the project. The Steer report made clear it was Rod who took the bull by the horns at a December 1969 meeting of the convention centre committee and announced the federal contribution of $2.5 million, a provincial contribution of $1.5 million, and the prospect that at least one developer (Tankoos-Yarmon) was still in play to put the project together on one block.

Steer's report suggested the scheme was allowed to drift until April 1970, when Rod again took control and pushed for a resolution of matters. It was

self-evident, Steer said,[8] that the one-block proposal would benefit Palliser
Square that Rod had developed while with Marathon, but Steer also noted
that Rod had cut all ties with Marathon. "I am satisfied, therefore, that Mayor
Sykes was entirely bona fide in the steps he was taking." Steer also accepted
evidence that Sykes and other officials reached out for other proposals, but
by the July 1970 deadline, a consortium of Tankoos-Yarmon, Marathon, Four
Seasons Hotels, and Western Realty had made the only concrete submission.
"That was only because of confidence in me personally," said Rod. "The City
itself had no credibility at all." In other words, no other interested developer
was in sight.

The consortium plan called for the City to own and operate the convention centre, while Four Seasons ran its hotel and did the food catering for
conventions. The whole matter came to council in October of that year.
Commissioners said the proposed project "had a great deal of merit."[9]
However, a number of knotty issues still remained unresolved. Cross-leasing
of space, and catering and staffing arrangements between the Four Seasons
and the Convention Centre were among them. Because economic analyses
projected annual operating deficits of up to half a million dollars and because
Rod had promised regular homeowners they wouldn't pay for the facility's
costs through their taxes, he pushed successfully for a special tax surcharge
on downtown businesses to cover these deficits. An unexpected boost for the
one-block scheme was the decision by the Province to pay for and include the
Glenbow Museum and Gallery in the plans.

While Rod brought the project to fruition, obviously with the help of other
determined and committed players, just about the only public recognition
for the centre's completion was a plaque with his name on it and those of
his fellow aldermen of the time. Also on the record was a brief letter from
the then Calgary Convention Centre Authority chairman Charlie Smith to
Rod and two other people involved with the project three years after the official opening. The letter simply advised Rod of a recently approved motion
"to express grateful appreciation and earnest gratitude for their exemplary
service."[10] That's it. That understated, stiff statement was the sum total of
acknowledgment for all that slogging over all those years.

More shameful is the lack of accurate historical record relating to what is
now called the Calgary Telus Convention Centre. The centre's website pays no
tribute to Rod's role in the centre's creation. It merely refers to the allegations
of wrongdoing that led to the Steer Inquiry.

There is no hint that Mr. Justice G.A.C. Steer, in his 1976 report, exoner-
ated Rod of any wrongdoing. Regarding the campaign contributions to Rod
from some of the major companies developing the centre, Steer stated, "My
conclusion is that the contributions listed were purely political contributions.

No inference of wrongdoing can be drawn on the part of either the donors or the receiver."[11]

Steer noted, "matters did not proceed at all speedily." [12] Wrangling by the people Rod liked to call the old guard impeded progress. Some aldermen charged "the developers may have obtained ... benefits they ought not to have obtained and that these were improperly obtained by the intervention of Mayor Sykes." Steer's response was, "This advantage was implicit in the scheme from its inception, and council itself must have known and appreciated that fact."[13] This project had been batted around for years. After all the dithering, why wouldn't Rod want to deal with principals he knew well and could trust would get the job done? Besides, the administration had produced no alternatives.

In a confirmation of Rod's leadership role in steering the project through, Steer agreed that during negotiations, Rod "intervened from time to time." Rod's obvious rationale was, "I was trying to keep things moving." Steer noted in support, "There's not a shred of evidence to indicate Mayor Sykes was trying to influence City negotiators to abandon their position." The project went through an incredible thirty-two plan revisions, causing pounding headaches for architect Albert Dale, whom Rod knew well and with whom he had worked on projects while with Marathon, and who was one of Calgary's most successful practitioners.

The pressures mounted. If there was no formal agreement by the end of 1972, costs would be invalid, and the deal would collapse. Meanwhile, a Pittsburgh-based consultant hired by the City warned the proposed catering deal with Four Seasons was too favourable for the hotel. Other leasing charges by the hotel were deemed above market value. The project was indeed in danger of coming apart. Steer heard evidence from the consultant of "ungentlemanly" questioning of him by the mayor at an April 1972 meeting. Rod's later comment was, "If calling someone totally incompetent is ungentlemanly, then that's what it was."

There were questions as to whether Rod fired the consultant or he quit, but the result was he left Calgary quickly with his ears stinging. Steer's response was further reinforcement of Rod's leadership role. "I believe the mayor's intention was bona fide trying to get things moving." Council finally approved the development and associated costs at a June 1972 meeting. Capital costs to the City were pegged at $7.2 million [about $32 million today], and that's what Calgary paid for its convention centre and the redevelopment of the whole block. That should merit consideration for bargain of the century, especially when you place that amount in the context of the hundreds of millions of dollars in additional benefits to the city during the four decades since.

To consolidate the centre's success, a second building with additional display and meeting space was opened in May 2000.

Then there was the bugging incident involving Ralph Klein. The most humorous assessment of this saga came from local wit and well known defence lawyer Chris (C.D.) Evans in his book *The Western Flair* about another famous Calgary lawyer Milt Harradence. The formidable Harradence, whom Rod also considered a friend, was Convention Centre Authority chairman at the time of the inquiry.

"In 1975, during the reign of Sykes I," Evans wrote, "a furor erupted—probably media-inspired—over the awarding of the contracts for the construction of the convention centre facility. As with all such humdrum city scandals, this was the usual tempest in a pisspot." The allegations of impropriety "were all the expected nonsense, and the principal event in the whole debacle was the alleged bugging at a January 20, 1975, in-camera meeting of the authority by an informer or mole ... Alberta's beloved rubber-faced, loquacious Ralph Klein was playing his early life as a crusading television reporter with a specialty in City Hall issues ... Harradence was convinced that the alleged bugging was an artless rumour, that is, until Klein broadcast the fact of the surreptitiously taped meeting in a controversial documentary on the Convention Centre aired on CFCN-TV. Harradence had to eat his words about 'media-concocted rumours.' "[14]

Police investigated, and Klein was charged with allegedly breaching the Protection of Privacy Act because it is illegal even to reveal the existence of unlawfully intercepted private communication. The defence mounted by lawyer C.D. O'Brien was based on freedom of the press. "To the immense relief of everyone concerned," wrote Evans, "Klein was discharged after the preliminary inquiry by Judge Thurgood, there being no evidence upon which a jury, properly instructed in the law, unless insane, might return a verdict of guilt." So the matter died. Almost a decade later, Rod called the pony-tailed, bearded Evans "quite bright, in a lunatic way," and, "a good man behind all the hair and whiskers."

Despite the difficult years, the centre's official opening in 1974 was a satisfying event for Rod. It was purely his decision to invite former Conservative Prime Minister John Diefenbaker to be the headliner guest and cut the ribbon. That was a controversial choice, in that Rod had developed a good relationship with the then Liberal Prime Minister Pierre Trudeau. Customarily, Trudeau, or his housing minister Bob Andras, who had funnelled all that federal money into the project, would have been the obvious choices. Inviting the maverick and long-retired Diefenbaker was a provocative move that required considerable explaining by Rod. "I hope this will not be taken amiss," Rod wrote to Trudeau.[15] "The fact is that I believe that Mr. Diefenbaker has reached the stage where questions of party can hardly apply, and he is certainly a Prairie institution." Rod clearly liked Diefenbaker and figured he'd received a raw deal when he was booted from his party's leadership at the notorious 1967 Conservative convention. Diefenbaker worked hard during his terms as prime minister from 1957-63 to include Canadians of all ethnic backgrounds in the country's affairs. Representing the Prince Albert, Saskatchewan, riding, he also raised the West's profile throughout Canada.

In his invitation letter to Diefenbaker, Rod outlined his version of the centre's history. "It was dead as a project when I was first elected to office in 1969 and I have revived it and made it happen," Rod told him. "Rather than the normal kind of opening … we would like to use the occasion to honour somebody who has devoted a lifetime of service to the Canadian West and particularly to the Prairies … we can think of nothing more appropriate than to request you to be our guest for a few days and allow us to use the opening of our new centre to pay you a tribute of appreciation for the work of these many years." It was a generous gesture that Diefenbaker surely valued.

A visit by Diefenbaker to the mayor's office less than two months after Rod was elected undoubtedly helped Rod's positive impression of the theatrical and populist politician. He kept with pride a letter Diefenbaker wrote to his Calgary friend George Cloakey about that visit. "He is an intelligent, able, and aggressive person and has ideas and the ability to elucidate his views with clarity. He should go a long way in public life," Diefenbaker wrote about Rod.[16] Diefenbaker's ego was notorious, and one of Rod's favourite stories about him resulted from them sharing the same vehicle during the Stampede Parade one year. They were riding in the back of wealthy oilman Bill Herron's monster convertible car. Rod was wearing the brown and white calfskin jacket and mauve shirt Herron had donated to him to spice up his western image. As they drove down Ninth Avenue, the adulation and the applause from the tens of thousands lining the street grew louder. Diefenbaker, eyes bulging and jowls trembling, turned to Rod. "You realize, some of this may be for you."

After the grand opening, the controversies didn't let up. The authority hired Doug Goadby, purportedly with extensive experience in trade show marketing and exhibition management, to be the new manager. He was not an administrator, though, and the complex terms of the contract between the convention centre and the Four Seasons Hotel caused frictions, including authority meetings ending in anger, management critiques, and unhappiness with the budgets, particularly on Rod's part. This eventually led to Goadby's bitter departure two years after his hiring. Goadby had told the Steer Inquiry that the mayor was hostile to him and didn't support him. Rod's response was that Goadby didn't handle his responsibilities adequately. A demanding mayor may have been at the centre of Goadby's firing, but others clearly approved of the action.

Similar to the low-key credit Rod received for getting the convention centre built was the praise going his way for initiating light rail transit in Calgary. Conventional wisdom, encouraged by *The Herald*, consistently offered the narrative of Ralph Klein as the prime mover behind the C-Train. "Elected mayor in 1980, he brought the 1988 Winter Olympics, light rail transit, and strong financial growth," reporter Eva Ferguson wrote in 2010, for example.[17] More accurately, however, the Olympics were secured during Ross Alger's term as mayor, the commitment to LRT clearly occurred back in the 1970s, and the soaring City debts under Klein and then mayor Al Duerr could hardly be described as strong financial growth. Klein was front and centre with his twisted grin when it came time to cut ribbons and launch facilities and events like LRT and the Olympics, but it's a perversion of reality to suggest he did the heavy lifting. Some *Herald* reporters socialized with Klein from the time he was elected. They were much tighter with Klein than even lax principles of journalistic independence would suggest were appropriate. Klein was their man, and their relationship with him flourished. Rod, meanwhile, was considered the bad guy, and that attitude seemed to be passed on from one generation of reporters to another. *The Herald* did once refer to the Convention Centre as "an urban treasure,"[18] but no recognition was given to Rod.

Less than a year into his first term, Rod was lambasted by council for his active promotion of rapid transit as a solution to Calgary's traffic tangles. For placing priority on rapid transit over what he called "destructive" expressway and freeway plans, he was accused of playing "instant politics" and eroding vital, long-range planning for downtown Calgary. "If the city is to preserve its environment, it must accelerate the completion of rapid transit," Rod was quoted as saying in a *Herald* story.[19] "Rapid transit will make much of the road building planned by engineers unnecessary." Rod also downplayed the problems of financing rapid transit, saying, "the money intended for freeways, expressways, and interchanges can easily be diverted into a rapid transit system." Soon after, he reinforced his commitment to mass transit, saying that a balanced transportation system for the city would include an improved Calgary Transit System. "The transit system has been the poor relation of City Hall," he told council.[20]

Two and a half years later, Rod was still prodding the provincial government, council, and his administration to prepare for rapid transit. His intentions were clear in a letter to Municipal Affairs Minister Dave Russell regarding provincial grants. "My own opinion is rather in favour of devoting increased transportation grants to the improvement of public transit. I believe public transit ought to have higher priority in our plans than construction of freeways, for example."[21] Calgary's bus system enjoyed important upgrades before LRT came along. In 1971, for example, the exact fare system was introduced to speed up boarding and reduce operating costs. A year later, the system officially became known as Calgary Transit, and Blue Arrow express service was introduced. The last of the trolley buses were phased out in 1975.

Even though Chief Commissioner Geoff Hamilton warned funding for rail transit was "totally beyond the capability of the city,"[22] Rod forcibly made the case that a rearrangement of spending priorities would make it possible. "It's well within Calgary's financial grasp," he said. At that same meeting, he managed to persuade aldermen to protect a possible rapid transit alignment in southeast Calgary. By the end of that year, Rod helped gain council's backing for the City's transportation department's major report, a *Balanced Transportation Concept*. That report included plans for rapid transit, and made the point that implementation would occur within two years—and that's what happened.[23]

In 1974, Calgary received $45 million of a $220 million provincial plan to assist public transportation in Alberta cities.[24] Rod's persistent prodding had paid off. Transportation Director Bill Kuyt said part of the money would go toward laying the groundwork for a future rapid transit system by buying up potential right of way. That sounded like a commitment to rapid transit.

Because Edmonton was already proceeding with its own form of mass transit, and by 1978 had become the first city in North America with a population of less than one million to build a modern light-rail system, Calgary rode their coattails by deciding to purchase the same make of rolling stock as their northern neighbours. Originally designed for and used by the Frankfurt underground system in Germany, the model of car, called a Siemens-Duewag U2, was also adopted for light-rail transit use in San Diego, California. A consortium of Siemens, Wegmann & Co., and Duewag built the cars in Krefeld, north of Bonn in central-west Germany. A minor fuss occurred when a minority of aldermen wanted the City to look at cars made by Urban Transportation Development Corporation of Ontario. Transportation manager Kuyt scoffed at claims the UTDC cars would be cheaper. The company was still months away from testing prototypes, Kuyt said, noting the operational benefits of the Siemens-Duewag cars.[25]

Before he left the mayor's office, Rod was able to announce, "The project is now committed beyond recall. "The LRT system "represents the single most important feature in the future of transportation in Calgary."[26] Despite Calgary's relatively low population density, the C-Train system, as it came to be called, became one of the busiest light-rail systems in North America. In 1978, the construction of the first southern leg began. Mayor Klein officially opened it in May 1981. The northeast leg was completed in 1985, and the northwest leg in 1987. A western leg was completed in 2014. Klein received most of the accolades, but this was a major legacy project for Rod.

13
HIGH-FLYING CONNECTIONS

Although professing shyness as a boy and despite the torments he described from his school experiences, Rod appeared in later life to enjoy meeting people and participating in social, business, or more formal activities. Rarely at a loss for the right words and despite an austere demeanour, he had talent for putting people at ease. During his career as a chartered accountant, then with CPR, and later as mayor, he demonstrated an uncanny ability to engage with a rich variety of people, from the shy Ukrainian waitress at a banquet he was speaking at or the soft-spoken Chinese-Canadian doorman at the hotel he was entering, to high-powered business tycoons, political leaders, and even British royalty. He maintained a consistency of style no matter whom he was chatting with. He spread his dry wit and erudite ways around even-handedly. His carefully enunciated speaking manner, with the hint of an English accent, never left him, whether he was talking about complex business deals or retelling a ribald tale.

"I had many, varied friends – as long as they held true to their character," Rod said. The types of projects he took on reflected his ability to relate to the gamut of issues landing on his desk. He appeared similarly comfortable advising a corner-store owner on a rezoning issue as he did discussing annexation complexities with the head of an international development company. This facility came in particularly useful in his final months as mayor. The occasion involved the official re-opening of the Calgary International Airport expansion in October 1977 after extensive renovations.

A priority for Rod from the beginning of his term was the re-establishment of the Calgary airport as a well-used international hub. By the time he resigned in 1977, Calgary had one of the best and most convenient airports in Canada. It was also the third busiest. Politically, "the airport was my baby," he said, although he never enjoyed much public acknowledgment for his efforts and foresight.

In the 1960s, when the then city-owned facility was known as McCall Field, after the distinguished First World War pilot Fred McCall, there was little recognition of the importance of the airport to a growing city, according to Rod. A potentially scandalous aspect of the airport was that Calgary's entrepreneurial spirit of the day had engineered the building of hospitality and sleeping rooms at the airport for business people and other itinerants passing through. Thanks to an alleged council blind eye—a most overworked portion of the civic anatomy, as Rod called it—other supplementary services began to be offered. Somebody dreamed up the idea of operating an undercover bordello there, leading inevitably to the unofficial renaming of Calgary's airport among those in the know as McCall Girl Field. The city's aeronautical good name was dropping faster than a stalled Boeing.

Many breathed sighs of relief when the federal government bought the airfield in 1967 and ended these "undercover" activities. However, in Rod's view, the Calgary Transportation Authority at that time received only weak enthusiasm from city leaders. City Hall barely recognized the airport's significance as Calgary's link to the rest of the world. Consequently, federal authorities in the Department of Transportation showed scant appetite to invest in and promote the airport.

Further, around the time Rod became mayor, the Feds were encouraging economies on airport development by building super-airports far away from urban areas to serve two or more population centres. The idea was also to avoid problems of growth on the boundaries of airports and increasing noise complaints. Two for the price of one was a further obvious incentive. The first of these super-airports on the drawing board was Mirabel, planned about forty kilometres outside Montreal to replace Dorval, then the poster-boy for airport growth problems. Mirabel was intended as a major gateway into Canada. Because of its distance from Montreal, however, it met with resistance from carriers and passengers. Shortly after its 1976 completion, it was branded a white elephant, and its status was reconsigned to cargo airport. But even before Mirabel, similar plans were being devised for Pickering outside Toronto and for central Alberta to build a massive regional airport.

In Alberta's case, even though land assembly had not begun, the department of transportation was considering plans for an international airport at Red Deer to serve Calgary and Edmonton. As Rod pointed out, travellers to Calgary or Edmonton would be expected after landing to face a further journey of 130-150 kilometres south or north. No airline wanted to be sentenced to service the wilds of central Alberta with miles to ferry passengers and freight to their real destination, he said. The costs and the aggravation would be horrendous.

While relatively toothless, the airport authority did have a farsighted, imaginative businessman as chairman. Jack Pierce, president and owner of Ranger Oil, already had a reputation for getting things done. The Daily Telegraph Book of Canadian Obituaries, *Canada From Afar* described Pierce as a "tough-talking Canadian oilman whose early hunch about the North Sea

oil paid off in 1974 with the discovery of the 1-2-billion-barrel Ninian Field."[1]
He was wiry and weather beaten, with an egocentricity that bemused British
oilmen—exactly Rod's kind of guy. Pierce once provocatively noted that the
Canadian government comprised ministers with zero industry experience.[2]
His view of the Alberta government was that it "operated at the IQ level of
taxi drivers, though this might be an insult to cabbies."

Learning to fly at fifteen, Pierce later piloted his own planes, including a
Lear Jet he put at Rod's disposal in 1974 to lead a Calgary "trade mission" to
Toronto. He died in 1991, aged sixty-seven, from a heart attack while round-
ing up cattle for branding at his southern Alberta ranch. That's the way, of
course, iconic Albertans should pass on.

The dynamic duo hit it off "wonderfully well," according to Rod, and
they quickly prepared to scuttle the Red Deer proposal. The authority's only
employee was Don Brownie, who came from the oil patch and for whom Rod
had positive words. Rod branded the other authority members as "useless,
chamber of commerce blowhards." Rod and Jack recognized the importance
of the airport if Calgary were to grow. A land-locked Prairie city needed excellent air services to prosper. From Rod's logical business perspective, and likely
his maritime background in Victoria, "the airport was our seaport." Despite
his scornful sentiments about government, Jack Pierce was well-connected
with Ottawa. Also, Rod shrewdly noted, Ranger Oil was dynamic and successful, "so there was money for expenses." Pierce turned out to be a pillar
of strength in lobbying senior managements of international airlines to back
their plans.

Rod had also quickly forged a good, friendly relationship with Prime
Minister Pierre Trudeau and with the federal minister of transport, Otto
Lang. Through his CPR and other business ties, he had an inside track to
CP Air. "We couldn't lose," Rod enthused. After several years of relentless
work, spread over Rod's terms as mayor, they got their new airport. Ottawa
committed $120 million to the project. That would be about half-a-billion
dollars today.

After the new airport was built, figures showed Calgary chalked up more
air travel, freight service, and carriers than any other airport in Canada except
for Toronto and Montreal. This was mostly thanks to the efforts and foresight
of Rod and Jack Pierce, with people like Don Brownie. It was done without
council involvement. However, the sparkling statistics soon fizzled after Rod's
time as mayor. The main factors were the early 1980s recession and lack of
subsequent City Hall sustained effort with airlines. Consequently, U.S. and
European carriers reduced, and in some cases, abandoned services.

Because final completion of the airport would occur after Rod had left City
Hall in 1977, Pierre Trudeau and Otto Lang decided, with little prompting,

they would not open Canada's most expensive airport without him. This meant the ribbon-cutting took place two months before construction was done.

Rod then had a bright idea for adding appeal to the opening ceremonies. With a nudge from Jack Pierce, he wanted to arrange for a visit to the airport of the sexy supersonic aircraft, the Concorde. In April 1977, a memorandum from the so-called Fun and Games Committee, which organized the official opening program, noted, "Concorde is the most important single feature of the whole event." The product of a remarkable Anglo-French government treaty, combining the manufacturing prowess of the British Aircraft Corporation and Aerospatiale of France, Concorde had gone into service just over a year before. Twenty of them were eventually built, flying mostly trans-Atlantic routes in half the time, and sometimes at least twice the cost, of other airliners. A devastating crash at Charles de Gaulle Airport near Paris in 2000, when debris from another aircraft led to a ruptured fuel tank and subsequent explosion right after Concorde's take-off, marked the beginning of the end for the venture. Because of its sonic booms, the aircraft had long faced problems flying over inhabited areas. A combination of factors, including economic ones that had dogged Concorde for more than two decades, led to operations ceasing in October 2003.

Yet, in the fall of 1977, Concorde was a daring symbol of British and French pride and a source of wonder and excitement wherever it flew. How could the mayor of a landlocked prairie city of about half a million people persuade senior Concorde authorities to showcase their star product here? The answer lay partly in the hands of a powerful British citizen, Earl Mountbatten, who had taken a shine to Rod and who felt motivated to help him. Earlier in his term, Rod had been introduced to Mountbatten during a visit by this famous former British admiral of the fleet, statesman of German descent, and uncle of Prince Philip, Duke of Edinburgh.

The introduction resulted from Rod's long-time association with the military establishment. Remember, Rod's father served in the Canadian Scottish Reserves, and other family members had strong military ties. In his teens, Rod served as an army cadet, and his later affinity for the military, particularly the Calgary-based Princess Patricia's Canadian Light Infantry (PPCLI), was understandable. The specific connection with Lord Mountbatten came through Mountbatten's eldest daughter, Baroness Brabourne, colonel-in-chief of the PPCLI, who came to Calgary on several occasions to celebrate her association with the infantry regiment. Baroness Brabourne was the goddaughter of Princess Patricia of Connaught, a granddaughter of Queen Victoria. The regiment had been named after Princess Patricia. Even after the Provisional Irish Army (IRA) assassinated Mountbatten in 1979 when they planted a bomb in his boat at Mullaghmore, County Sligo in the Republic of Ireland, Rod and Baroness Brabourne continued to exchange letters and Christmas cards.

"Lord Mountbatten was a remarkable man," said Rod. "He became very friendly and he did me favours." Furthermore, Mountbatten was close to Prince Philip and to Charles, Prince of Wales. "I got on well with all of them," said Rod. When he and Mountbatten spent time together, they rarely talked politics, but rather history. Rod's voracious reading and retentive powers helped him engage with Mountbatten in discussions on such topics as the history of India, where Mountbatten had served as the last viceroy and then the first governor-general of the independent Union of India (1947–48), from which the modern Republic of India would emerge.

"I really must thank you again for your splendid luncheon at the Wainwright Hotel in the Heritage Park," Mountbatten wrote in May 1977, in a letter he appeared to have typed himself on crisp, cream letterhead with his Romsey, Hampshire, home address and his personal insignia at the top. "I much appreciate the kind things you said and I certainly meant all the things I said about you. I know how deeply the Patricias [the PPCLI] feel about your wonderful support of the regiment and how grateful they all are, particularly the Colonel-in-Chief [his eldest daughter]."[3] Through their exchange of personal letters, Rod offered advice and information that Mountbatten passed on to Prince Charles before a 1977 visit to Calgary and participation in the Stampede Parade.

When the Concorde proposal started to percolate in Rod's mind, he asked Mountbatten for his help. He quickly replied to pledge his support, and was true to his word. "I enclose a copy of a letter I have written to your chairman about the proposal that the Concorde should make a special visit to Calgary to mark the opening of their new International Airport," Mountbatten wrote in a letter to Gordon Davidson, director of Concorde Operations for British Airways.[4] "Rod Sykes has tremendous power in that part of Canada … it would be a great pity if he was left with the impression that British Airways are not doing everything in their power to enhance their own reputation."

Rod flew to London to meet with British Airways officials himself. By design or unintended coincidence, British Airways had planned a Concorde flight to the Persian Gulf during the couple of days Rod was there as part of their "reputation enhancement" plans and offered him a seat. Rod's attuned ears naturally picked up on that potential opportunity. However, he also discovered Alberta's deputy minister of transportation was in London as well, and only one seat was available on the Persian Gulf flight. Ever the shrewd calculator, Rod gave up his seat for the Alberta official. "I did the political thing," he explained. The official could not help but be impressed by the gesture and the perks of the flight. He might end up recommending that his political masters back plans originating with Rod and Jack Pierce for a regular Calgary to Houston, Texas, Concorde route, befitting Calgary's role as Canada's dominant energy centre. Although Concordes have long disappeared, Calgary now takes for granted its regular, direct connections with Texas and other southern U.S. destinations.

As a result, Rod was left to cool his heels in London over the weekend. According to his original account, he decided to contact Karlheinz Schreiber, then forty-three, and not yet on the radar of the Canadian public as a lobbyist, fundraiser, armament salesman, and all-around wheeler-dealer. Schreiber would gain much notoriety decades later for his extensive and apparently fruitful lobbying efforts with Prime Minister Brian Mulroney Conservatives to persuade Air Canada, then a Crown corporation, to purchase $1.8 billion worth of aircraft from the European-based Airbus Industrie, on whose behalf Schreiber toiled. The matter gained notoriety as the Airbus affair. Schreiber's handing over of cash-filled envelopes, containing at least $225,000, to Mulroney during clandestine hotel meetings, just as the curtain fell on the prime minister's political career, became the subject of further investigation under the 2009 Oliphant Inquiry. The result was a scathing, if understated, report by Mr. Justice Jeffrey Oliphant, castigating the inappropriate actions by Mulroney in this affair.

Schreiber launched his Canadian lobbying career in Alberta during the 1970s, setting up trust accounts here for wealthy Germans and investing mostly in real estate. Rod maintained good relations with Calgary's large German-Canadian community, so it was quite natural that the gregarious Bavarian would, following introductions from community members, drop by the mayor's office early in Rod's term as a courtesy visit. "I liked him. He was another person I got on well with," said Rod. As a result of his contacting Schreiber from London on his Concorde visit, Rod was invited to spend a quick visit to Schreiber's comfortable Kaufering Estate near Munich for a relaxing, low-key day in the Bavarian countryside.

Rod retained a casual friendship with Schreiber for many more years, and when Schreiber was finally extradited back to Germany in August 2009 to face eight years in jail following his conviction on serious tax evasion charges there, Rod was among the few Canadians who had sympathy for him. While Schreiber was widely reviled for his insinuating ways with Canadian politicians, Rod argued that Schreiber was merely doing his job as a lobbyist and salesman. Offering inducements to elected officials and their staff was not wrong in itself, he argued. The real sin was committed by those succumbing to the temptations. From extensive writing and television programs about Schreiber, plus Oliphant's report, it's clear he crossed many paths—and palms—during his Canadian lobbying career. But Rod retained most of his scorn for the politicians and officials who milked what they could from their relationship with Schreiber, then dumped on him when their dealings were exposed.

Long before Schreiber hooked up with Mulroney and friends, he practised his political schmoozing in Edmonton.[5] His activities there helped prompt a judicial inquiry into the biggest scandal of Peter Lougheed's years as premier, involving purchases of land that was later annexed by the City of Edmonton. The 1981 inquiry by Mr. Justice William Brennan into these matters found no fault, formally at least, with Schreiber's behaviour. In his decision a year later, though, Brennan warned of the potential for "an ugly cloud of suspicion of impropriety" descending on those involved. Evidence showed that Schreiber played a central part in the big land play surrounding Edmonton's 1979 bid to expand its boundaries. Any land that would fall within the new city boundaries would skyrocket in value, of course. Schreiber managed to buy 350 hectares just south of the city, part of which somehow ended up inside the new boundary. In a similar coincidence, Schreiber bought 480 hectares near the city's northeast, two-thirds of which ended up within the new city boundary[6]

How he made that guess was not determined. However, Schreiber was a close friend of Horst Schmid, a member of Lougheed's cabinet. On the board of Schreiber's company, A.B.S. Investments Ltd., were former provincial cabinet ministers Hugh Horner and Bill Dickie, and former Conservative MP Bill Skoreyko. Horner and Skoreyko soon resigned their board positions, before the boundary decision was announced. The judge found no proof that Lougheed's cabinet members shared secret information, but this episode certainly raised suspicions.[7]

Such matters were still a long way off when Rod returned to London from his brief Bavarian trip with his Concorde hopes high. British Airways people told him they would do what they were told regarding the Concorde appearance in Calgary for the airport opening. Earl Mountbatten of Burma had unequivocally gone to bat for his Calgary friend, a man whom he described in one letter as a "great go-getter."[8] The whole experience set Rod to considering the extraordinary influence a senior member of the royal family could still exert over large business institutions. The prospect of later appointments and royal honours for the business leaders making the big decisions were likely at play here, he thought.

So, in the week or so before the full-scale airport opening ceremony, Rod was able to confidently inform local media Concorde would be at the party. Then, with just days to go, the deflating news came out of the blue: Concorde would not be flying to Calgary. Calm and focused, working closely with Jack Pierce, Rod put an urgent call through to Mountbatten. The royal warrior's concern was clear. "That won't do. I will speak to the British Airways people," Rod heard him say. "They would not want me to have to refer to Her Majesty." That was not an empty threat, Rod knew well. If British Airways were to pull the rug from under the feet of Earl Mountbatten of Burma, they might find other feet on the rug, he said later.

Considerable scrambling went on in London. Mountbatten contacted British Aerospace to suggest that if British Airways couldn't divert a Concorde off a scheduled route, then perhaps they could send out one of its test models. After urgent messages back and forth, Mountbatten was able to tell Rod, "In view of my urgent plea, British Airways are again reconsidering the whole matter." Rod then received word that British Airways would indeed be sending the Concorde to Calgary. "There is little doubt that but for your persistence and getting me to lobby … this whole idea would have been discarded by British Airways and a marvellous chance to show the British flag in a really dramatic way would have been lost," Mountbatten wrote. "You are one of the few men in the world who could have pulled off such a coup." With a touch of humour, respect, or irony, the letter is signed, "Your sincere Sykes Servant, Mountbatten of Burma."[9] Heady praise for our Cowtown mayor.

The official opening day on October 12 went well, even though the plane had been delayed in Washington, D.C., during a visit there and did not grace Calgary skies until the next day. A Boeing 747 did a flyover, as did some F104s. The Canadian Reds and the Snowbirds performed aerobatics. An official plaque was unveiled, and tasty food and refreshing drinks were served. Rod, of course, was front and centre, as he deserved to be.

He was also at the airport for the arrival of Concorde. Many Calgarians still recall Concorde slowly circling the city, showing off its sleek lines and belying its reputation as a noisy beast. Reporters in helicopters estimated a quarter of a million people packed vantage points on hillsides and rooftops as the jet swept low over the airport three times. An estimated forty thousand spectators were on hand at the airport to catch a closer look and welcome the crew after the landing here. With the latest in aeronautical technology on display, the city basked in the prestige this visit would generate for its growing world-wide connections. The incredible enthusiasm still bubbled the next morning when hundreds of cars filled the airport's perimeter road to watch Concorde's 5 a.m. take-off.[10]

Rod remembered one of the pilots, Captain Brian Walpole, and other members of the flight crew descending the aircraft's steps and asking almost immediately, "What happened? How did you manage to pull this off?" At 5:00 the previous day, they were told the Calgary flight was cancelled, only to be informed three hours later it was reinstated. "I told him I must have a guardian angel," Rod said with that often-seen wry smile. Guardian angels were not infrequent in his sometimes charmed life.

As a footnote, the Calgary Airport Authority has owned and operated the airport since 1992, initiating further extensive terminal rebuilding and expansion of services, particularly in the past decade. But, in the late 1970s Calgary had the then newest and best airport in Canada—all at federal expense. "No boasting, but Jack Pierce, his assistant Don Brownie, and I did it all," said Rod with obvious glee. He could appropriately throw in the impact from some Royal and guardian angel interventions too.

14
BUDGET BATTLES

Three months after Rod became mayor, *Herald* cartoonist Tom Innes drew a cartoon depicting a hulking goon with "Taxes" on his shirt ready to attack a preppy-looking Sykes with "S" (as in Superman) on his shirt. Rod liked the cartoon, and he did indeed take on the ugly taxation behemoth. After all, keeping taxes down was one of his most significant campaign promises when he first ran, and this chapter will examine how well he did. Despite the odds, he had that assailant in a stranglehold for his first few years in office. In his final years, he had more trouble keeping his grip on the big-gutted monster, and suffered some blows.

Because Rod had an inside track with the Social Credit government during his first two years in office on government financial policies for municipalities, one could say he received provincial help in those hold-the-tax-line years. But, as inflation soared to double figures, it became tougher to ward off the economic assaults. Rod, therefore, liked a lot less an Innes cartoon from four years later depicting him with a sailor hat, glasses akimbo, thrusting his apoplectic face right up to another character who has "City Council" on his sailor's headdress and a look of inebriated bemusement. "Mayor accused of spending money like a drunken sailor," said text inside the cartoon. The caption had Rod snarling, "Who are you calling a ... hic ... drunk?"

Rod rode a balancing act between keeping peace with the unions, maintaining good, basic services, and putting the brake on City Hall spending. He frequently accused council members of spending like drunken sailors and voiced homilies about the need for good housekeeping. This wasn't just talk, though. Throughout his eight years, he kept a sharp eye and a sharp pencil for budgetary excesses and the systemic kind of overspending that governments incline towards. His chartered accountancy background allowed him to see both the big picture as well as delve into details of the City's balance sheets. But, that doesn't count for much without a steely ability to say no or publicly pounce on misspending.

Joseph Yanchula, a member of Calgary's Citizens Budget Advisory Commission, made a significant comment regarding Rod's contribution to the budget process. A chemical engineer who ran unsuccessfully as a provincial MLA for the New Democrats and who was no friend of Rod's, Yanchula remarked, "It is painfully obvious that the mayor was the only council member on the budget sub-committee who really knew what was going on. Only when he was present did I get the impression that the budget was actually scrutinized … From personal observation of the council's performance to date, the present mayor appears to be singlehandedly responsible for saving the taxpayers about $10 million per year."[1]

On a personal level, Rod was consistent with what he acknowledged as his "tightwad" approach to finances. He sought to keep a short leash on his personal spending and that of his family. During most of his mayoralty years, he owned a slightly rusting 1960s station wagon. Later in life, when he had fewer cares about material security, he still drove a twenty-two-year-old Nissan around Calgary. His wardrobe as mayor was modest. He liked to buy etchings or books, and he continually added to his Boys' Own, Chums, and stamp collections. Unless he was hosting dignitaries, he mostly avoided upper-end restaurants. He was careful to remain sensibly frugal.

Realizing balancing budgets was as much a revenue as a spending issue, Rod directed considerable efforts to finding additional revenue sources. One target in his first term were the agreements the City signed with developers, and intended to cover the costs of City servicing to new areas. At the same time, Rod zeroed in on a matter that still bedevils municipalities today, that of the imbalance among municipal, provincial, and federal revenue sources and taxation powers. Taking advantage of hearings in Calgary of a House of Commons-Senate committee on the constitution, Rod's clear message was that constitutional reform was not the answer. Instead, he told the committee, the nation's problems were inter-governmental financial issues "arising out of a mismatching of revenues and responsibility for expenditures."[2]

His solution, therefore, was not to change the constitution, but to revamp the financial arrangements between cities and the other government levels. The City's revenue sources were not adequate or predictable enough to meet the increasing demands of health care, education, transportation, social services, and housing, he said. Unfortunately, property tax remained the principal means of revenue for local government, while the Feds and the Provinces could access broader areas of taxation. Besides, Rod pointed out, tax revenues that went to other levels of government came mostly from cities where most people lived, so why shouldn't cities enjoy a greater share of their contributions? This remains today the lament of big city mayors everywhere, and we're hardly closer to solving the dilemma.

During his second term, Rod kept up his push for the federal government to administer some of its financial aid programs directly to municipalities rather than through the provinces.[3] The underlying message was that Canada might function better without all-powerful provincial governments. The Feds dealing directly with city states would be a more efficient way of running Canada. Of all three levels of government, the provinces were the most superfluous, Rod argued in the 1970s. When Prime Minister Trudeau asked Rod to represent Canada at a meeting of the Organization for Economic Co-operation and Development (OECD) in Paris late in October 1976, Rod broached that theme as a keynote speaker for a three-day conference on local government.[4]

On several occasions, Rod raised the question of a special provincial sales tax, the revenues from which would be proportionately directed to municipalities. "There is no sense in Albertans being proud of being the only province without a sales tax that could provide the municipal services they need," he said in one sally. "All across Canada, people accept the sales tax as a part of life." Rod proposed exemptions for food, drugs, children's clothing, reading material, and other essentials. He believed the tax could apply to luxury items like new cars, boats, and recreation equipment.[5] Despite Rod's entreaties, the Province has since stuck to its stance of never introducing a sales tax.

Caught in the fierce jurisdictional wars of the 1970s over oil and gas revenues between the federal Liberals and Alberta's Tories, Rod took a reasoned approach to defending Calgary's interests at a conference on revenue sharing. He pointed to the threat this bitter dispute imposed on the city, and the importance of a stable and unfettered environment for the industry if it were not to leave Alberta. Otherwise, he said, "you have an invitation in unmistakable terms to find a better place to do business."[6]

He also took a brave stand against the theatrical outrage arising from the National Energy Program, gripping Alberta with Lougheed's active encouragement. "Sharing is what this meeting is all about. Do you realize that quite a lot of people here don't want to share?" he told the conference. "The talk about separatism for Alberta is nonsense, of course; negotiating nonsense. But the greed, the selfishness, that is real. There is a sense of isolation here, and a profound ignorance of the rest of Canada, especially the East … And there is a desire to hold on to what we've got, even if we're not using it right now."[7] That was a reference to massive surpluses accruing to the Province from resource revenues.

Although he had made keeping taxes down a big part of his first election campaign, Rod surprised many early in his term by announcing he would hold the tax line, not for one year, but for two.[8] What clinched Rod's goal of balancing the first budget were increased provincial funds to school boards. It should be explained that, at this time, the school and hospital boards derived a large portion of their funding through supplementary requisitions to the City that helped determine the tax rate set by council. City Hall had to collect on their behalf, so school board spending, out of council's direct control, had considerable influence on the final mill rate establishing how much taxpayers actually had to fork out.

The Albertan's Fred Kennedy was ambiguous about Rod fulfilling his campaign promise. "Social Credit to the Rescue," said the headline to his regular column. "School boards are now in a position to reduce their supplementary requisition to the city by a sizeable amount," Kennedy wrote. "Rodney will not only be able to hold the tax line, but actually reduce the mill rate … if there is a moral to this story, kiddies, it is this. If, when you grow up and decide to run for mayor, be sure that your politics are aligned with the senior government then in power … The fact that Rodney is a Social Crediter provincially, and a Liberal federally, undoubtedly helped him to pull off his great coup."[9] Meanwhile, *The Herald's* City Hall reporter, Vern Simaluk, attributed the no-tax-hike good news to deliberate depressing of the city's service standards.[10]

We can only watch and admire the high-wire act by Rod and council to maintain services and hold down costs in subsequent years. In 1971, council conducted six successive votes on different combinations of mill rates and financing arrangements before approving a compromise measure that Rod was able to cobble together and once more demonstrate his negotiating skills. The 5.5-mill-rate increase agreed to translated into a $40 hike for the average taxpayer. Rod and council were aware, however, the newly-introduced provincial homeowner grant would provide a $75 return for each taxpayer, meaning net payment by homeowners would drop slightly. This was good news for everyone the second year in a row.

The next year's tax debate was similarly convoluted, due in part to sky-rocketing spending on parks and recreation facilities.[11] Rod unveiled a budget that would bring an average $28 tax increase if the Province absorbed the rising requirements from education and hospital budgets. When council got around to establishing the actual tax rate, Rod was away in Germany. Despite lots of infighting, the majority of council, led by Alderman Peter Petrasuk, agreed with Rod's previously introduced idea of a split tax rate of 64.5 mills before June 30, with a further 4.1 mills to be added on December 1, if that was necessary. Rod based his strategy on the possibility of the school board cutting its requisition further and the Province contributing more financing by the end of the year. Constructing the mill rate this way neatly put more pressure on the board to exercise restraint and on the Province to provide more help. They could be fingered as the culprits if the additional mill rate had to be levied.

Unfortunately for taxpayers, the December additional mill rate became necessary. The original proposal was, however, consistent with Rod's philosophy of imposing taxes only to the extent necessary. When the school board failed to reduce its requisition, Rod called on the Province to review the board's fiscal policy. "Why should people pay higher taxes than they need to?" His consistent campaign was to prevent overtaxing and get that message out to the people he sought to protect.

Rod's frugal ways led him in 1974 to resist a Calgary bid for the Commonwealth Games that some local business people were promoting and instead boost an Edmonton bid. "Calgary is not bidding for the Commonwealth Games," he told an anxious Edmonton mayor, Ivor Dent, seeking to bring the Games to his city. "We have less money than you and we have no intention of bankrupting our city while I am here. We don't need the Games because we are already on the map. However, we are your friends and we would like to help you," he said. It was important for the provincial government to stand behind Edmonton now. "It is the credit of Alberta, not Edmonton, that is at stake," he said, adding with characteristic guile, "and we look to the Province to treat Calgary as fairly as it does Edmonton, no more no less." He'd already met with the Games-for-Calgary group, he added, and "I am not interested. I am supporting you. This is no time for Edmonton to start wetting its pants." [12] He had fun dictating that letter. Although many Calgarians would have liked their city to bid for the Games, there were then as today others aware of the seemingly inevitable cost overruns that afflict the hosts of major athletic events

For Rod's fifth budget, the City approved a complex three-level tax structure that would see an average increase of $63 over the year for a single-family homeowner. In an unusual departure, three different tax rates were proposed for single family residences, apartments, and industrial/commercial property. Because of the provincial tax rebate program now in place, an average homeowner would pay only $330 of an average $480 tax bill. [13] This was again good news for taxpayers, thanks partly to the Province.

Rod's sixth budget in 1975 was tougher to swallow. Higher municipal costs and soaring school board supplementary requisition led to proposals for a whopping twenty-three per cent hike for the mill rate. The taxation schedule, which set out different levels of taxation for three categories of property, as it had the previous year, would boost taxes by about $100 for the average single family home. [14] This prompted Rod's letter to Premier Lougheed noting the irony of the Province being able to boast an all-time high in its operating budget surplus—estimated at $350 million—while the City of Calgary had to raise taxes at a rate unequalled in its recent history. Rod warned of "spectacular hardships."[15]

There was more lecturing in Rod's 1976 pre-budget letter. This time he blasted the budget committee for abandoning its review responsibilities. He singled out Alderman Ed Oman as one of the most reprehensible members, a move some observers considered unnecessarily negative. But Rod still believed that isolating the miscreant aldermen was effective in modifying what he saw as destructive behaviour. "What City Hall needs," Rod said, "is a strong dose of good housekeeping, and a few more tightwads. It is too easy to spend other people's money, and it's time we faced facts. We can't go on this way." Some aldermen understandably hated these letters and what they saw as the preachy, condescending tone. However, Rod left no doubt he was defending taxpayers with a ferocity that has seemed such a rare attribute since.

By his seventh budget, Rod was quoting *Apophthegms* from the *Essays of Lord Bacon*, an esoteric exercise that went over the heads of most aldermen. Council was at the time provisionally committed to a ten per cent raise in the mill rate. Rod's customary pre-budget letter offered ways to handle the budget through a more dispassionate analysis of City operations. He offered templates for determining how efficient and effective City operations really were. As in other years, council missed the meaning of the missive. It was a valiant effort to put a brake on assumptions that budgets should endlessly continue to rise in concert with population growth.

For his final budget debate in 1977, Rod accused the administration of inducing council to overtax Calgary property owners by about $5 million. "I believe we have been overtaxing, and our huge surplus shows that to be the case," said Rod in his pre-budget letter.[16] "That is wrong, absolutely wrong, and the administration knows it. This attitude, at all levels of government, is the root cause of inflation." He was indeed defiant to the end, if not always successful, when it came to defending Calgary taxpayers' dollars.

15

MEDIA MACHINATIONS

Apart from a brief assignment when I worked for The Lethbridge Herald, my first contact as a reporter covering Rod was just before and after his election in 1969. I like to think I maintained appropriate journalistic objectivity with my stories on City Hall. But I increasingly respected the stands he took and questioned what I considered hostility toward him on the part of my bosses at *The Herald*. When Rod asked me to join his staff as an executive assistant in 1972, I jumped at the chance. Rod delighted then and in subsequent years in likening my departure from the paper to "the whore leaving the whorehouse." I was clearly contaminated and needed protection from my former handlers. Well into his second term, Rod had little respect for the grandly named Fourth Estate and many of its practitioners. As we'll see, he had a particular hate on for *The Herald*.

In his remarkable learning and building period during the 1960s, Rod wrote a regular advertising column in *The Herald* on behalf of Marathon. Called *Palliser Square*, it conveyed a perky style, confirmed by the jaunty photo of Rod that accompanied it. It launched a direct association with the press, as he usually called it then, which lasted for decades.

After his first election, he quickly became disillusioned with the media and the role practitioners played. During his eight years as mayor, relations with the media zig-zagged between hostility, contempt, and affability. Although he never considered himself one of them, he did incongruously join the ranks of the great unwashed during the 1980s as a regular *Calgary Sun* columnist. Since then, he's written occasional articles for *The Herald* and other publications.

Just as Rod became mayor, television, specifically television news, was staking out a major role in the reporting of public affairs. Sharp, angular features and a sometimes austere presentation didn't make him naturally suited to television, but when the camera lights turned on, Rod did too. As movie critics have said about actors, the camera liked him. His normally expressionless eyes, widening and sparkling, peered straight into the camera as he ignored requests from interviewers that he look at them when he was answering questions. His voice was clear and unwavering, and he was rarely lost for words. He also made a subtle point after an interview of always acknowledging the cameraman and exchanging friendly words with him (Camerawomen were a rarity then).

The result of his self-taught approach to television was a strong sense of engagement with viewers. After 1971, when Peter Lougheed became Alberta premier, Rod loved to contrast his own accessibility and spontaneity with the premier's rigid stage-managing and controlling approach. Lougheed took private lessons and carefully cultivated his television style. Lougheed's political persona, along with his relations with the media, were carefully choreographed and controlled. He did this with a tight hand in "the timing and flow of government information, and the access given to journalists." [1] He had a huge public affairs bureau under him to help him with this, of course. ·

While aware of the need to stick to an agenda, Rod reacted mostly extemporaneously to media. Even when written press releases were prepared, he often ignored the script. He had great confidence in his ability to find his way through the media jungle without a map. He was caught out the odd time, but his fluency and clear thinking usually prevailed. When confronted with a notepad, microphone, or camera, he rarely resisted making a comment. He teased the media more than many realized and sometimes carried on conversations with them more openly and longer than advisers thought he should. He befriended some reporters, and dismissed others scornfully. People like Andy Phillips of CHQR even drew affection. When he felt boxed in or was disinclined to meet with the media at all, he simply disappeared and became unavailable.

His interest in journalism was apparent from an early age. He maintained that fascination throughout his life, offering sharp commentary on traditional media into his later years. Once asked by a Calgary student newspaper how he felt about the noble sentiments the press were inclined to apply to themselves as protectors of the public truth, he offered a concise answer. "Sometimes they're not worth a pinch of coon shit," he said. [2]

Many of this book's footnotes clearly show how intimately the news media were linked with the narrative of Rod's life. I liken the media to the oxpecker birds riding around on the backs of cattle, feeding on parasites and even warning the cattle of approaching predators. Rod and the media enjoyed a symbiotic relationship; one needed the other to fulfill their function and flourish. The metres upon metres of archival clippings at the University of Calgary and City Hall contain a wealth of material about Rod, and while many journalists feared or disliked him, a hungry fascination consumed them.

Rod's particular venom directed at *The Herald* and, to a lesser extent, *The Albertan,* is obvious. The CBC drew its share of criticism too. The break with *The Herald* came almost immediately in Rod's first term. He described it this way.

As a new mayor, he may have carried some illusions about the media. One naïve assumption related to its integrity. "I soon found out *The Herald* had none," he said. Right after his election victory, *Herald* City Hall reporter and columnist Vern Simaluk accosted him with the assertion that the paper assumed they would be able to continue their special relationship with the mayor's office. "We have a deal with the mayor," Simaluk was supposed to have said. "You look after us. We look after you." In other words, give *The Herald* the inside track on City Hall business, and the paper handles the mayor favourably in its news stories and columns. "I was absolutely shocked," Rod related later. "I gave him a very dusty answer."

The paper's city editor, Merv Anderson, then met with Rod and presented matters with a smoother approach. In an obsequious manner, according to Rod, Anderson insinuated how advantageous it would be for Rod to accept such an arrangement. It had worked well for his predecessors, so why would His Worship not want to enjoy similar benefits of office? Anderson proposed it as a regular social interaction. "We can meet over Scotch and cards, and discuss City issues," Anderson said, presumably with the intention of Rod laying down his insider-information aces in the process. "We've always had this arrangement with the mayor's office. We expect you'd like that to continue."

For Rod, the whole conversation was shocking and disappointing. "I was sickened. Anderson was like a snake." The rookie mayor had considered the media as the guardians of honesty and objectivity. "I thought I was a seasoned businessman, but I was still full of young idealism. There was no free press; instead, it came across as quite corrupt." Mike Horsey, Rod's media-savvy assistant, reinforced Rod's resistance to this attempt to reshuffle the deck. But former mayor and campaign supporter, Harry Hays, was dumbfounded when he heard Rod hadn't bought the deal. "Why wouldn't you do it? They keep the bastards off your back," Hays told him. Now Rod believed this arrangement had helped suppress all the wrongdoing and administrative incompetence from the previous mayor's term in office he was beginning to uncover at City Hall and that had led to the Morrow Inquiry. "They [*The Herald*] had allowed theft and fraud to go on at City Hall without anyone knowing about it," said Rod.

Thanks to Rod's clear spurning of their courtship, relations with *The Herald* remained icy. By writing so-called news columns and opinion pieces, Simaluk seemed to put himself in a conflict of interest. While reporting on the news from council meetings on a regular basis, Simaluk then had the freedom to criticize in his columns the conduct of those meetings. He could lambaste, for example, what he described as the lax way Rod handled debate, the aldermen, and himself. Mayor J.R.W. Sykes, as he sometimes referred to him, "also stretches out the meeting with his elucidation process that is interrogation, exemplification, clarification, and summation by the chair." From that, you can also tell the belligerent Simaluk liked big words.

The more anonymous *Herald* editorial board, headed by the mean-spirited and ill-humoured Richard Sanburn, reflected their boss's character. After just over a year in his first term, Rod offered further proof of a wicked sense of humour by publicly asking *The Herald* to give him a weekly column in which he could list the paper's "appalling" errors in its City Hall coverage. Remember that by this time, CHQR Radio had given Rod a half-hour spot every Sunday with a lot of freedom to tackle just about any issue he wanted.

Under the headline, "No Thanks," *The Herald* published an editorialized response in suitably snooty fashion. "Well, we have news for the mayor. He's not going to get any such thing. If there's anything this city does not need, it is another vehicle for the mayor's seemingly endless supply of vituperation … The mayor's hysterical desire to damage this newspaper in the eyes of Calgarians has led to some quite amusing things, if you like sick humour. He has, on at least one occasion, damned us for something which appeared in another newspaper. This, note, from a man who is constantly harping about newspapers getting their facts right … This newspaper will continue to cover City Hall to the best of its ability, with precious little help from the mayor, it can be said. And, of course, we expect to hear his self-martyred whine every time we support something he doesn't want reported, or we report something in a manner he doesn't like. No, there will be no mayor's column in *The Herald*, for which thousands will be grateful. He can go and beg for his free advertising somewhere else, and keep his giggling venom for the air waves. I felt *The Herald* took the bait in this spat too seriously. There's no denying, though, the paper's lack of regard for the mayor.[3]

Rod was not shy in offering criticisms of the media generally. In one poke at all media, he said accounts from citizens made council meetings seem like a kindergarten. "The media—press, radio, and television—have got to take a share of the blame." The colourful way events are presented do not present the complete picture, he explained, and the public knows this. "I am not complaining … I'm just pointing out that this is so."

This book quotes *Albertan* columnist Fred Kennedy quite extensively. After praising him initially, Kennedy, through his thrice-weekly columns, became quite consistently cranky with Rod. With his close ties to the Stampede and traditional Calgary figures, Kennedy grew more uncomfortable with the notion that when Rod said he was going to change the power structure in Calgary, he meant what he said. Tired of the frequent rants, Rod, in typically provocative manner, decided to act. He wrote to Robert Malone, head of the *Free Press* in Winnipeg, the *Albertan* owners, to voice his displeasure. "*The Albertan* has a columnist named Fred Kennedy who has reached an advanced age and is apparently in poor health," Rod said. "For the past eighteen months, Kennedy has used his columns to attack me in a highly personal and frequently vicious manner. I do not object to criticism on issues, but this is quite a different thing. These attacks, which are so frequent as to be systematic, reflect on my personal integrity."[4]

Rod said he had tried to ignore what he hyperbolically called this "hate campaign," but the paper hadn't published retorts from readers. Even staff members complained the columns reflected on the integrity of the newspaper, according to Rod. He pointed to other censoring activities—for example, he was told that no letters critical of Kennedy were to be published. His source for most of this alleged information was Don Peacock, once a member of the Ottawa staff for Pierre Trudeau, about whom he wrote a book. Peacock was at the time of this flare-up *The Albertan*'s managing editor.

In language Rod thought Malone would particularly appreciate as a military man, he compared public service to serving in the forces. "It's something that every man has an obligation to undertake at some time in his life, and I have made it clear I intend to stay in City Hall for two terms (if the people want me) because the job that needs to be done can't be done in less time. Beyond that, I think it is well known that I do not like politics and that I have no political ambitions nor any interest in continuing in public life." In view of later political involvements, this assertion was disingenuous.

Rod concluded, "I am now faced with what appears to be a sustained, systematic, malicious, and vindictive campaign of abuse that is apparently encouraged and protected by *The Albertan*—because that is what protecting Kennedy from normal editorial control amounts to. I've discussed this with the managing editor, but he has no authority over Kennedy, it seems." Warning that he had "ample grounds for defamation action," he added, "I am not asking favours. I do not want immunity from criticism. I want fair play, and I want a remedy for what has happened so far."[5] This was a classic, full-court Sykes press against the doddery columnist who had come to loathe the city's mayor.

Note Rod's condemnation of the press after his second election victory on October 14, 1971. "The attitude of the newspapers [toward him] was sick, hysterical, and vicious, but it has been for a long time," he told a news conference after the results were in.[6] "They have taken one more step toward destroying their credibility with the man on the street. I discount the newspapers as formers of public opinion. They have lost their credibility."

The editorial departments of both papers had certainly taken a stand against him being mayor again. If *The Albertan* was trying to mitigate ill feelings when it stated, "this newspaper opposed Mr. Sykes' re-election out of conviction, not out of personal prejudice," it may not have been doing itself any benefit. The rhetoric on all sides was part of the pull and push with a political figure who may have been thin-skinned, but who was also adamant about not kowtowing to what he considered the papers' misguided, arrogant take on issues that was subservient to the Calgary establishment. His harsh responses to people like Fred Kennedy, who didn't last much longer anyway, was his way of thumbing his nose at the media.

His pushbacks against the papers in particular reflected his ability to insert barbs where they would create the most pain and the greatest rage. Like a skilled matador, he knew how to maintain his posture while sweeping the red cape over the snorting bull's head. Take his decision, just before Christmas, to invite Fred Jones, executive secretary of the Toronto Newspaper Guild, to organize journalists in Calgary. "Certainly you will have all the help that this office can give you, particularly with respect to the newspapers," he said.[7] "I find great willingness to join your organization, combined with a great fear of lack of personal protection against management retaliation. I will be glad to set up a meeting. My interest in this matter is the community interest. Staff turnover is very high and morale very low, and the product is what you would expect. My observation is that there are better papers and better people where the guild operates."

This was a provocative move against two dailies, the publishers of which would have gulped black ink by the gallon to prevent their editorial staff from forming a union local. As part of its strategy to keep out a newsroom union, *The Herald* had an unofficial policy to pay its staff within ten per cent of salaries earned by unionized newspaper employees in places like Vancouver. An air of intimidation certainly loomed over anyone who broached the remotest hint of organizing the newsroom.

"The open warfare between the mayor of Calgary and the daily press has hit a new pitch," said the *Globe and Mail*.[8] Adding insult to injury, Rod announced his plan during a television interview.

The Herald quoted Rod as saying the representative from the guild would be in Calgary the next month, and in the meantime, "I will try to set up some contacts with people he can talk to."[9] On previous occasions, the mayor argued that a guild in Calgary would "improve the standards of responsibility, integrity, and quality of city newspapers by establishing adequate pay and working conditions" for reporters. "My only concern is to help the newspapers improve. The city is not well served by its newspapers, and proof of this in Calgary is the growing circulation [here] of *The Globe and Mail*." A guild might help make the newspapers the responsible operations "they claim to be and are not."

Nothing substantial came from this initiative. Ironically, *The Herald's* newsroom employees did organize almost three decades later, leading to an eight-month strike when the company sabotaged the prospect of a first contract agreement (an affair in which I was directly involved). During that period, *The Herald* published a letter from Rod saying it had become a much better paper since most of its regular employees had hit the picket lines. Rod showed again his tendency to gore people who'd been loyal to him.

Tensions flared with the CBC when Rod stalked off a radio interview, and "relations between the people's network and the people's choice reached a new low."[10] The mayor had long criticized the lack of a CBC television station and related production facilities in Calgary. This particular incident started when the interviewer suggested a number of Rod's recent appointees to civic committees had been active volunteers in the recent civic election campaign. The interviewer even provided names. He also referred to Rod's real estate connections. According to the news report, "The mayor became angry, called down the reporter and left the interview with four minutes left on a live interview show."

This incident may suggest that relations with the media were irreparable, but a few months later he offered his greetings for the Calgary Press Club's year-end annual bash. "In closing my good wishes for this year, let me say that I am pleased to see that the media continue to honour the classic maxim that you can slide further on bullshit than on sand. You've had a darn good slide in '72!" [11]

When Rod early that spring tarred and feathered Herald writer Don Whiteley with the sobriquet "chicken-shit operator," punning headline writers could not resist "Mayor uses fowl language on reporter." [12] The peck at Whiteley occurred after a squawking news scrum in City Hall when reporters seemed interested in asking questions only about Rod's proposed ten-day trip to Scandinavia, where he planned to view social housing projects, among other activities. Part of the visit would be in his capacity as Honorary [that is, unpaid] Finnish Consul in Calgary, he explained. Several aldermen had publicly belittled the trip, and Rod was exasperated over repeated questions about the City's financial contribution to the trip [it turned out to be $400]. Alderman Adrian Berry predictably said Rod's "chicken shit" outburst was "disgusting".

Conflict with *The Herald* never let up. After a trip to Germany where Rod looked at housing and mass transit, among other activities, a *Herald* reporter called up the aldermen he knew would have some negative comments about the trip. He thereby set up the opportunity for *The Herald* to describe the trip as purely a holiday, and according to a letter of complaint Rod sent to editor-in-chief Richard Sanburn, "attack me for attempting to do my job." The visit, Rod pointed out, had been arranged by the Federal Republic of Germany. This in turn led to another carping editorial stating, "We say it was a waste of time and money. There is no common interest between the City and the Federal Republic of Germany that is susceptible to mayoral interpretation. Mr. Sykes was on a junket, nothing more. Calgary taxpayers paid for his time, and thereby wasted their money. The West Germans paid for his ticket and therefore wasted their money." [13] No matter that the City ended up buying many millions of dollars' worth of equipment and the Siemens-Duewag U2 cars that helped form Calgary's light-rail transit system. Disregard, too, the large Canadian-German population in Calgary that played a significant role in the city's economy. *The Herald's* position demonstrated once more its obsession with undermining the mayor at every opportunity.

Despite appreciating that the mass media gave him a valuable platform for putting his side of issues to the public, Rod demonstrated many times he was not a patsy for them. Because he performed so well in live interviews, he received invitations to appear on many national programs. He never let himself be enthralled by his interviewers, though.

Rod's off and on relationship with the CBC continued until the end of his third term. Tom Kennedy, an earnest and mostly friendly reporter at *The Albertan* who freelanced extensively with the CBC told Rod at a function he was distressed by the lack of contact between the CBC and the mayor, and he wanted to make the relationship warmer. After considering the matter, Rod laid out his feelings quite succinctly in a letter to Kennedy. "The CBC reporters in City Hall have not earned the respect or confidence of the administration in general nor my office in particular. They have often been discourteous; they have often been shallow, and they have sought sensation regardless of truth and accuracy," Rod said.

Kennedy wanted to interview Rod extensively about City Hall operations. Rod noted that the objective approach had never been taken by any of the news media, including CBC. "The fact is the CBC coverage of civic affairs is pathetically superficial, frequently grossly inaccurate, and generally highly unreliable. It is also true that many CBC people are rather arrogant and thoughtless in their dealings with their employers, the people of this city. Rudeness isn't necessary, and the casual, scatter-brained attitude toward responsibility that says, in effect, 'I don't need to be informed, I don't need to check with somebody else, I don't need to research and learn the facts,' can only lead to poor performance. As a secretary of state recently told me, what he objected to with the CBC was not their socialist tendencies and their left-wing bias, it was their incompetence. Well, that's off my chest, Tom."[14]

These comments summed up well how he considered most of the media at City Hall. Journalists frequently operated as a pack, with radio, television, and newspaper reporters all following each other around and watching each other like hawks, or maybe chickens, to make sure they didn't miss a story. They also spent considerable efforts teasing negative, critical comments out of aldermen and other players at City Hall. Rod branded it the "Let you and him fight" approach to news, although he sometimes seemed like a willing participant in the game.

The disappointment of Rod with the local media, as he expressed it in later life, related in part to what he considered their reluctance to pursue people they considered their friends, an approach he first spotted at *The Herald* and which he later believed permeated much of the media here. As an example, he cited the prevailing protective attitude to Ralph Klein during his political career during which, Rod alleged, there was compelling evidence of Klein's mistreatment of his first wife and other bad behaviour that remained unreported.

16

FROM STRING QUARTETS TO SMACKDOWNS

A mong Rod's incongruities was his position on arts and culture. While participating in a forum on the future of the arts in Calgary about five months after his first election, he proposed a wide range of leisure-time activities that could come under the definition of the arts. "At one end of the spectrum you have TV, wrestling, and beer; at the other, chamber music or something equally esoteric," he told a Local Council of Women gathering.[1] Despite the appearance of an aesthete, he seemed as much at home in a dingy, working man's tavern quaffing beer from a stained table as sipping sherry in the subdued, black-tie environment of a concert hall reception with a quartet performing Mozart concertos. Many a Friday evening, he went alone to join the screaming and unruly masses at the Victoria Pavilion in Calgary's Stampede Grounds, and later, the Stampede Corral to watch professional wrestling. It's true that, as mayor, he fell into the role of chairman of the boxing and wrestling commission, but his interest predated that.

Although full symphony concerts had no particular appeal, Rod did enjoy chamber music performances. As part of his culture portfolio, he possessed a prodigious knowledge of English literature and could debate the finer points of classic books with the most erudite. Over his lifetime, he also took great pleasure in amassing a collection of etchings, and postage stamps, for that matter. If he had to choose, though, he might have even preferred the honest unsophistication of the Victoria Pavilion crowd to the vain poseurs sometimes found at the Jubilee Auditorium or other concert venues.

However, he had one major and unrelenting proviso in his role as mayor: Art and culture had to prove it could pay its way. Council could only help those cultural groups that helped themselves. "No organization can expect council to finance its initial steps. First, the organization must prove it is worth something in the community," he said.[2] "A small group of dilettantes has no right to expect the taxpayers to support them. You must earn your status." That position put him in early conflict with those in the Calgary arts and culture scene who were frequently on the steps of City Hall with their manicured hands out.

An early and fascinating tussle involved the Allied Arts Council. Depending on whom you talked to, descriptions of Calgary's art scene at that time ranged from cultural wasteland to nascent incubator of creativity. Despite a strong visual arts community by the 1970s,[3] the height of cultural experience for many Calgarians was still watching the perky Young Canadians do their corny song and dance routines. It's true that the naked, twenty-one-foot-tall, definitely avant garde "Family of Man" statues, bequeathed by developer Robert Cummings and rescued from the 1967 Montreal Expo, were erected in the Calgary Board of Education grounds. However, most art still comprised traditional mountain scenes or contemplative cowboys on the range; long hair, bare feet, and sandals were viewed with suspicion.

Carmen Wittmeier delightfully put her finger on prevailing sensibilities when she described the traditional greeting visitors were supposed to recite during welcoming events called White Hat ceremonies. As an example, she quoted the greeting that Tourist and Convention Bureau representative Jack Herman made to a national seminar on the visual arts in early 1969. "We're a bunch of rhubarb and haywire cowboys," Herman yelled to the stunned audience. "I, havin' pleasured myself considerably in the only doggone genuine Cowtown left in Canada, namely Calgary, and havin' been duly exposed to excessive amounts of heart-warmin', backslappin', tongue-losenin', thirst-quenchin' western spirit, do solemnly promise to communicate this here Calgary brand of horsepitality to all folks and critturs that cross my track hereafter, honest Injun."[4] Rod failed to eliminate this cringe-inducing salutation, a version of which could be heard more than four decades later when Naheed Nenshi was mayor.

When Rod became mayor, a cultural gulf lay between the city's political and business establishment and the city's arts community. Some, including Rod, might have used the term 'arts clique' rather than community. One of the first run-ins for the new mayor came in the form of a panicky ultimatum from the Calgary Regional Arts Foundation: Unless the City came up with $232,000, the Allied Arts Centre doors would close by December 31, halfway through its busy season. When council agreed to offer them just $10,000, Rod was unapologetic. "I'm satisfied the banks won't seize the Allied Arts Centre because they won't know what to do with it," he said, suggesting the centre return to the use of volunteer staff as a way of saving money. Despite fury from the arts lobby, he asked why taxpayers should dump money into "a private organization which has spent $250,000 having fun for themselves." He said he had never seen "such a pressure campaign whipped up so quickly to shake the City down for a quarter of a million dollars."

Behind the scenes, two of the wealthiest, so-called arts patrons in the city, Carl Nickle and Harry Cohen, approached Rod directly, metaphorical tin cups in hand. The two had signed guarantees with the bank for the arts centre and they now wanted to safeguard their money. Remember that Nickle, who founded Nickle's Daily Oil Bulletin, formed his own oil and gas company, was elected as an MP for two terms, served on many boards and charitable organizations, and became known for his major collection of ancient coins, was not short on cash. Likewise Cohen, who, with other brothers, formed General Distributors with interests across Canada, later expanding into other retail, real estate, and oil and gas exploration ventures. Rod essentially sent them scurrying with a stern warning they'd be in a fight if they brought their request to council.

During a later meeting with the manager of the bank holding the guarantees, it was suggested the City should pick up the debt. Rod rejected that idea quickly and asked why the guarantors, Nickle and Cohen, both millionaires, wanted to place the burden on taxpayers rather than meet their obligations. When Rod warned of publicizing their position, the manager backed off. The public purse was safe for a while from the demands of wealthy arts patrons.

At the same time, recall that Rod, with particular efforts from his executive assistant Tom Yarmon, responded favourably to a proposal in 1971 to renovate the old Variety Theatre, just east of City Hall on Eighth Avenue Southeast. With a colourful history dating back to the heydays of vaudeville, the Variety Theatre had been vacant for a while, caught in the middle of an unfinished urban renewal program. After determining it would still be serviceable and could be refurbished at reasonable cost, Rod, with Yarmon's help, obtained the consent of the federal and provincial governments to put it to use.

Among the arts community favouring the renovation was Christopher Newton, the English-born founder of Theatre Calgary about three years earlier. Costs were estimated at between a quarter and half a million dollars for the venerable east Calgary building. The issue remained unresolved for several years, however, with the majority of council dragging their feet on the financial commitment. "I thought rejuvenating the Variety Theatre was a good thing. It could show this neighbourhood could be brought to life," Rod said. Opponents fretted, however, that it would attract lay-about hippies to this part of the city; there would be lots of weird, young people having fun. Rod was convinced that Nickle, Cohen, and their hangers-on undermined the plans because they feared a refurbished Variety Theatre would detract from their hopes for an ambitious downtown theatre complex west of City Hall. They envisaged spanking new buildings with their names on them in suitably large letters. They got their wish years later with the Centre for the Arts, and the old Variety Theatre was eventually demolished.

As significantly, Christopher Newton, by then celebrated here for his the-atrical productions, got fed up with the infighting over the Variety Theatre and left the city, a big loss for Calgary. After his appointment in 1979 as artis-tic director for the Shaw Festival at Niagara-on-the-Lake in Ontario, he went on to enjoy an illustrious career, bringing fresh vitality to the famous festival. Who knows what he could have done for Calgary if he had stayed even a few more years?

With his literary and musical background, Rod had a strong interest in the arts—just not in burdening the taxpayers with all the costs. He remembered welcoming Maurice Handford from Manchester, England, as a clearly up and coming conductor with the Calgary Philharmonic Orchestra in 1971. "We were lucky to have him," said Rod. "He was the only musical director to make a courtesy call to the mayor's office." Handford enjoyed an enthusiastic fol-lowing in Calgary until he left in 1975. "I thought he was the kind of man, like Christopher Newton, who would help build a solid arts foundation here, but he couldn't stand the politics and returned to Britain."

At the time, Rod made sincere and thoughtful efforts to intervene when the Calgary Philharmonic Orchestra Society was undergoing one of its regular periods of unhinged disharmony, and a rift with Handford was quite apparent. Noting the improvements Handford had instilled in the orchestra, he pleaded with members to mend relations with their renowned conductor, even though he appeared "uncompromising in his determination to produce a high quality of music."[5]

In other correspondence, Rod suggested personal feelings must be sac-rificed for the common good. His quest for humble reconciliation by the society with its conductor is a rare public example of Rod the negotiator at work. It was far from the scorched-earth approach he was often vilified for. Unfortunately, his entreaties fell on deaf ears. Hurt pride and grievance won the day, and Handford left town for good.

Rod and Handford enjoyed their association during the four years he spent here. Handford even helped Rod add some missing years to his *Chums Annual* collection. They also discussed the possibility of encouraging the establishment of a chamber orchestra in Calgary, but too many people opposed the idea. "Most of them probably thought chamber music came in a pot," Rod said. During part of Handford's term as conductor, Talmon Herz was principal cello in the CPO and had expressed ambitions to form a trio. The conventional wisdom, however, was that a trio would be too small and detract from the success of the full orchestra. Herz still went ahead with his plans and ended up leaving Calgary to play around the world and make many popular classical recordings with his sister Yaela Herz, and with Dale

Bartlett. One of the few places he wasn't well received unfortunately appeared to be Calgary.

As far as his interest in the boxing and wrestling commission was concerned, Rod clearly got a kick out of a world where people called Abdullah the Butcher, Sweet Daddy Siki, and Archie the Stomper strutted the stage. Wrestling was good practice for council meetings, Rod liked to joke; only the rules were fairer and the fighting seemed much cleaner. The blood and guts of this dramatic, no holds barred display of physical aggression, with its fakery on its sleeve, served as an antidote to the suppressed hypocrisy of his daytime interactions at City Hall. "It was so relaxing," said Rod.

Through experience, he figured out the best seat where he wouldn't get spat upon was near the corner post. Abe Belzberg, a member of one of Calgary's prominent Jewish families, used to sit around the same spot with his walking stick when he was in his late eighties. One Friday, a wrestler was thrown right out the ring, landing near him. As Abe started slashing at the man with his stick, the wrestler took it from him, snapped it in two, then in two again. The crowd roared its delight. Rod recalled the place was almost always full, with aboriginal people, particularly women, making up the majority.

Friendship with Stu Hart in the 1960s first lured Rod into wrestling when he was still with Marathon. Hart was the promoter who originated the Friday night Stampede wrestling back in 1948 for live and, later, for television audiences. He was the city's uncontested Mr. Wrestling, and created an impressive dynasty for the city. With his colourful wife, Helen, the couple had twelve children, almost all of whom became professional wrestlers or were associated with it. From 1952, they lived in a Victorian-era mansion up on Broadcast Hill in southwest Calgary by the television station. In the basement gym, he trained his sons and scores of others who went on to successful wrestling careers.

From modest beginnings, Hart made his own way in life. He began wrestling and weight-training at fourteen, developing in the process a twenty-two inch neck, twenty-one inch biceps and, according to a Ralph Klein quote, hands as big as toilet seats.[6] He became an outstanding, all-around athlete, playing professional football with the Edmonton Eskimos, and participating in a range of other sports. As a wrestler, he qualified for the 1938 Empire Games in Australia, but lack of funds in the Depression-strapped Canadian government stopped him from going. Despite a serious bicycle accident in 1941, Hart competed in various exhibition matches to entertain the troops in the Second World War before realizing a long-held dream to wrestle professionally in New York. His two years there launched a long and eventful career, in which his many adversaries included a tiger and a grizzly bear.

By the time Rod met him, Hart was approaching middle age. He seemed to walk with difficulty from all his injuries and spoke slowly in a rasping voice, sometimes hesitating to find the right words, but he was still very much on the ball. Despite his rough profession, he exuded a beguiling gentleness and good humour that drew others to him. He and Rod seemed to get on well, although the broomstick and the bull made a fascinating physical match. Rod usually tried to cover Hart's broad back when matters became a little over the top at Stampede wrestling. Hart gave some of Rod's sons part-time jobs. Henry distributed the programs, for example.

The boxing and wrestling commission, of which Rod, as mayor, automatically became chairman, frequently had to deal with transgressions by the wrestlers in and out of the ring. Before Rod's first year was up, Hart was hauled on the commission carpet for lax supervision over the wrestlers by two of his regular referees, R.B. Frank and Gordon A. Graystone. The referees were suspended. The commission wanted to demonstrate that it had the power to put the Stampede wrestling participants in a headlock. When a penitent Stu Hart, who perfected this role of head-bowed sorrow quite skillfully, came before the commission to have it lift the refs' suspensions, Rod had fun with his response. "I have come to the conclusion that the referees are suffering from defective eyesight, and I think the least the commission can do before renewing their licences is request a medical certificate with respect to the condition of their eyes," he said.[7] Examination of eyesight thus became a condition of renewing their licences.

The commission had to tackle an epidemic of wrestlers taking into the ring what became known as "foreign objects." Archie the Stomper became notorious for using coat hangers, or pulling other objects out of his pants. String for choking opponents, ice-cream sticks, chains, and straps seemed to become part of the required equipment. Despite the commission handing Archie and other well-known wrestlers frequent suspensions, there was no let-up. One of Stampede wrestling's regular and incongruous fans was a Calgary medical doctor who also noted the deteriorating behaviour of the wrestlers. "It is my observation that wrestling ... has come to mean, more and more, a rougher and more violent form of exhibition with almost a seeming return to the days of the Roman gladiators ... i.e. attempting to win by striking an opponent against the post either by the head being smashed into the post, or the scrotum or testicles by leg-pulling."[8]

A full-scale brawl outside the ring after a match between Archie Goldie, or Archie the Stomper as he was better known, and Les Thornton also came under the scrutiny of the commission. Criminal assault charges were laid against the Stomper and against others arising from the July 27, 1973, incident. Flamboyant defence lawyer Milt Harradence was legal counsel for Goldie.

During its hearing, the commission heard from twelve witnesses about the pandemonium that followed the fight, with people "grabbed by the throat" and "kicked in the head." A wheelchair and occupant were also knocked over in the free for all, and a metal chair was waved at police representatives in the arena.[9] After other incidents, the commission banned Goldie from Calgary, but the action provided an exhilarating outlet for the audience, including, the mayor, apparently.

Hart eventually dismissed some of the wrestlers giving him the most trouble. Things had become quite different since he first opened up wrestling in Edmonton in 1948, "when life was simpler, the fans less jaded, and the wrestlers didn't resort to such tactics as they do now."[10]

The threat by another promoter to seek a wrestling licence in the city provoked a highly poignant response from Hart. In an impassioned letter to the commission,[11] he outlined the course of his career and his contributions to wrestling in the city. "Wrestling is my livelihood," he pleaded. Another promoter in Calgary "would be the kiss of death." The competition never came, and Hart continued his domination over wrestling until 1984 when promoter Vince McMahon and the World Wrestling Federation (WWF) bought him out before the business was sold back to the Hart family the following year and run by one of his sons, Bruce Hart, and prominently featured another son, Bret Hart. Cultural or not, wrestling entertained multitudes of Calgarians during its long run here.

Rod enjoyed friendships with several big-name local athletes. Gene Filipski, former Stampeder football player and a Stampede wrestler, was a loyal supporter throughout Rod's mayoralty. It didn't hurt that Filipski owned a sign and bus bench advertising company that came in useful during elections, as pointed out earlier. Hulking Don Luzzi, all-star defensive tackle and offensive guard for the Stampeders for twelve seasons, also kept his imposing but good-humoured presence close to Rod through all his campaigns. Luzzi made a run at provincial politics himself, representing the Alberta Social Credit Party in the 1971 election, losing by only five hundred votes to Ron Ghitter. As we have seen, Rod's friendships in the fields of culture and sports were varied.

17
QUEENS AND KNAVES

This chapter takes a further look at some of the characters who played alongside Rod in the City Hall theatre. You realize by now that several aldermen served frequently as wearying irritants to Rod's aspirations, like mosquitoes that had somehow found their way through the screen door and were whining around his head as he lay in the dark. They were persistent, they were not going away, and they'd get under his skin before morning. We've noted some of the antics of Aldermen Ed Dooley, Adrian Berry, and Eric Musgreave. It was fascinating, therefore, to hear that Dooley, for example, showed up at the 2011 funeral for former Alderman John Ayer that Rod also attended. As did Peter Petrasuk, then going under the last name Peterson. Their conversation after the event was reasonably convivial, according to Rod, with Dooley even expressing low-key contrition for his behaviour several decades previously. He took this approach, he said, because of a belief that, toward the end of life, one should try and tie up loose ends and seek forgiveness for earlier transgressions.

Looking back, there's a mix of pleasure and wonderment in realizing what strange and varied characters with whom we've shared the spotlight during life's unfolding drama. Most of the council cast from 1969-1977 occupied a prominent place among the hundreds of other actors replaying their disparate roles in Rod's mind into his old age. Enough has been said about Dooley, Berry, or Musgreave, and for Don Hartman, Tom Priddle, John Ayer, Jack Davis and Roy Farran.

Petrasuk was an enigma to the end. Although Rod may not have formally endorsed him when he ran for mayor against Ralph Klein in 1980, he certainly hung out with him during the campaign. I saw them together several times. Considering their hostilities during the previous decade, that connection seemed quite discordant. Aware that Petrasuk felt vulnerable about his modest Ukrainian background, Rod took cruel delight when he was on council in accentuating the last syllable of his name when referring to him— as in Pet-ra-SUCK. At the same time, he still respected the alderman's knowledge of civic affairs. "Petrasuk could have been a competent mayor," Rod said later in life. When Petrasuk lost badly to Ralph Klein in that 1980 mayoral race, he complained it was because he was Ukrainian. Rod's blunt rejoinder at the time was, "No, it's because you're short." What he said he meant to impress upon Petrasuk was, "You have a chip on your shoulder. People are not at ease with you." Though they may never have been warm with each other, it was not in Rod's character to shun him as others did. And there they were, more than thirty years later, having a lively conversation after a funeral.

Also in attendance at that funeral was former Alderman Bob Greene. A direct and compassionate man, Green was among three ordained ministers who served on council during Rod's tenure. He became known as the "happy warrior." The other two ministers were Ed Oman and Bob Simpson. Oman has already been discussed. Simpson, who served on council from 1971 to 1980, was relatively quiet and well meaning, but not always effective.

Gordon Shrake, mentioned early regarding his vote swapping and enticing gifts from developers, was another former alderman who kept in contact with Rod into his later years. When he first won a council seat in 1971, he was just thirty-four. Although seemingly naïve, he was, in the John Kushner mold, "dumb like a fox." Like Kushner, he served the Forest Lawn area of east Calgary as an alderman and then as a Conservative MLA.[1] He became practised in the art of community politics, sticking like a burr on jeans to his grassroots constituents. He was prone to veer off occasionally on erratic tangents, making Rod consider him a not always reliable ally, similar to John Kushner. Shrake retained his garrulous and genial tendencies into later life. He famously called Rod "the most interesting person I have ever met. You can be called many names, but never boring! It has been a pleasure to have known you." Considering their history of council spats, that was generous.

Pat Donnelly also remained complimentary about Rod. With an oil executive husband, she was a busy community volunteer before her election to council in 1974, representing a northwest Calgary ward. Among her volunteer activities was service on the Citizens Open Government Study that Rod initiated to encourage citizen input into City Hall policy-making. During her three terms, she was an earnest and articulate alderman. Rod appreciated her talents and kept in touch with her until late in life.

The profiles of other players in later councils are fuzzier. Leone Wellwood, Harry Huish, and Pat Ryan were among others with whom Rod served. Barbara Scott and Rod never hit it off. Harbouring suspicion about her motives, Rod was dismissive toward her. Mental images remain of Rod showing his patient, chivalrous side with Virnetta Anderson, elected in 1974 as Calgary's first black Alderman and the wife of former Stampeder football star Sugarfoot Anderson.

I discussed in chapter 13 Rod's ability to engage with an eclectic range of characters. The visit of Queen Elizabeth and the Duke of Edinburgh to Calgary in July 1973 as part of a tour of Canada to celebrate the RCMP's centennial, provided a revealing example of Rod's ability to bridge with skill and grace the social and economic chasms that separate people.

When Rod learned of his responsibilities to host the royal visit, he opted for a luncheon with a twist. The invitees would not comprise the traditional conglomeration of big-wigs, political hot shots, sycophants, or royal hangers-on. Instead, he assembled 150 guests from other distinct and unexpected segments of Calgary society. As he explained in his address at the luncheon to the royal couple, "Our guests today represent two of the most important elements in our city: the cultural groups and volunteer workers."[2] He made the point that Calgarians, like other Canadians, came from all over the world. About half the city's population was not of English origin, he said. He eloquently added an observation he'd often made before: "But this land is now their land, no matter where they came from and no matter when they arrived, for the true status of a man is not determined by either length of residence or by money in the bank, and there is only one class of Canadian."

Those present representing varied cultural identities within Calgary must surely have beamed proudly as Rod continued, "Calgary is a better city because they have come to live here, and we should not think of them as minorities unless we remember that we too are a minority. Canada, for that matter, is a community of minorities."

Introducing the volunteer guests, Rod then noted the many institutions that existed for the relief of human suffering could not function effectively without the help of a "very special kind of person." Thus, he used this chance to thank them publicly and warmly. Shining a royal light on regular Calgarians, most of whom had never participated in a function like this, was a coup for his commitment to open citizen participation.

However, when plans first emerged regarding his hosting role, opposition arose from quite unexpected sources. According to Rod, Premier Peter Lougheed, in his prickly way, called Prime Minister Trudeau in Ottawa to explain to him that he, as premier, outranked the mayor, and he should be the host while the mayor should be told, as Rod put it later, to get lost. Trudeau related the details of the exchange some time afterward with great relish, Rod explained in later life. Lougheed, after all, had made his political career out of attacking federal authorities in general and the prime minister in particular. Aware of Rod's own cool relations with the premier, Trudeau thought Rod would be amused to hear of Lougheed's attempts to "sandbag me [Rod] and dump me in the nearest swamp, so far as a royal visit was concerned." In any event, Trudeau supposedly told Lougheed he could not interfere in the hosting process; the arrangements had been made and this was not a political matter.

After other failed attempts to assert his role in the process, the undeterred Lougheed contacted Buckingham Palace to explain to the Queen "where she had gone wrong." A polite yet long-suffering secretary told Lougheed nothing could be done to change the arrangements. According to Rod, these details all came from Trudeau, who had a long history of having to deal with this "odd Prairie person [meaning Lougheed] and his strange views on royal protocol and his own importance." Rod and Trudeau both agreed that Lougheed was a pushy, vain man.

At the special luncheon, while Rod sat beside the Queen and conversed, she asked him if he knew that the Alberta premier had tried to scuttle this pleasant occasion. She said, "ever so nicely," as Rod related the story, that the premier should have known that her family had been dining with mayors for a thousand years, much more so than with premiers. Throughout the luncheon, she was friendly, talkative, and funny, said Rod. Lord Louis Mountbatten, with whom Rod had already formed a good relationship, had "clearly made known to her that I was not dangerous—meaning, I think, that I didn't run to the press to recount everything said in a private conversation."

Three years later, Rod played host to another royal visit with similarly pleasant memories. This time, Charles, Prince of Wales, and younger brother Prince Andrew were the guests of honour for a special luncheon Rod arranged in the Garden Terrace, an elegant enclosed area that was then still a part of the convention centre amenities. Rod recounted "they bickered just as brothers often do in the most ordinary of families. I felt I was complimented in a funny sort of way that they would do it in front of me. This was clearly the Mountbatten connection since the family knew of his good opinion of me and our fairly frequent communications."

Rod had invited Peter Lougheed to this luncheon, but at the last moment, Roy Farran called Rod to say the premier would not attend. "No regrets, no apology, no message of sorrow to the princes," said Rod. "That was the way, I had noticed, that the premier seemed to think important people behaved. Very odd." When Rod asked Farran to represent the province instead, Farran said he had been instructed not to do so. A shame, thought Rod, because Farran's remarkable and well known war record, as well as his literary skills, would appeal to the princes.

With a place of honour right next to Prince Charles still to fill, Rod called on another invitee from another table and put him there. Rod soon realized that Rabbi Lewis Ginsberg was an inspired choice. "Rabbi Ginsberg and Prince Charles got on like the proverbial house on fire," said Rod. "The rabbi had once been a professional wrestler in New York. He had both experience and a sense of humour." Rod also later learned that Lougheed had not appreciated Rod's choice of replacement, "but I also heard that some of the guests were amused."

He had other recollections of Lougheed's clumsy intrusions into royal visits. That included an airport reception for Prince Charles. Although the premier's office had instructed the mayor's office not to present flowers, to Rod's amusement, there was the premier rushing toward the advancing prince with a tot in tow bearing flowers.

Relations between Rod and Lougheed were frequently hostile. Hugh Horner, who held cabinet posts from 1971-75 in the Lougheed government, used to joke with Rod that whenever his name came up in cabinet meetings, the premier would refer to him as "that bastard." As was outlined in chapter 8, Rod disagreed vigorously with Lougheed's decentralization plans for the province. He lambasted Lougheed for his "high expenditures and huge failures." That included, according to Rod, the Heritage Trust Fund, Lougheed's supposed great legacy to Alberta. "The premier was good at pouring money down rat holes," was Rod's assessment. This criticism was drowned out, of course, in the tsunami of praise that swept over Lougheed's name after he died in 2012.

During his involvement with a major project to build a new city hall and parking structure for the City of Brampton, Ontario, during the late 1980s and early 1990s, Rod came to know William Davis, Progressive Conservative premier of Ontario 1971-1985 and sometimes known as Brampton Billie. He was born there and represented the constituency of Peel for a decade and a half. Davis, also famously known for once remarking that "bland works,"[3] considered moving to federal politics by running to lead the federal Progressive Conservatives in 1983 after Prime Minister Joe Clark received lukewarm support during a leadership review and stepped down. Davis decided not to do so when he realized he would not receive endorsements from western Canada because of his lobbying for the patriation of Canada's constitution and his refusal to outright condemn the National Energy Program so hated in Alberta. Lougheed, he said, had strongly opposed his candidacy.

It was no surprise that when Rod and Davis got together, the conversation included discussion of Alberta's premier. Davis recalled Lougheed's ambitions to lead the federal Progressive Conservatives in 1983 when the party's leadership convention was being planned. However, Lougheed soon realized he would have little to no loyalty from the East. The nail in the coffin of his leadership aspirations came when Davis told him bluntly, "If you run, I will run too." As we know from history, Lougheed never formally entered the race that Brian Mulroney won. "Lougheed has run a relentless campaign of self-promotion throughout his career," was another cutting judgment from Rod. "It's extraordinary how a man could be so concerned with his image." *Herald* columnist Gary Park scored a bulls-eye with his comment that Rod's dislike of Lougheed was not discreet. "What started as a brooding lack of communication between Sykes and Lougheed in the last few years has come close to open antagonism," he once wrote.[4]

The influence Ernest Manning had over Rod will be touched on later as we look at Rod's short-lived bad dream as leader of the Alberta Social Credit Party. They had first met during the 1960s when Rod was still with Marathon and building his reputation as a go-getter. Rod found Manning open to ideas, true to his word, and as honest a political leader as he ever met. Brian Brennan's book on Manning, *The Good Steward*, quoted a *Calgary Herald* reporter, Doug Sagi, as noting in a piece on the premier that one important factor in Manning's political success was his willingness to take decisive action whenever a hint of wrongdoing threatened his government. "He won't take nonsense from anyone," Sagi wrote. [5]

Rod saw Manning's political philosophy as being honest and being seen as honest. Brennan's book on Manning offered another viewpoint, though, when it quoted Canadian novelist Arthur Hailey as believing "Manning had been lax in policing areas of conflict of interest and 'proximity to influence' affecting cabinet ministers." [6]

Manning's son Preston, who eventually became leader of the Reform Party and leader of Canada's Official Opposition, did not receive the same glowing praise from Rod. When Rod was Social Credit Leader, he found Preston reserved and not fully committed to the cause of reviving the party. At the time, operating a consulting company that did considerable work with Alberta's First Nations peoples, Preston was viewed as far more concerned about maintaining his contracts from the provincial government than dedicating his skills and energy to the Social Credit struggles.

In the context of Rod's regard for Ernest Manning, it's quite odd to reconcile that with his friendship with Prime Minister Trudeau. Manning was on record as having described Trudeau as "the worst political leader in years from the standpoint of the Western provinces." Manning hated federal policies such as the Official Languages Act, giving French equal status to English in the Canadian confederation. [7] Yet, in a move that had mouths gaping, it was Trudeau who offered a senate seat to Manning in 1970 that the former premier accepted.

Trudeau called Rod "my only friend in Western Canada," according to Rod. They could both be described as fearless mavericks. They had other common ground too. Rod's wife, Gisele, and her family history in Montreal going back numerous generations, augmented Rod's legitimacy with the PM. Rod's links with Jesuitism must also have also endeared him to Trudeau, who was raised as a Jesuit in Montreal.

"Trudeau was a very bright man ... a cultivated man," said Rod in later life. "He was quite secure in his own skin. He was a rebel." The latter point undoubtedly helped seal their friendship. Rod added with customary and forthright lack of bashfulness, "He liked to talk with people who had thoughtful, intelligent ideas." Often when Trudeau would fly to Western Canada for political functions, he would try to arrange a meeting with Rod at the Calgary airport. "He would stop for a chat," is how Rod explained the get-togethers. Rod had his direct number and would call him when necessary.

"I liked him very much," was Rod's simple judgment of Trudeau. They had disagreements, though. The PM's statement in the early 1970s that he had "wrestled inflation to the ground" didn't sit well with Rod. When a reporter asked Rod what he thought of Trudeau's position on inflation, Rod cleverly responded, "I see he has wrestled it to the ground, but he doesn't say who's on top." Trudeau likely appreciated that kind of tight-rope walking.

The memories many Albertans retain from Trudeau's visits here during the 1970s are tainted with images of arrogance, outright scorn, and a defiant middle finger. Rod tried hard to combat the hostility that bristled among so many Westerners, and to bridge the fractious relationship between Trudeau and this region. "I was delighted to welcome you in Calgary during Stampede," he once wrote to Trudeau. "Practically all the problems of misunderstanding between the East and the West can be resolved with more visits such as yours. It was very obvious that your support cut across all party lines. The many remarks that I heard were generally of this kind: 'Well, I've been a Conservative all my life, but I sure do support the prime minister.' "[8]

A year later, Rod was less diplomatic about Calgary's response to Trudeau. "I don't know if you saw or heard the local news reports of your visit. If you did, it may have occurred to you that the highly imaginative and wildly inaccurate accounts can be explained by the simple fact that this is still cattle country. Good luck in the election."[9] Trudeau's luck was compromised—he beat Bob Stanfield's Progressive Conservatives, but could only form a minority government. Rod's derogatory comments on cattle country seemed to suggest an ambiguous attitude toward that industry. His relations with the Stampede board crowd may have tainted his regard for ranchers. But when you consider his friendly relationship with people like Senator Harry Hays, whose many accomplishments included a successful cattle breeding operation, and his later dealings with ranchers around Calgary to protect their interests against Calgary's empire-building annexation plans, you realize his views varied.

Rod had Calgary's interests in mind when he congratulated Trudeau on his 1973 delegation to China. "The reception you received reflects tremendous credit on the achievements of your government and on your personal standing abroad," he said. "Our Chinese community is delighted." He then acknowledged an "ulterior motive" in writing along these lines. Reports suggested the Republic of China was planning to open a consulate in Western Canada, presumably in Vancouver. However, Rod's pitch was that Vancouver may not be the most logical place. "Consider Calgary," he argued. With possibly the second largest Chinese population in the country and certainly the healthiest and most aggressive, "Calgary is well placed to serve Vancouver and all Prairie cities. We would be delighted to encourage the Republic of China to locate its consulate here." Ever the bulldog that never lets go of the trouser leg, he added that if the commitment had already been made to Vancouver, "it is entirely logical for a country of the status of China to have more than one consulate in Canada."[10] This ambitious representation on behalf of his city made sense because of his closeness with Trudeau. Although the consulate didn't put down roots until several years later, Rod believed he helped sow the seeds for its establishment here.

Trudeau expressed his gratitude for Rod's loyalty in the otherwise mostly Tory-blue province. "I have found a good friend and a stronger supporter in the West!" he wrote with obvious enthusiasm. "Allow me to congratulate you also for some 1973 achievements: for making splendid arrangements for Her Majesty's visit to Calgary last year … For being a positive force at the Edmonton National Tri-Level Conference [dealing with federal and provincial funding issues], and for courageously experimenting with new housing and urban development policies in your city."[11] I have heard people say Rod exaggerated the closeness or influence with Trudeau, but there's no denying the prime minister kept up frequent communications with him throughout Rod's three terms. He signed his "Dear Rod" letters with a pen and ink sweeping flourish like the tracks of a daring skier in deep powder

After Trudeau won back his majority in the 1974 federal election, Rod congratulated him on his "magnificent personal victory." He said, "Your conduct of the campaign was excellent, and the professional naysayers are all routed, if not discredited." He noted, too, the positive role that Margaret his new wife had played. "Exactly what it should have been … an understanding wife can be a great asset to any politician."[12] A few years later, the "understanding wife" scenario took a wrong turn as the prime minister and Margaret Trudeau parted ways after a public and messy marital breakdown that lead to formal divorce in 1984.

When Trudeau had asked Rod in 1972 to run against Conservative Eldon Woolliams in Calgary North, Rod had declined, citing his unfinished business as mayor. "I can fully understand your predicament and feel your primary responsibility to the City of Calgary must be fulfilled," was Trudeau's response. "Your decision not to run robs politics of a great campaign."[13] Senator Keith Davey, the prominent architect of Liberal campaigns during the 1970s, again put the heat on Rod before the 1979 election, with strong hints he would receive a cabinet post if he won his seat, just as Senator Hays had in the previous decade. A Senate post was also held out, Rod claimed, but he turned Davey down again. He needed financial security, and the prospect of life in Ottawa still didn't thrill him.

Another example of Rod's positive efforts on behalf of Calgary came to the fore in his lobbying of Trudeau for a commemorative stamp for Calgary's 1975 Centennial. "I would like to impress upon you the pleasure you could bring to many Calgarians by issuing such a stamp," Rod wrote.[14] Trudeau's response showed a shared tendency for weak puns and exclamation marks: "You are, no doubt, as happy as I am that we have this matter licked!"[15] The announcement delighted Rod, who replied, "I am now working with Sam Nickle, who is a member of your design committee, in an attempt to get an engraved stamp of the calibre that Canada used in its issue in the 1930s. I have the impression that you are not a stamp collector, but Canadian stamps from that period are recognized to be among the best designed and most beautiful in the world."[16] That prompted Trudeau to respond, "I must correct the impression you have of me: I am in fact a stamp collector of sorts."[17] So, they had another shared interest. The stamp was unveiled on July 3, 1975, with a presentation to Rod from Postmaster General Bryce Mackasey in a ceremony at the Calgary Stampede.

Through his own personal experiences, Rod was also able to show empathy with the PM on another issue that dogged Trudeau: criticism of his travelling abroad. "I am sure that you appreciate that the news media does not represent the people of this country in any conceivable way. I am sorry to see the personal attacks that have been made on such trivial matters as questions of travel. It seems to me that we are encouraging personal attacks on people in any position of responsibility to the exclusion of their conduct in the responsibilities of office ... I find this whole subject rather depressing, as I suspect Madame Trudeau must do."[19]

On a personal note, he added, "Gisele and I send best wishes to you, Madame Trudeau, and your children. From my own experience, I would say that my political life such as it is at this level creates far more problems for my wife than it does for me, but I am fortunate in my choice, and her patience seems to be inexhaustible (although there are times when we both wonder)."

After retiring as mayor, Rod continued to talk about the "little guy." He kept up the propensity to tackle those he believed abused their powers, but, while retaining the gift of setting people back on their heels with his vehemence and self-certainty, he never again regained the ability to influence public affairs to the extent he did at City Hall. Despite the challenging ventures of the next two decades, Rod's years as mayor represented the apogee of his life's journey. The return to earth was not always smooth, and these decades provided their share of fascinating collisions, as we'll see in the next chapter.

18
END TO POLITICS

I n his return to civilian life after retiring as mayor, Rod hit the ground in a rush. The day after his final hours at City Hall, he was back taking on the planning department by representing Carma at an annexation hearing. This was a dramatic and bizarre turnaround for Rod, who had expended effort battling Carma in his last years in office. It also occurred without the cooling-off period one might have expected from a public official who was often critical of elected people's close ties with development. Rod saw no anomaly in this new relationship. He had, after all, remained on good terms with Roy Wilson of Carma, who had helped him in his first mayoral contest, and with Ralph Scurfield of Nu-West, which worked closely with Carma. Rod saw sense in Carma's revised plans for development in the proposed area to be annexed, and, as Rod noted, "they knew I would be competent in advancing their case." As head of Sykes Property Consultants, Rod's explanation for accepting the contract was, "I had no trouble working with Carma if the end result was a real mix of housing in different corners of the city." A different kind of adventure was immediately under way.

A steady rudder for keeping Rod's affairs on course during the 1970s was Barbara Tate. After joining the mayor's office in 1973, she became an indispensable staffer. Efficient, cool under pressure, and diplomatic, she was able in her subtle ways and in her role as a personal assistant to keep Rod on track during stormy weather and keep lines of communication open with others. After sticking with Rod right to his last day as mayor, she joined him as he continued the launch of his venture as a development consultant and project builder—activities he had excelled in while with Marathon almost a decade earlier. Tate remained at City Hall for about three months after Rod left to help with the transition to the new regime, before joining Rod in their two-person office in the downtown Grain Exchange building owned by Larry Ryder.

In the next two years, Rod assumed a partnership position with Vic Burstall in some apartment buildings in southwest Calgary, and became partners with a Frank Longinotti in the construction of a twenty-four unit apartment block near the former Holy Cross Hospital, among other projects. He also remained busy with his consulting activities in Edmonton with Tom Yarmon. Without soliciting or advertising, the work poured in. "I had more work than I could handle. People knew I was competent in advancing a case," he said. "I was well known and could be trusted."

As she watched Rod getting sidetracked into other political activities after his retirement as mayor, Tate sensed that Rod "never settled after City Hall." Tate stayed with Rod until 1979. She then pursued successful careers at Nova Corp as vice-president of human resources before taking an executive position with the United Way in Calgary and later the presidency of the Calgary office of the Canadian Mental Health Association.

Apart from his more lucrative consulting work and his project developments, Rod still couldn't resist taking on causes where he perceived injustice. "I made some mistakes financially speaking. I didn't know how to say no because I knew nobody else would take on these matters" he said. "I felt that by saying no to desperate people, I would be helping put families out on the street."

A case in point concerned the plight of a family-owned business close to the Centre Street Bridge called DeGreeve Auto Upholstery Inc. Planning to expand on the property or sell their land and move to another larger location, the company met only resistance from an obdurate planning department. Because planners had it mind to buy the land for the City and other riverbank development, they froze the ability of the owners to increase the use of the property or sell it at market value. "The planning department was actually trying to devalue the land," said Rod. Backed by his wherewithal as a former mayor, he made an appointment with City Commissioner Charlie Howarth, who, to his credit, saw the unfairness of the situation and intervened on behalf of the company to let them sell the land in question and move to the southeast Calgary location where they still operate today. "This was legalized robbery," Rod said. "I've always been shocked to see injustice from people you pay taxes to for justice."

He continued to take on these types of cases for the rest of his working life and into retirement. The rewards included the satisfaction of beating the system on behalf of a defenceless citizen in a squeeze from powerful bureaucrats, even when the cash rewards were distinctly modest.

Although he wanted to be more involved in actual land development and resume the kind of success he'd enjoyed with Marathon, it was the consulting projects that occupied most of his time. That side of the business included contingency projects in long-term industrial development in other cities. As befitted his experience, his main contribution was guiding these and other projects through the bureaucratic maze of the local authority approval process.

Rather than regular monthly fees, he was more likely to receive agreed-upon commissions when projects were completed. To his consternation in that highly volatile period in the early 1980s when interest rates reached almost twenty per cent, many companies experienced financial trouble. Some succumbed completely to the calamitous economic conditions. Rod

estimated he lost at least half a million dollars from unpaid bills. One client
offered to pay him in diamonds. "They were investment-grade diamonds, and
I knew they would be worth nothing if I opened them up." He once asked
Balzac farmers to pay him with rocks and eggs when he later represented
their interests in Calgary annexation hearings. Even in the forbidding world
of business, he could demonstrate an idiosyncratic and humorous approach
to his dealings.

Pursuing what he most wanted to do—real property development—would
have required considerable speculative borrowing. After retiring as mayor,
he still had relatively little capital at his disposal. In those volatile years, Rod
was reluctant to assume too much risk and insecurity. His motivation, after
all, was to provide for Gisele, his growing family, and himself. "I saved and
invested what I earned. I didn't fritter money away," was his guiding philosophy — unlike that of many business contemporaries of that era who lost their
shirts, trousers and socks in the economic wash-out.

You may remember the large consulting contract with CNR to prepare
a redevelopment study on the company's Edmonton downtown tracks that
Rod, with partners Tom Yarmon and Chris Graefe, secured before his term as
mayor ended. That work continued after Rod's return to private life. Yarmon
recalled fondly the occasional lunch invitations to the private CN rail car
when it was moored at the Northern Alberta rail yards in Edmonton. "They
were a treat for me, and Rod was always very interested in railway operations." From his previous CPR connections, that was understandable.

Sykes Property Consultants did produce a comprehensive redevelopment
plan, phased over a lengthy period. "I am gratified to see that our plan is actually nearly complete with all the development that has gone on over the yards
east of the CN Office Tower," Yarmon said. "Development is still taking place
today." Chalk up another success for Rod's record of getting things done.

But, once more, the thrill of the political high-wire act beckoned. Rod
had enjoyed the highs and lows of the political circus as mayor—despite
his protestations to the contrary. There was for him an irresistible element
to wielding political power, making a difference in society, or enjoying the
spotlight that political high-wire artists attract. Even as Rod left City Hall and
set out on a new course as a private entrepreneur, he still left the door open to
running provincially for the Social Credit Party.

When the Socreds won only four seats in the 1979 election, with just
twenty per cent of the vote—they had been reduced to four seats in the 1975
election too—they were little more than stubble on the political chin. Rump
was too grand a term for the once-mighty Socred caucus and leader Bob
Clark, almost a decade past the end of their glorious thirty-six consecutive
years in power. Earlier chapters discussed Rod's outstandingly successful

relationship with the ruling Socreds of the 1960s, particularly with Premier Ernest Manning.

The evangelical Christian and the converted Catholic with the Jesuit leanings certainly seemed to hit it off. Both studious, stern yet friendly, and unathletic looking, they shared an obsession for responsive, clean government. Manning, who had mused about other forms of federal political alignment after retiring as premier, still viewed with dismay the precipitous demise of his once dominant party. After that 1979 election, he clearly felt motivated, in a discreet, behind the scenes way, to help initiate a final, make or break strategy for the party. An important aspect of that strategy would require new, dynamic, and bold leadership. Bob Clark, leader since soon after the Socred's first disastrous drop in the electoral polls in 1975, had been one of Manning's original Cabinet young Turks of the 1960s when he served as youth minister. Clark later became education minister under Premier Harry Strom. By the end of the decade, however, Clark had lost his aura as the Big White Hope with his apparently growing distaste for the action in the ring.

Manning turned to Rod in the late 1970s, and with flattery and persuasion, courted him for the leadership role. The first clear public acknowledgment of such a courtship came with Rod's attendance at Social Credit's 1979 convention in Calgary. In the shadow of the party's plummeting electoral popularity, this was a bizarre convention. In the lurid description of Ted Byfield's *Alberta Report*, "a white-skinned, red-haired belly dancer provided the entertainment," and oglers at the event stuffed dollar bills into the dancer's girdle and top.[1] Trying to spice up some excitement in the party that way would suggest it was not only on its last legs; it was flat out, belly down on the floor. This, after all, was the party that had ruled Alberta for decades with its odd social credit monetary policies and its strict conservative Christian social values.

Still, there was Rod, a convention speaker, talking up Social Credit's stand "for supporting and defending and promoting moral standards." He reminded the party delegates that Social Credit stood for "respect for religion—a religion that is brought into your business, your daily life, and your government … It stands for free enterprise, for small business, and working men who've got a chance to make something of their lives and stand on their own feet … it is a compassionate government policy that helps people who need help—not on a hand-out basis, but on a human survival basis, on a brotherhood basis."[2] The latter sentiments were vintage Rod Sykes. The religious references, though, were new in their explicitness. Rod's political statements were taking on a sermonising tone.

Time spent with Ernest Manning and other Socred pillars such as long-time party secretary Orvis Kennedy appeared to wield an influence on Rod. In his subtle but single-minded way, Manning did not let up on his recruitment of

Rod for party leader. "I felt so complimented and overwhelmed by Manning's apparent regard for me," said Rod. "I wanted to tell him, 'I'm not the man you think I am.' " Manning, however, tightened his hold with challenges such as, "You are the only person who can lead the party ... I will help you." And then the kicker, "You'll regret the rest of your life wondering whether you could have done it." Rod succumbed.

Despite Manning's hard sell and Rod's uncharacteristic vulnerability to flattery from the revered politician, it is difficult to understand more than thirty years later how Rod was drawn into a cause that turned sour so quickly. It is especially incomprehensible in light of his ability to resist Trudeau's entreaties to run federally. But, it's worth remembering how precipitously he decided to run for mayor and how idealistically he approached that challenge. As I've described, that move quickly turned rancid, but sheer will power drove his ongoing career as mayor. Besides, we've seen his propensity to take on what looked like hopeless causes and still turn lemons into lemonade. With long hindsight, Rod in later life saw his decision to stand for the Socred leadership not so much as a miss-judgment. "It was an error in priorities," he said.

Reporter Frank Dabbs astutely defined this after an interview in October 1980, just days before Rod was to finally make public his decision on whether to run for the Socred leadership. "By any rational judgment, Rod Sykes had grabbed the brass ring," he wrote. Rod was enjoying a prosperous development and consulting business, time for his family and his voracious reading habits, and mostly peace and quiet from the rough and tumble of public life. "On this evening, however, he is wrestling with passions that have marked his life and set him apart from most of the people he has known well: the passions of politics." Dabbs explained that the day after the interview, Rod and Gisele were to meet Manning and discuss further the wisdom of committing themselves to pursuing the leadership of the party. With a flicker of indecision—and insight too—as he related this to Dabbs, Rod added, "It must be my vanity, because there's no rational reason to do something which doesn't pay and is so destructive to one's family—who needs it?"[3]

Who indeed. But he was, after all, the man who taught himself to handle the toughest of challenges without backing down; who, in his fierce independence, relished the battle against the odds in the name of righting wrongs and bringing his version of justice and hope to ordinary folk. Add to that the belief that Albertans were tiring of "the Lougheed government's tight, clubby little clique, and the way it has stopped listening to ... its ordinary people who do not have the power of access to government."[4] Rod's mind was made up.

Besides, another prerogative impinged on his decision-making. He'd experienced *noblesse oblige* before. Rod had long believed that people with the knowledge, energy, and wherewithal to run for public office, particularly people from the business sector, had an obligation to serve for a period in political life. "Although I'm a Catholic, growing up in Victoria I was saturated with Protestantism," he told Dabbs with some irony. "I learned that life is a duty and a responsibility. One should not expect to be happy on this earth." He then added a lament he had used before: "My, how politics has fulfilled that expectation."

Rod prepared a more direct path to the Socred leadership than his interview with Dabbs suggests. Earlier in the summer of 1980, he wrote a stern letter to the Social Credit board to let members know where he stood on its current state. "In my view, Social Credit has made mistake after mistake in recent years, and now it proposes to make some more." [5] The party was more than $250,000 in debt and falling deeper every month with income far behind expenses. The board had not heeded advice he'd offered regarding its finances in particular, prompting him to warn, "I, as many thousands of other Manning Socreds have already done, will have to find another political party to work for if Social Credit continues to head for self-destruction." These words may leave hurt feelings, he noted, and he was at the time "not a candidate for anything." Then a big "but" that if MLA Ray Speaker "were not to run for the leadership, and political common sense took over, then I would have to reconsider my position." Speaker was a long-time representative for Little Bow in southeast Alberta. With his ranching background, he had been another of Manning's young cabinet Turks in the 1960s after being first elected in 1963 at age twenty-seven.

Rod based his critical attack on the board on several issues. First, he warned Bob Clark couldn't remain as interim leader because of the party's abysmal showing in 1979, combined with Clark's earlier promise to quit if he didn't improve Socred standing in the polls. That made Clark a duck with no wings. Worse, Clark wanted to wait until the spring of 1981 to introduce a new leadership selection process before a permanent leader was elected. Social Credit would have been out of business for more than two years of drifting, Rod pointed out.

Rod also took aim at the financial situation and the large debt that Clark had run up in the 1979 election. This left even salaries and pensions of staff in arrears, with nothing for the future. "A disgrace," Rod called it. Also under the critical spotlight was the poor shape of the organization and membership numbers. Rod's rallying messages was to get on with the change in leadership, now.

While the board he was so forcibly addressing couldn't or didn't change much else, it at least voted to push up the date of the leadership vote to November 29, 1980, and give Rod the motivation to announce a few days after the Dabbs interview referred to above that he would seek the top job.

Rod's aggressive, take charge, hard to misinterpret approach had indeed cleared away the tangled path ahead.

In his announcement statement, Rod realistically portrayed the challenges ahead as truly formidable, "rather like setting out to climb Mount Lougheed on foot from the bottom—without the help of the taxpayers' helicopter!" That was a shot at the free ride Premier Lougheed took a few years earlier to the top of the peak in Kananaskis Country named after his family.

He laid out his credentials as a Manning Socred. He believed in small government that would not interfere in people's lives. He sought a climate that would encourage private initiative; he would not tax unnecessarily or build up surpluses; he promised help for people who needed it, but avoid the handout programs that create a welfare state. More specifically, he would sell Pacific Western Airlines, which Lougheed had proudly created, and put the Heritage Trust Fund under the control of Albertans by giving them direct shares in the fund. Social Credit, he said, was "a workingman's free-enterprise party." His conclusion was, "Alberta needs effective opposition."[6]

Most of the statement was consistent with views he articulated as mayor. However, it also reflected his hardening against what was known as tax-and-spend liberalism. At the time, Rod's enthusiasm for U.S. presidential candidate Ronald Reagan was palpable, signalling his ongoing leaning to the right of the political spectrum. Economic conservatism was cascading over the western world at this time, led by the election in the U.K. of Margaret Thatcher in 1979 and the success of Reagan in the U.S. a year later.

In the build-up to the Socred leadership convention, Rod still found time to accompany Peter Petrasuk on some campaigning as he made his second bid for the Calgary mayoralty. Ralph Klein also sought Rod's backing. Rod told the media he thought Klein could "come up the middle" and beat both Petrasuk and Ross Alger. Many people, Klein included, interpreted this as a nod to the electorate, whereas it was merely an observation. The CFCN reporter and high school dropout did find that sweet middle spot, winning the mayor's seat and launching a political career, the length and success of which are still sources of utter bewilderment to some observers, including Rod.

The Socred leadership convention, meanwhile, was set for November 28 and 29, 1980, at the Red Deer Lodge in Red Deer. While Rod was the clear favourite, Bob Clark and other less friendly party members had recruited Edmonton businessman and former City Councillor Julian Kinisky to oppose him. Ray Speaker was Rod's campaign manager, and I was a member of the campaign committee. The gist of the campaign was that Alberta badly needed a free enterprise political alternative, and Rod brought to the table a winning record as former mayor, a deep understanding of private business, and a twenty-year association with Social Credit.[7] With balloons, band, and boisterous demonstrations among the three hundred or so delegates, Rod won handily.

The huge task of raising money and rebuilding the organization began in earnest in 1981. Rod made speaking tours across the province, and held press conferences in the legislature and other locations. Not having a seat was an obvious handicap, but he hoped to address that soon. One theme during the National Energy Program crisis of the time was that the 'do it my way' approaches of both Trudeau and Lougheed were destroying the country. Rod and Ray Speaker had harsh words for the provincial Tories' projected budgetary deficit for 1980-81 and the growth of unauthorized expenditures, which were all solid Opposition points.

A new Socred executive was in place, and Rod worked closely with House Leader Speaker and the other three elected Socreds, Walter Buck, Clark, and Fred Mandeville. Tall, diffident, quiet, and seemingly affable, Speaker seemed at first an excellent ally for Rod in the legislature. Meanwhile, Reagh Burgess, who called himself a real estate developer and who first had dealings with the mayor's office during the early and mid-1970s as southern Alberta co-ordinator for the federal Opportunities for Youth program and other federal initiatives, came on board as a full-time organizer. At thirty-four, with a reputation as a fun-loving socializer, he seemed an odd choice for a role with the driven Rod and a still rather prim party, despite the belly dancer a year earlier. Another bright spark who belied the party's sedate image was Dwight Bliss from Duke University, Durham, North Carolina, who, as Speaker's executive assistant, brought pizzazz to legislature proceedings. I was hired as an assistant in the legislature, serving as Rod's eyes and ears.

During the first year or so, Speaker's office, with Rod's encouragement, initiated several innovations to attract public interest. Initiating surveys of Albertans indicating dissatisfaction with the Tories' handling of the Heritage Savings Trust Fund was one. The creation and placement on Alberta stations of a critical television advertisement, paid for by Opposition funding, were among other unprecedented and creative initiatives originating from the Opposition. The ad portrayed a young child and his grandfather puzzling over a piggy-bank savings container they couldn't open as a symbol of the Lougheed Tories' failed accountability for the provincial trust fund. The printing of Social Credit's own *Opposition Speech from the Throne* was another brainwave from the energetic, red-headed Bliss.

A major legislature event late in 1981, with the participation of all the Socred caucus, was the so-called Alamo filibuster. In reality, the filibuster drivers were NDP leader Grant Notley and then-independent Calgary MLA Tom Sindlinger, booted from the Tory caucus for his tough questioning on spending accountability. Using procedural delaying tactics, such as maintaining debate through the night, the six MLAs working as a team held up regular legislative business for more than a month in an effort to force the Lougheed Tories to produce more information on the Heritage Trust Fund and release a letter from the independent auditor general indicating his concerns about the fund and an apparent $60 million short-term loss. In practical terms, Rod was only peripherally involved in this effort that produced newspaper headlines through November into December and that indicated the tiny Opposition, including the Socreds, could lay a heavy punch on the puffed-up Conservatives.

There were other more ominous signs, however, that Rod was stepping into a quagmire. He remained convinced Lougheed consciously avoided holding a by-election where he could run and establish a presence in the legislature. But, with well-honed cunning, Rod announced in August 1981 he would run in Calgary Mountain View, in the city's east side, when Lougheed called the next general election, which could come as early as 1982. The seat, as newspaper reports noted, had many ethnic and blue-collar voters; the kind of people who had been Rod's most ardent supporters when he was mayor.[8] The only trouble was, the seat was held for the Tories by Stan Kushner, son of John, an erratic ally of Rod's for many years when they were on council together.

Further, John himself had represented Mountain View before running successfully for the federal Tories in Calgary East. In Rod's version of events, John Kushner had warned him to stay out of his son's riding so his son could win a second term and thereby qualify for an MLA's pension. Rod called Stan Kushner so bad an MLA, "I'm sure the Tories will do their best to prevent him from running again." As *Herald* writer Nino Wischnewski put it, "Stan Kushner had better brace himself for a brutal fight."

During Rod's first full year as leader, relations with *The Herald* descended again into anger and mistrust. Rod became weary of what he described as the unrelenting campaign on the part of the paper to undermine, twist, and ignore initiatives by the Socreds or Rod as leader. Misrepresenting Socred policies, repeated references to the "moribund party" or the "down and out political force" were examples.

The *Edmonton Sun*, through a column by Fraser Perry, once a *Herald* writer, added to the weariness. When Rod announced his plan to run in Mountain View, Perry wrote a vituperative, hate-filled column. "For most, the death of Social Credit was confirmed when Sykes, an outsider, was able to walk in and take the leadership," he wrote. "For many, especially those who used to call him Rod Syko when he was mayor of Calgary, his decision to do so confirmed their opinion that the man's head never was wrapped too tightly ... If Sykes were half as bright as he and his supporters believe, he would have sensed something wrong from the fact that only one other man in the province was willing to take the job … I, for one, hope the people of Mountain View do not send him to Edmonton. I hope his political career will end next election day."[9]

Despite attempts to create political excitement and attract more media attention, the small crew in the engine room of the good ship Social Credit sensed a spluttering motor and an approaching gloom about where the enterprise would end up. Isolated from the legislature and juggling competing pressures even before the first full year was up, Rod was becoming increasingly frustrated with the slow pace of change, the lack of money, the challenge of attracting new, competent people on board, and his irregular contact with caucus. A festering sore was the failure of anyone to close the party office in Edmonton, even though he'd made clear he wanted this done. As well as hauling the leadership weight on his back, he tried to continue his business and consulting ventures. They were, after all, his only sources of income.

According to Rod, Ray Speaker had agreed to direct the extra pay he earned as house leader [more than $15,000 a year] into a fund to pay Rod. He never honoured that agreement. Rod was expected to make regular appearances in the legislature and at meetings across Alberta for no pay, while trying to support himself and his family. Speaker's failure to follow through on his promise demoralized Rod. The ongoing negative spin by some of the media on Socred initiatives infuriated him, and he made himself less available to meet with them.

In my position as liaison between the legislature office and Rod, I too became discouraged by Rod's outbursts of frustration, his withdrawal from availability, and what I saw as a lack of co-ordination between him and party members. In a rambling and emotional letter to Rod, I gave notice of my intention to resign early in 1982.[10] I concluded, "Life is too short to do lots of handwringing."

In the meantime, the party had to prepare for the end of October annual convention in Edmonton. Reagh Burgess rounded up his contacts—educators, economists, and small-business owners—to help lead workshops on various policy topics at the convention. He and Dwight Bliss were still determined to keep party business as up-beat as possible. Just two hundred delegates showed up for the convention, which was abbreviated to one day, October 31. In the spirit of the day, Burgess dreamed up a Halloween theme for the delegates, the great majority of whom had grey or blue-rinsed hair, if they had any hair at all (they were mostly an elderly crowd). For the evening dinner, where Rod was to deliver a keynote speech, Burgess rented a theatre device for pumping out dry ice to create the illusion of mist and add Halloween magic to proceedings.

However, Burgess had not calculated the impact on frail respiratory systems, and a chorus of confused coughing greeted Rod's opening words.

In the spirit of Socred leaders long past and their oratorical powers, Rod prepared twenty-six pages of notes. The dozen younger participants in the event sat at one table. With forty-five minutes elapsed and still no apparent end to Rod's rambling address, word circulated at the youth table of liquor and recreational drugs available in one of the hotel rooms. Almost as one, the youth wing spirited themselves as quietly as possible out of the dining hall, leaving Rod still in full voice and an empty table as blatant as a missing front tooth in a grinning contest. More than thirty years later, this abandonment of ship at a difficult time for Rod still lingered in my mind as an embarrassment and shame.

The media were relatively kind about the convention, though. They noted, for example, the significance of Senator Ernest Manning's appearance there during the day. It was the first time he had attended a Socred convention for ten years. Son Preston was also there and spoke briefly. It's funny how *The Albertan* had Rod "looking to the past for Socred priorities," as one headline put it,[11] while *The Calgary Herald* headline read more positively but still enigmatically: "New, young faces offering faint hope for revitalization of Socred party."[12]

MacLean's Magazine ran a fair piece under a subheading, "The Alberta Social Credit Party is making a valiant effort to rebuild before it is too late," suggesting hope rather than desperation characterized the party. Gordon Legge, a former *Calgary Herald* staffer, even offered the view that Rod's aggressive policies, which some saw as counter-productive, "are just what the Socreds need."[13] Soon after the convention, Gordon Jaremko of *The Herald* wrote a piece noting that many Socred members "still believe the wiry, sharp-witted property development consultant and undefeated ex-mayor of Calgary can end the party's decade-long coma."[14]

From early in his leadership, Rod assumed much of the responsibility for fund-raising. I recall accompanying him for a cup of tea with former Edmonton entrepreneur and Oilers owner Peter Pocklington in the latter's penthouse office. Sitting elevated above his audience of two before a clear-glass table, the gnome-like, bearded Pocklington bore a Cheshire-cat grin as he alternated between offering unlimited funds to the party and worrying about the impact on his business investments if a vindictive Peter Lougheed found out. Rod held up his end well, but the image stuck of a cat playing with a mouse.

After a mercurial career, in which he ran for the federal Progressive Conservative leadership, fought hard to break the union at his Edmonton meat packing plant, and famously traded Wayne Greztky from the Oilers,

Pocklington ended up declaring bankruptcy, abandoning loan obligations with Alberta Treasury Branches, moving to Palm Springs, and facing bankruptcy fraud charges. In 2010, a judge agreed to a plea bargain of probation and house arrest. For Rod and for Social Credit in 1981, Pocklington was a dud, a damp squib, a miniature caricature of contrived cleverness and bombast. He never handed over a penny to the Socreds.

Similar disillusionment arose from requests for financial contributions from the four Ghermezian brothers, Iranian Jews who had emigrated with their father from Iran in the 1960s and had become Edmonton's largest landowners. They built the West Edmonton Mall, then described as the largest shopping centre on the planet and a colossal monument to conspicuous consumption. They too ended up in controversy over loans from Alberta Treasury Branches. When the multi-millionaires sent a cheque to the party for $200, Rod, to his credit, had it returned with a note saying that if this was the value of their enthusiasm for the Socreds, then everyone would be better off if they kept their money.

As the party's 1981 year-end board meeting approached, glummer prognostications gnawed at the principal players. "No significant progress has been made in the past year at the constituency level," said Rod in his familiar, straightforward manner. With the debt now at more than $300,000, "the party suffered from a serious case of financial mismanagement ... there has been for a considerable time a reluctance to face the unpleasant facts of life." On the other hand, as far as the Legislature Office was concerned, "this is working better than ever." From a political perspective, "the picture is brighter than it has been for years."[15]

In hindsight, that was rash and unjustified optimism. Under the roiling waters were hidden political rocks that would sink the Socred ship quicker than even the most pessimistic would have imagined. A by-election in Olds-Didsbury resulting from Bob Clark's formal retirement as an MLA was expected in the New Year. Even before Lougheed set the date for February 17, 1982, the Socreds were ready with their nominee, Lloyd Quantz, a thirty-four-year-old beef producer from near Didsbury and the general manager of the Canadian Charolais Association. A native of the Didsbury area, with a master's degree in agricultural economics and experience working as an economist for Richardson Securities in Winnipeg, he seemed just the ticket for the Socreds, even if he was a bit bland.

Clark still controlled the constituency, Rod said, and had earlier indicated he would oppose Rod running there. "I couldn't challenge that. It would have been an ugly fight." So, for the good of the party, he stayed out of the race. There was sufficient optimism that Quantz would carry the day against the Conservative, Liberal, and New Democrat candidates.

Alarm bells remained initially mute when the Western Canada Concept, a fledgling separatist political party, announced it would also contest the election. Recall that separatist sentiments were rising in Alberta at this time. The Liberals' National Energy Program (NEP) produced a gush of hatred against Pierre Trudeau and his party that lingers today. Premier Lougheed did his part in fanning the flames of dissension with such outlandishly paranoid pronouncements about the federal government stepping uninvited onto the porch of provincial autonomy, ready to smash down the front door.

In this environment, along came the Western Canada Concept (WCC) with its principles including the establishment of just one official language in Canada, a halt to metrification, opposition to firearms restrictions, and the recognition of God as the Supreme Power. Most importantly, the WCC stood for "an Independent Nation of Western Canada, comprising ... British Columbia, Alberta, Saskatchewan, Manitoba, the Yukon, and North West Territories." As well, it decreed, "the major function of our government is to protect property and freedom of the individual." Other specific policies included the requirement that people should have to "earn the right to be Western Canadians."[16] Many thought it was the deluded dream of a fringe, right-wing party.

Few, including Rod and Ray Speaker, predicted what they witnessed in stunned silence on television the evening of February 17. The WCC candidate, Gordon Kessler, an oil scout, rodeo rider, and quiet-spoken, God-fearing citizen, beat Lloyd Quantz by more than 1,300 votes. As political commentator Richard Gwyn wrote later, "The voters of Olds-Disbury became the first Canadians to bellow out loud in rage."[17] They had reason to be angry, he said. The oil industry was on its back laying off staff, and drilling activity was in a dive. Interest rates higher than the Calgary Tower loomed over the economy and overshadowed prospects for farmers and ranchers.

Any hopes the Socreds may have entertained for a political comeback evaporated under the blast of the by-election bombshell. Within weeks, Rod resigned as leader. Socred House Leader Ray Speaker, in a unilateral move soon after, announced a decision not to run Social Credit candidates in the next provincial election. Speaker also initially gave tacit support to the WCC.[18] In fact, Speaker had lengthy, behind the scenes conversations with Gordon Kessler, an action Rod considered as a betrayal that tarnished his feelings about Speaker for the rest of his life. He saw Speaker's role in the quick denunciation of Social Credit and a nimble readjustment to the WCC as reflecting a pattern of political expediency and self-preservation above all else that became a hallmark of Speaker's political career. At almost the same time he was talking with Kessler, Speaker and the other two remaining Social Credit MLAs, Walter Buck and Fred Mandeville, were also discussing ideas

for a new free enterprise party.[19] "The three are determined not to go down
with their debt-ridden party," said a *Herald* story.[20]

Herald legislature columnist Geoff White interpreted Speaker's actions in
a similarly negative light as Rod did. "Opposition leader Ray Speaker shows
no shame as he proposes to bolt to the separatist camp," he began in one
column. Five months previously, White pointed out, Speaker enthusiastically promoted the "feelings of commitment and patriotism" arising from the
constitutional agreement under Trudeau among nine provinces and Ottawa,
and now he was "ready to cast his lot with a party that condemns it absolutely." With a strong hint at what Speaker's motivations might be, he added,
"Speaker's unprincipled flight to the WCC raises the real possibility that the
party will attain the prestigious status of official opposition and its $400,000-
plus budget as early as next fall." Speaker was already indicating a willingness
to lead the party, prompting White's conclusion that, "It's no wonder people
become cynical about politics." In an earlier column, White once described
Speaker as an economically ultra-conservative, "though open to change when
faced with pleas like those of equally conservative ranchers seeking a beef
price support program."

In the meantime, Rod was wrapping up his ties with the party. That
included seeking payment of expenses still outstanding from the previous
August, plus a parting shot at Speaker about his failure to follow through on
his commitment to hand over his house leader's pay through a trust fund
they had set up together. "You will certainly recollect offering to pass on the
leadership portion of the house leader's salary when you were persuading me
to take the party leadership," he reminded Speaker. "As you know, that is a
commitment you never came to grips with after my election as leader." Then,
more ominously, "It may be that there are grounds for an interesting claim."[21]
Speaker sat on his hands, and his wallet, and the two never spoke again.

Rod followed with cynical amazement Speaker's continuing career in politics. Following his flirtation with the separatists, Speaker and Walter Buck ran
as independents in the 1982 election and won their seats. The down and out
Socreds lost all representation in the legislature. In order to qualify for legislature funding again, the two MLAs formed the Representative Party, of which
Speaker became leader. In 1987, after making no progress with his fringe
right-wing party, he crossed the floor to join the Progressive Conservatives
under Don Getty. In 1989, his loyal Little Bow riding re-elected him with a
seventy per cent majority, and he was named minister of housing and urban
affairs. Speaker ran for and won a House of Commons seat in the 1993 election as the Reform Party of Canada MP for the federal riding of Lethbridge.
He served as finance critic and then house leader of the Reform caucus. He
retired from politics before the 1997 election. After the Conservative Party

won a plurality of seats in the 2006 federal election, Speaker was appointed to the prime minister's transition team. He also was the chair of the Conservative/Alliance merger. He came across as honest and upright, with an air of modest idealism. Yet to Rod, he was a chameleon, changing colours and adapting to whatever conditions seemed most advantageous for his advancement. Rod claimed that money he'd helped raise for a Social Credit war chest—about $30,000—was never accounted for. "The money simply disappeared," said Rod. Orvis Kennedy, who served for decades as the party's loyal secretary, was left without a pension because he had lent the funds to the party. "The whole affair was a dismal story," said Rod.

These were hard times for Rod. As the bitter disengagement from the Socreds unfolded, Gisele was diagnosed with colon cancer. Rod took her on an emergency trip to the Mayo Clinic in New York for surgery. "By the grace of God it worked," said Rod. "We had twenty-six more good years together after that."

After all he had been through, it challenges credibility that less than two years later, Rod accepted yet another plea to put his neck on the line for another election campaign. The buzz over the prospect of a high-profile involvement in politics once more lured Rod from his routine of buckling down for his career. This time it was Liberal leader and new Prime Minister John Turner coming to him on bended knee for him to run in Calgary East, John Kushner's former riding, in the 1984 federal election.

Dubbed the silver fox with his head of gleaming white hair, and considered competent from his years as minister of finance, Turner helped Liberals eye the prospects of a 1984 general election with confidence. They would be taking on the Tories, led by Brian Mulroney, who had won the leadership from Joe Clark. Mulroney, already with a successful business background, had harboured prime ministerial ambitions since the mid-1970s. Rod and Mulroney enjoyed a long, convivial chat in the mayor's office in 1975 when Mulroney took himself on a cross-Canada tour to promote his name, meet with Canada's movers and shakers, and lay the groundwork for a possible leadership bid. An abiding image is of a chain-smoking, affable but fidgety character sitting in the reception area as Rod kept him waiting while talking with another visitor.

With hopes of picking up more seats in Western Canada, the newly minted Turner put the heat on Rod to run in Calgary East and be in line for a possible cabinet position. "Turner made many visits ... he was very forceful," said Rod. He promised to pull the Liberals back from their leftish tendencies to middle of the road, or in other words, be more fiscally conservative. "I felt challenged by the opportunity," said Rod. Gisele, recovering from her bout with cancer, noted that whatever resulted, "we win." That is, Rod would continue a political career with a national profile, or he would be out of politics for good and resume his private career.

His opponent in the election was Dr. Alex Kindy, a Calgary physician, who counted John Kushner among his patients. That is the same John Kushner who had been more or less a friend during Rod's mayoralty years, but with whom relations were more strained after Rod had told him he was going to contest the riding of Kushner's son Stan in Mountain View when Rod was Socred leader.

As history tells us, Turner turned out to be a stumbling, stuttering failure. Mulroney gave him quite a beating, showing him up as weak and indecisive. Rod lost his bid to be an MP, and ambitious political hopes were dashed for the second time in two years. The campaign had begun positively enough. When Rod was first nominated as Liberal candidate, the whole PC executive quit their party and came to work for him, he said. Premier Lougheed stepped in and provided some of his own people to help Kindy, though. Lougheed also urged Kindy never to appear on a debate platform with Rod, a strategy Kindy seemed to gladly embrace. Years later, Rod could only laugh at the anomaly. "Kindy won by not appearing anywhere I was. He stayed completely out of sight."

For Rod, "John Turner was the final straw." As leader, he hadn't kept promises made during his leadership campaign, and the Liberal message became "incoherent and wishy-washy" as the party continued its move to the left. Turned excused himself to Rod by saying, "I can't go ahead of my caucus. I have to go where they lead." The result was not that he left the Liberals, but "the Liberals left me," said Rod

So ended a relationship with the federal Liberals that had begun so warmly a decade and a half earlier through Rod's friendship with Pierre Trudeau. At least Rod was purged of any residual desires to enter the political arena again, and he was able to resume what became a successful and lucrative career as a development consultant, land developer, and stock market investor.

He did take another surprising public detour. This time it was into the field of journalism, writing a regular column for the breezy and sometimes irreverent *Calgary Sun*, aiming to topple *The Herald* off its perch as Calgary's number one paper with its big stable of columnists, Sunshine Girls, and extensive sports coverage. *Sun* publisher Hartley Steward asked Rod to write a weekly column by saying simply, "I think you can write. Like to try?" Soon it was three columns a week, touching on all kinds of political issues. He wrote—critically, of course—about service on airlines, and Alberta's economy; he expressed liking for the National Citizens' Coalition and for the downsizing of governments. There were columns about immigration policies and the lack of qualifications needed to run for public office. He wrote them all with customary sharpness and sarcasm.

Although in the "whore house", the term he used years earlier for the media, he wasn't a neophyte. He scored well in the *Sun's* readership polls. One survey in 1984 showed Rod at third spot with eighty per cent support from readers—just two per cent behind top columnist Jack Tennant.[22] Initially the *Sun* featured him in promo ads. "Look for Rod Sykes' incisive columns three days a week on Page 11," said one message under his photo.[23]

The *Sun* gig came to an end when the haughty William Gold, who, feeling his talents were not appreciated, had quit *The Herald* where he worked for many years, defected to the *Sun,* and assumed the title of editorial director. Gold and Rod had long rubbed each other the wrong way, so there was no surprise when Gold cut him adrift. Another factor was that Hartley Steward, who had hired Rod, was no longer at the *Sun.* "There is no easy or cosmetic way of saying this, so I will plunge right in. I am afraid that the time has come for us to stop publishing your column," said Gold's letter. "Although I have sensed of late that your heart is not in the column to the extent that it once was, the change we are now making is dictated by much broader considerations which do not reflect upon you or your work in any way."[24] Under the heading, "All good things come to an end," Rod's last column appeared the day before New Year's Eve, 1986. He went out with head held high, noting Hartley Steward's insistence when he hired Rod that it was "particularly important that political columnists bring the authority of direct and credible experience to their opinions." According to Rod, Steward had told him he had "helped establish the *Sun* in Calgary, and that I had shared in its success."

There was plenty of consulting work for Rod to do, and that's what he turned his hand to once again as he approached his sixties. During the late 1980s and early 1990s, Rod joined a small group and helped form a company that ended up developing a new city hall and parking structure for Brampton, Ontario. One of Rod's primary responsibilities there was to navigate the project through the stormy waters of the city bureaucracy and then through council. Obviously, his Calgary City Hall record was a big help. Although he found the mayor of Brampton co-operative, the politics otherwise were challenging, but he got the job done. Completed on target, the project was a financial success.

The Brampton project ended sourly, though, when one of Rod's partners wanted to roll over the profits from the City Hall project into another development in town. By that time, Rod was ready to return to Calgary and had to sue his partner for his share of the proceeds. In the end, payment was handed over on the courthouse steps, just before legal proceedings were to begin. A significant project for Rod around that time was an apartment development in Medicine Hat in partnership with a German builder. "Again they needed me to put plans in place for the political machinery," said Rod.

As he was proud to point out, Rod invested proceeds from his business activities wisely and shrewdly. He did well on the stock market over the years, and by his seventies, had established an impressive financial portfolio—all the result of his individual effort and acumen, plus, of course, good fortune.

The inner drive that found no political outlet after 1984 did sublimate into the many issues he took on at no charge where he felt injustice was being perpetrated. He had trouble resisting those kinds of challenges. Interested in digging around in the earth from boyhood, he also channeled energies and knowledge into an almost obsessive pre-occupation with gardening. For a while, he was totally out of the public eye. Rod recalled a woman approaching him on the street in the early 1990s and exclaiming, "I thought you'd croaked." That prompted his retort that "people think I'm either dead or in hiding if I'm not in a fight." I wrote in a *Herald* article that if Rod had any fights at that time, they were more likely with the rocks and plants adorning his Elbow Park garden.[25] Then sixty-four, he considered himself "as retired as I want to be."

Rod received many compliments for his garden. As he entered his eighties, it became increasingly difficult and a source of frustration for him to maintain it as he wanted. While his body became frailer, his mind remained sharp. If he couldn't be out in his garden, he could still dig through the memories that crowded and shone through his intellect like jewels in an ornate keepsake box. He was ready to spread them out on the table, sort through them, re-arrange them and relate their singular stories.

19
EPILOGUE

After putting the life of such an unusual man on the public record, I'm still mystified that Rod disavowed himself from the project. Even though most of our conversations over three years until 2012 focussed on personal aspects of his life, he called the results too personal and lacking in historical and institutional perspective. "What you have produced ... is not at all what I had understood we were to collaborate on. The story of Calgary City Hall in the 1970s ... has become what purports to be a personal biography!"[1] There was no acknowledgment the reader might even consider this book overly generous. Rod still emerges as a larger than life character, who had considerable and positive impacts on Calgary and Alberta. Many of the tangible projects he initiated and presided over are described in detail. The admiration of a one-time acolyte are there to see.

I share the human drive to search for explanations as to why people behave the way they do. The results can still be misinterpretations or wrong. No individual demonstrates entirely consistent and unchanging characteristics (well explained by David McRaney in his recent book, *You Are Not So Smart*). Real people, as opposed to fictional characters, manifest inscrutable nuance and defy facile definition. I am aware how characteristics change according to prevailing circumstances, yet I am tempted like anyone to apply predictable labels to individuals like Rod.

A strong motivation for this book was my estimation that the will, the nerve, the strategic skill, the hard-wired intelligence that led Rod to the successful completion of projects still benefiting people today have not earned him sufficient acknowledgment or even celebration. The fearlessness to tackle the toughest and most entangled of issues, the willingness to take on causes without apparent allies, the instinct to ferociously and publicly challenge what he saw as wrong-doing, are rare and refreshing attributes. Corruption in all levels of government and in the private sector is likely as prevalent today as it was decades ago. Few have spoken about it as openly as Rod. However, tackling it the way he did—largely on his own—may seem like spitting into the wind.

Yet Rod could demonstrate a surprising subtlety and sensitivity to people and issues. Granted, he was often clumsy and alienating too. I hope I've been able to show that the sum total of his abilities is more important and more impressive than the individual components of his character with which some felt uncomfortable.

The broader response to Rod's achievements since he retired as mayor has been too mute. There has been little to no public or institutional recognition of his place in the region's history. This book hopes to fill that void and encourage mitigation of that neglect, despite Rod's disassociation from the project. Not that Rod has promoted his candidacy for any public honours. At this stage of his life, he couldn't care less. That's what he says, at least.

He still mentions, though, the fact that when the CPR sent him to Calgary in the early 1960s, he was one half course short of an economics degree at Sir George Williams University. The half course he didn't have time to complete was in public speaking. In 1970, after winning the mayoralty and having already made hundreds of speeches and presentations with the CPR, Marathon, and as mayor, he asked the University of Calgary to give him credit for that half course to complete his degree. The university declined, and he has not followed the matter up since. In fact, for all his profile and public service, no university, let alone the U of C, has seen fit to award Rod any kind of honorary degree.

The desire for acknowledgment was obvious in his initial encouragement for the writing of this record. Although they were tough years as mayor, he often in later years spoke nostalgically, almost wistfully about them. Like the aging former sports star sitting at his corner table of the pub and eager to chat about his big-league glory days to anyone who would listen, Rod glowed when he reminisced about his City Hall times. Even though he didn't actually grab your arm, there was the Ancient Mariner's sense of urgency having to tell his remarkable tale to anyone he could. Stories were repeated at length, and they occasionally changed in emphasis and detail. Of course, they usually reflected well on the story-teller.

In the end, though, the purpose of the book comes down to retelling a good story. Apart from reliving a dynamic period of this region's history, or learning more about the evolution of local municipal government, I hope the reader also takes away impressions of a highly unique character. Rod Sykes was during his professional life an oddball, a maverick, a performer, and a warrior. In other words, he was a character quite different to anyone most of us will meet again in our lives. Like Joseph Campbell's archetypical hero, he set out on adventures into the unknown and virtually on his own. On those adventures, he tackled formidable demons, weathered stormy seas, and climbed steep mountains with varying degrees of success. The adventures certainly changed him, and the man he became in older age is, at least to me, still an enigma. At the same time as his attitudes harden, he also grows weary of conflict. In one breath, he exudes patience; in the next, testiness. He shows more humour and yet sermonizes more solemnly. I'm left with thanking him for punching above his weight for so long. Thin power made its mark. Let's celebrate that.

END NOTES

CHAPTER 1

1 *The Albertan, May 28, 1970*
2 *The Alberta Business Journal, May 1, 1970*
3 *Albertan, Nov. 30, 1970*
4 *Calgary Herald, Aug. 5, 1977*
5 *Albertan, Nov. 18, 1980*
6 *Calgary Herald, Oct. 26, 1977*

CHAPTER 3

1 *Urban History Review, Sept. 22, 2005, goliath.ecnext.com*
2 *Ibid*
3 *Ibid*
4 *Ibid*
5 *Calgary Herald, Dec. 29, 2010*
6 *Calgary Herald, Jan. 15, 1968*
7 *Urban History Review, Sept. 22, 2005, goliath.ecnext.com*
8 *Ibid*
9 *Memo to Candis McLean, Dec. 4, 2000*
10 *Alberta in the 20th Century, Vol. 10, Published by United Western Communication Ltd., 2002, Page 229*
11 *Good Morning, Your Worship, Century Calgary Publications, 1975, Page 119*
12 *Letter to Prof. Michael McMordie, University of Calgary, April 13, 2000*
13 *Memo to Candis McLean, Dec. 4, 2000*
14 *Expansive Discourses, Urban Sprawl in Calgary, 1945-1978, by Max Foran, Athabasca University Press, 2009*
15 *Asia Pacific Foundation of Canada website, asiapacific.ca*

CHAPTER 4

1 *Albertan, July 25, 1969*
2 *South Side Mirror, Sept. 4, 1969*
3 *Memo to Ald. Priddle, Jan. 19, 1973*
4 *Albertan, Sept. 4, 1969*
5 *Albertan, Sept. 6, 1969*

6   *Albertan, Sept. 10, 1969*
7   *Calgary Herald, Sept. 8, 1969*
8   *Calgary.ca Corporate Records*
9   *Calgary Herald, Sept. 30, 1969*
10   *Albertan, Oct. 10, 1969*
11   *Calgary Herald, Oct. 10, 1969*
12   *Calgary Herald, Oct. 16, 1969*
13   *Ibid*
14   *Ibid*   '
15   *Ibid*
16   *Calgary Herald, Oct. 20, 1969*
17   *Ibid*
18   *Albertan, Oct. 17, 1969*

CHAPTER 5

1   *Albertan, Oct. 17, 1969*
2   *Albertan, Nov. 10, 1970*
3   *North Hill News, May 20, 1971*
4   *Calgary Herald, Oct. 22, 1969*
5   *Ibid*
6   *Turcotte Report, July, 1959, Page 191*
7   *Calgary Herald, Oct. 20, 1969*
8   *Calgary Herald, May 21, 1971*
9   *Letter, May 30, 1973*
10   *Calgary Herald, Oct. 24, 1969*
11   *Albertan, Jan. 7, 1970*
12   *New York Times, March 11, 2011*
13   *Albertan, Nov. 11, 1970*
14   *Calgary Herald, Nov. 26, 1969*
15   *Albertan, Jan. 7, 1970*
16   *Albertan, Jan. 8, 1970*
17   *Westminster, B.C., Real Estate Board
     Newsletter, June/July, 1977*
18   *Albertan, Jan. 9, 1970*
19   *Calgary Herald, Feb. 10, 1970*
20   *Calgary Herald, March 3, 1970*
21   *Albertan, March 24, 1970*
22   *Calgary Herald, March 24, 1970*
23   *Albertan, March 28, 1970*
24   *Calgary Herald, April 4, 1970*

25 *Albertan, April 6, 1970*
26 *Toronto Star, Sept. 19, 1970*
27 *Albertan, July 27, 1970*
28 *Vancouver Province, Sept. 2, 1970*
29 *Albertan, Oct. 27, 1970*
30 *North Hill News, Oct. 29, 1970*

CHAPTER 6

1   *Globe and Mail, Oct. 9, 2009*
2   *Ibid*
3   *Governing Ourselves? The Politics of Canadian Communities, by Mary Louise McAllister, UBC Press, 2004*
4   *Globe and Mail, Oct. 9, 2009*
5   *Municipal Government Act, Section 154, As amended 1994, 1995*
6   *Municipal Government Act, Section 48, As amended in 1968*
7   *Calgary Herald, March 16, 2003*
8   *Calgary Herald, Feb. 13, 2003*
9   *Calgary Herald, Oct. 10, 2004*
10 *Naheed Nenshi, Alberta Views, April, 2010*
11 *Take Back City Hall, Ward 8 Press, 2004, Page 17*
12 *South Side Mirror, Sept. 4, 1969*
13 *Calgary Herald, Sept. 4, 1969*
14 *Albertan, Sept. 24, 1969*
15 *Albertan, Oct. 22, 1969*
16 *Calgary Herald, Oct. 20, 1969*
17 *Albertan, Nov. 24, 1969*
18 *Albertan, Jan. 10, 1970*
19 *Albertan, Jan. 8, 1970*
20 *Calgary Sun, Sept. 16, 1986*
21 *Albertan, March 28, 1970*
22 *Albertan, Nov. 29, 1971*
23 *Ibid*
24 *Memo to Commissioners, Jan. 18, 1973*
25 *Ibid*
26 *Memo to Commissioners, July 11, 1975*
27 *Memo to Commissioners, Nov. 16, 1973*
28 *Memo to Commissioners, July 12, 1974*
29 *Memo to Commissioners, July 5, 1977*
30 *Memo to Commissioners, Nov. 24, 1971*
31 *Memo to Commissioners, Dec. 28, 1973*

32   *Letter to D. Russell, Feb., 1974*
33   *Calgary Sun, Dec. 1, 2010*

CHAPTER 7

1   *Albertan, Jan. 11, 1971*
2   *Ibid*
3   *Ibid*
4   *Albertan, Jan. 12, 1971*
5   *Albertan, April 7, 1971*
6   *Albertan, Feb. 8, 1971*
7   *South Side Mirror, March 18, 1971*
8   *North Hill News, July 1, 1971*
9   *Calgary Herald, Sept. 4, 1971*
10   *Albertan, Aug. 31, 1971*
11   *Calgary Herald, Sept. 7, 1971*
12   *Ibid*
13   *Calgary Herald, Sept. 10, 1971*
14   *Calgary Herald, Sept. 14, 1971*
15   *Calgary Herald, Sept. 21, 1971*
16   *Calgary Herald, Nov. 27, 1997*
17   *Albertan, Oct. 15, 1971*
18   *Albertan. Oct. 22, 1971*
19   *Calgary Herald, Feb. 16, 1972*
20   *Press Release, July 17, 1973*
21   *Calgary Herald, April 1, 1972*
22   *Ibid*
23   *Albertan, Nov. 8, 1972*
24   *Albertan, Nov. 9, 1972*
25   *Letter to Ed Oman, Jan. 17, 1973*
26   *Calgary Herald, Jan. 19, 1973*
27   *Albertan, Jan. 19, 1973*
28   *Calgary Herald, March 24, 1973*
29   *Calgary Herald, March 29, 1973*
30   *Calgary Herald, March 31, 1973*
31   *South Side Mirror, Aug. 5, 1972*
32   *Albertan, May 3, 1973*
33   *Albertan, May 26, 1973*
34   *Memo to Brian Scott, Jan. 14, 1974*
35   *MacLean's Magazine, May, 1974*
36   *Calgary Herald, July 17, 1973*

37   *Calgary Herald, July 26, 1973*
38   *Albertan, April 17, 1974*

CHAPTER 8

1   *Albertan, June 29, 1974*
2   *Albertan, July 22, 1974*
3   *Albertan, Aug. 15, 1974*
4   *Ibid*
5   *Globe and Mail, Aug. 17, 1974*
6   *Albertan, Sept. 21, 1974*
7   *Albertan, Sept. 28, 1974*
8   *Life and Times of Jack Poole, July 3, 2009, www.bcbusinessonline.ca*
9   *Globe and Mail, Oct. 17, 1974*
10   *Ibid*
11   *Edmonton Journal, Nov.8, 1974*
12   *Medicine Hat News, Nov. 21, 1974*
13   *Letter to Premier, Jan. 22, 1975*
14   *Government and Politics in Alberta, Edited by Allan Tupper and Roger Gibbins, Page 170*
15   *Globe and Mail, May 10, 1975*
16   *Christmas Message, Dec. 17, 1974*
17   *Albertan, Dec. 30, 1974*
18   *Albertan, July 17, 1975*
19   *Letter to Century Calgary, Aug. 21, 1975*
20   *Albertan, Aug. 22, 1975*
21   *www.lieutenantgovernor.ab.ca 2008*
22   *Letter to Paul Godfrey, Sept. 18, 1975*
23   *Albertan, Sept. 18, 1975*
24   *Calgary Herald, Oct. 28, 1975*
25   *Letter to Dick Johnstone, April 6, 1976*
26   *Letter to Dick Johnstone, July 20, 1976*
27   *Albertan, May 14, 1976*
28   *Letter from Jack Gallagher, May 17, 1976*
29   *Letter, May 12, 1977*
30   *Memo to Council, Feb. 25, 1977*
31   *Calgary Herald, March 8, 1977*
32   *Albertan, March 28, 1977*
33   *Financial Post, May 14, 1977*
34   *Albertan, July 14, 1977*
35   *Globe and Mail, July 30, 1977*

36   *Calgary Herald, Aug. 5, 1977*
37   *North Hill News, Aug. 9, 1977*
38   *Saint John's Calgary Report, Aug. 12, 1977*
39   *Letter to C.D. Denney, Aug. 18, 1977*
40   *Calgary Herald, Aug. 29, 1977*
41   *Letter to Brigadier Shaver, Aug. 31, 1977*
42   *Memo to Chief Commissioner Cole, Aug. 31, 1977*

CHAPTER 9

1   *Memo to Commissioners, Dec. 22, 1976*
2   *Albertan, May 7, 1970*
3   *North Hill News, May 7, 1970*
4   *Albertan, July 21, 1970*
5   *Ibid*
6   *Calgary Herald, Oct. 28, 1970*
7   *Ibid*
8   *Year-end Statement, Dec., 1972*
9   *Memo to commissioners, May 30, 1975*
10   *Memo to Ron Brown, Oct. 18, 1973*
11   *Memo to Chief Commissioner, Oct. 18, 1973*
12   *Calgary Herald, Oct. 22, 1973*
13   *Albertan, Oct. 25, 1973*
14   *Calgary Herald, Oct. 22, 1973*
15   *Calgary Herald, Nov. 11, 1973*
16   *Calgary Herald, Oct. 30, 1973*
17   *Calgary Herald, Nov. 20, 1973*
18   *Memo, Nov. 8, 1971*
19   *Calgary Herald, March 1, 1972*
20   *Calgary Herald, Feb. 23, 1972*
21   *Ibid*
22   *Albertan, June 16, 1973*
23   *Calgary Herald, Feb. 23, 1976*

CHAPTER 10

1   *Memo to Commissioners, Feb. 13, 1974*
2   *Calgary Herald, April 27, 1976*
3   *Ibid*
4   *Letter, Feb. 16, 1976*
5   *Globe and Mail, Sept. 11, 1972*

6   *Calgary Herald, Oct. 30, 1972*
7   *Albertan, Sept. 8, 1971*
8   *Albertan, Jan. 18, 1972*
9   *Ibid*
10   *Letter, April 5, 1972*
11   *Ibid*
12   *Memo to commissioners, May 13, 1974*
13   *Published by Between The Lines, 1984, Page 114*
14   *Ibid, Page 116*
15   *Letter, July 29, 1976*
16   *Letter, Feb. 16, 1976*
17   *Memorandum, March 24, 1977*
18   *Letter, May 12, 1977*
19   *George M. Abouna; History of a Pioneer in Transplant Surgery, By Samir Johna,
     Listed on Amazaon.ca*
20   *Albertan, June 9, 1977*
21   *Ibid*
22   *Calgary Herald, Nov. 5, 1975*
23   *Letter to George Abouna, June 16, 1977*
24   *Edmonton Journal, April 16, 1980*
25   *Canadian Assoc. of University Teacher letter to P.A. Mackimmie, May 20, 1980*

CHAPTER 11

1   *Calgary Herald, May 20, 1994*
2   *Calgary Herald, Sept. 8, 1971*
3   *Memo from Medical Office of Health, March 19, 1970*
4   *Memo to Commissioners, April 2, 1970*
5   *Morrow Report*
6   *Might As Well, by Grateful Dead, 1976*
7   *South Side Mirror, July 9, 1970*
8   *Calgary Herald, July 6, 1970*
9   *Morrow Report, Page 67*
10   *Morrow Report, Page 89*
11   *Albertan, Nov. 24, 1972*
12   *Albertan, July 31, 1970*
13   *Fifth House, 2002*
14   *Letter to Ald. Dooley, Aug. 14, 1970*
15   *Letter to Police Commission, Feb. 7, 1971*
16   *Albertan, April 24, 1977*
17   *Albertan, Dec. 14, 1970*

18   *Letter from Jack Prothroe, March 13, 1972*
19   *Public Statement, Nov. 29, 1974*
20   *Letter, March 22, 1976, Globe and Mail, March 27, 1976*

CHAPTER 12

1   *Albertan, Sept. 6, 1972*
2   *Ibid*
3   *Ibid*
4   *New Release, Feb. 24, 1975*
5   *Steer Report, Page 16*
6   *Ibid*
7   *Steer Report, Page 17*
8   *Ibid, Page 24*
9   *Ibid, Page 32*
10   *Letter from Charlie Smith, Dec. 13, 1972*
11   *Steer Report, Page 104*
12   *Ibid, Page 33*
13   *Ibid, Page 37*
14   *The Western Flair, by C.D. Evans, Vile Publications Ltd., 2001*
15   *Letter to Pierre Trudeau, Nov. 15, 1974*
16   *Letter from George Diefenbaker, Dec. 8, 1969*
17   *Calgary Herald, Nov. 7, 2010*
18   *Calgary Herald, Feb. 1, 2011*
19   *Calgary Herald, Aug. 24, 1970*
20   *Calgary Herald, Oct. 15, 1970*
21   *Letter to Dave Russell, March 20, 1973*
22   *Calgary Herald, May 17, 1973*
23   *Albertan, Nov. 27, 1973*
24   *Calgary Herald, June 4, 1974*
25   *Calgary Herald, May 21, 1977*
26   *Letter, Aug. 9, 1977*

CHAPTER 13

1   *Canada From Afar, Published by Dundurn Press, 1996, Pages 252-253*
2   *Ibid*
3   *Letter from Mountbatten of Burma, July 7, 1977*
4   *Letter from Mountbatten of Burma, Sept. 21, 1977*
5   *Calgary Herald, Dec. 10, 2007*
6   *Ibid*

7   *Ibid*
8   *Letter from Mountbatten of Burma to British Airways, Sept. 21, 1977*
9   *Letter from Mountbatten of Burma to mayor, Oct. 7, 1977*
10   *British Airways News, Oct. 21, 1977*

CHAPTER 14

1   *Capital Budget Notes by Joseph Yanchula, 1972*
2   *Calgary Herald, Jan. 15, 1971*
3   *Regina Chamber Publication, Feb. 1, 1974*
4   *News Release, Oct. 20, 1976*
5   *Albertan, Feb. 3, 1972*
6   *Financial Post Conference Speech, Nov. 12, 1974*
7   *Ibid*
8   *Albertan, Feb. 17, 1970*
9   *Albertan, May 20, 1970*
10   *Calgary Herald, May 15, 1971*
11   *Calgary Herald, Feb. 23, 1972*
12   *Letter to Mayor Ivor Dent, released to media, Feb. 19, 1974*
13   *Calgary Herald, May 23, 1974*
14   *Calgary Herald, May 27, 1975*
15   *Letter to council, May 29, 1975*
16   *Albertan, Jan. 28, 1976*

CHAPTER 15

1   *Government and Politics in Alberta, University of Alberta Press, 1992, Page 202*
2   *Ibid*
3   *Calgary Herald, Dec. 14, 1970*
4   *Letter to Robert Malone, Sept. 7, 1971*
5   *Ibid*
6   *Albertan, Oct. 15, 1971*
7   *Letter to Newspaper Guild, Dec. 24, 1971*
8   *Globe and Nail, Dec. 28, 1971*
9   *Calgary Herald, Dec. 28, 1971*
10   *Albertan, Dec. 30, 1971*
11   *Letter to Calgary Press Club, Dec. 19, 1971*
12   *Calgary Herald, July 21, 1972*
13   *Calgary Herald, Oct. 24, 1975*
14   *Letter to Tom Kennedy, July 9, 1975*

CHAPTER 16

1   *Calgary Herald, March 17, 1970*
2   *Ibid*
3   *Alberta in the 20ᵗʰ Century, Chapter. 4, by Carmen Wittmeier*
4   *Ibid*
5   *Letter to Calgary Philharmonic, April 8, 1975*
6   *Alberta in the 20ᵗʰ Century, Candis McLean, United Western Communications Ltd., 2002*
7   *Board of Commissioner Minutes, Sept. 21, 1970*
8   *Letter to Commissioners, Dec. 1, 1970*
9   *Boxing & Wrestling Commission Minutes, Aug. 7, 1973*
10 *Letter to Boxing Commission, Dec. 11, 1974*
11 *Letter from Stu Hart to Commission, April, 1971*

CHAPTER 17

1   *www.Calgary.ca/corporate records*
2   *Remarks of Mayor Rod Sykes, July 5, 1973*
3   *Wikipedia.org 2011*
4   *Calgary Herald, Aug. 13, 1977*
5   *The Good Steward, by Brian Brennan, Fifth House, Page 145*
6   *Ibid*
7   *Ibid, Page 173*
8   *Letter to Prime Minister Trudeau, Aug. 4, 1971*
9   *Letter to Prime Minister Trudeau, Aug. 25, 1972*
10 *Letter to Prime Minister Trudeau, Oct. 26, 1973*
11 *Prime Minister Letter to Mayor, Jan. 7, 1974*
12 *Letter to Prime Minister Trudeau, July 16, 1974*
13 *Prime Minister Letter to Mayor, May 3, 1972*
14 *Letter to Prime Minister Trudeau, Oct. 7, 1974*
15 *Prime Minister Letter to Mayor, Nov. 1, 1974*
16 *Letter to Prime Minister Trudeau, Nov. 15, 1974*
17 *Prime Minister Letter to Mayor, Jan. 27, 1975*
18 *Letter to Prime Minister Trudeau, Nov. 15, 1974*

CHAPTER 18

1   *Alberta Report, Nov. 23, 1979*
2   *Ibid*
3   *Calgary Magazine, Nov., 1980*

4   *Ibid*
5   *Open Letter to Social Credit Board, July 23, 1980*
6   *Rod Sykes and Social Credit Statement, Oct., 1980*
7   *Rod Sykes Leadership Material, Nov., 1980*
8   *Calgary Herald, Aug. 15, 1981*
9   *Edmonton Sun, Aug. 18, 1981*
10 *Memorandum to Rod Sykes, Oct. 7, 1981*
11 *Albertan, Nov. 1, 1981*
12 *Calgary Herald, Nov. 1, 1981*
13 *MacLean's Magazine, Nov., 1981*
14 *Calgary Herald, Nov. 30, 1981*
15 *Board Meeting Memo, Dec., 1981*
16 *Western Canada Concept Platform, Nov. 28, 1981*
17 *Lethbridge Herald, March 16, 1982*
18 *News Release, April 26, 1982*
19 *Calgary Herald, March 17, 1982*
20 *Ibid*
21 *Letter to Ray Speaker, April 5, 1982*
22 *Calgary Sun, March 11, 1984*
23 *Calgary Sun, Nov. 14, 1984*
24 *Bill Gold Letter to Rod Sykes, Nov. 28, 1986*
25 *Calgary Herald, Aug. 9, 1993*

EPILOGUE

1   *Letter from Rod Sykes, May 31, 2012*